BEYOND THE LAW OF THE SEA

BEYOND THE LAW OF THE SEA

New Directions for U.S. Oceans Policy

George V. Galdorisi
and Kevin R. Vienna

Foreword by William L. Schachte, Jr.

Westport, Connecticut
London

Library of Congress Cataloging-in-Publication Data

Galdorisi, George, 1948–
    Beyond the law of the sea : new directions for U.S. oceans policy
  / George V. Galdorisi and Kevin R. Vienna ; foreword by William L. Schachte, Jr.
      p. cm.
    Includes bibliographical references and index.
    ISBN 0–275–95754–3 (alk. paper)
    1. Maritime law. 2. Maritime law—United States. 3. United
Nations Convention on the Law of the Sea (1982) I. Vienna, Kevin
R. II. Title.
JX4411.G35   1997
341.7′566—dc20   96–33197

British Library Cataloguing in Publication Data is available.

Library of Congress Catalog Card Number: 96–33197
ISBN: 0–275–95754–3

First published in 1997

Praeger Publishers, 88 Post Road West, Westport, CT 06881
An imprint of Greenwood Publishing Group, Inc.

Printed in the United States of America

The paper used in this book complies with the
Permanent Paper Standard issued by the National
Information Standards Organization (Z39.48–1984).

10 9 8 7 6 5 4 3 2 1

To our wives, Becky and Kathy,
for their patience, understanding
and support

CONTENTS

FOREWORD

As a member of the United States Delegation to the United Nations Conference on the Law of the Sea and, subsequently, as the Department of Defense Representative for Ocean Policy Affairs, I have had a unique opportunity to be involved in the formulation and implementation of United States oceans policy and the law of the sea. I also have seen the impact of this important segment of international law on both the United States and the world community as we grapple with the challenge of applying the rule of law to the over seventy percent of the globe covered by water. Additionally, during three decades of service in the Navy, I have observed, first-hand, the importance of the rule of law on the oceans and the pivotal role that the United States plays in formulating this body of law.

The importance of the law of the sea in general and the United Nations Convention on the Law of the sea in particular, is evidenced by the fact that the United Nations Conference on the Law of the Sea was the most extensive international negotiation ever conducted and the resulting Convention was the most comprehensive international treaty negotiated before or since. Accordingly, it is an area worthy of research, scholarship, and coherent analysis. Surprisingly, no previous books on the subject have addressed the many facets of the law of the sea.

This book combines, in a balanced way, the views of law, history, and policy as they relate to the law of the sea in general and to the United States participation in this area in particular. This interdisciplinary approach adds depth and detail to the subject and frames the subject superbly for the academic, the policy maker, the researcher, or the practitioner.

Although the 1982 United Nations Convention on the Law of the Sea (along with the companion Agreement) was signed by the President in July of 1994 and submitted to the Senate for its advice and consent in October of that year, as of this writing, the Treaty has yet to gain Senate approval. Even assuming Senate advice and consent, this text importantly emphasizes and demonstrates that the Convention on the Law of the Sea does not end the requirement for the United States involvement in the development of oceans law and policy. Rather, a universally adopted Treaty is the critical first step in oceans policy formulation and should serve as a springboard for continuing national attention.

Although it properly addresses all areas of the law of the sea, this text has a distinct national security orientation. A pivotal chapter of the book, chapter six, sets forth and defends the proposition that the Convention on the Law of the Sea is central to United States interests in the maintenance of stability and predictability in ocean spaces. Debate in this important policy area remains vital, and this book contributes immeasurably to shaping that debate.

During the current decade, some of the best scholarship in the United States and elsewhere on oceans law and policy has occurred in ephemeral form—such as Department of State Information Papers, Department of Defense White Papers, and papers presented at symposia sponsored by a variety of oceans policy groups such as the Center for Oceans Law and Policy, the Law of the Sea Institute, the Council on Ocean Law, and the Ocean Governance Study Group, among others. This book preserves a great deal of this scholarship in an enduring form.

The background of this book's authors is unique and contributes, in a synergistic manner, to the quality and utility of this work. Captain Galdorisi is an unrestricted line officer, has extensive operational experience, and has written extensively on the law of the sea. Captain Vienna studied under Professor John Norton Moore at the University of Virginia and has extensive operational law experience at sea as a fleet judge advocate and naval officer. Together, they have the perfect credentials to produce a work of scholarship that is of enduring value.

Beyond the Law of the Sea: New Directions for United States Oceans Policy is a critical link in the continuum of scholarship on the law of the sea. No other work combines the depth of research, focused analysis, and clarity of presentation that this book does. Policy makers, policy analysts, and mariners will all find this book equally valuable.

William L. Schachte, Jr.
Rear Admiral,
Judge Advocate General's Corps,
United States Navy (Retired)

PREFACE

This book is about the law of the sea. It examines the concept of "law" for the oceans within the context of international law and briefly examines the involvement of the United States in the historical development of the law of the sea. Next, it focuses on the way in which United States Ocean Policy has been affected by the 1982 Convention on the Law of the Sea and how future policy will be defined within the context of the Convention.

The book comprises three main sections. First, it examines the evolution of the concept of the law of the sea, reviewing important elements of the negotiations at the United Nations Conferences on the Law of the Sea, first in 1958, and ending with the conclusion of the Third Conference in 1982. Second, it "baselines" just what the 1982 Convention prescribes in areas most important to the development of U.S. policy. Third, it examines the oceans policy issues facing the United States as 1982 Convention achieves wider adoption.

This book is intended for several audiences. For those interested in the law of the sea, it should serve as a resource for understanding its development and effects. For those interested more generally in American foreign policy, it can serve as important illustration of how important issues challenge and shape the evolution of policy. Accordingly, the book should be useful to those interested in international negotiations and international security. For the informed public, generally, this book is intended to provide a thorough, yet readable, companion that provides insights into the 1982 Convention on the Law of the Sea, the most comprehensive international negotiations ever undertaken, which now provides the foundation for the rule of law over that 70 percent of the earth covered by water. Furthermore, the book examines the implications of this Convention for the United States as it develops policy to enhance its core political, economic, and security interests.

As with most works of this genre, the majority of the book is descriptive, in that it examines historical process and elaborates on rules. It concludes, however, with a consideration of ocean policy challenges confronting the United States and the means of addressing them. Finally, it urges a systematic, intelligent, and active approach in making and managing oceans policy to attain optimum results.

An effort of this scope would not be possible without the unselfish help from a number of people. Rear Admiral William Schachte, Jr., JAGC, USN (Ret.) provided encouragement, support, and invaluable advice from the inception of the project. His profound knowledge of the entire spectrum of law-of-the-sea issues and his experience in shaping its recent history served as "ground truth" as we refined the focus of this work. Captains Jack Grunawalt and Ralph Thomas, on the faculty at the Naval War College, provided early encouragement and direction and helped shape the outcome. Captain Dave Peace, JAGC, USN, the director of the Office of the Judge Advocate General of the Navy's International Law Division, and his capable assistants, Lieutenant Commander Pete Pedrozo and Lieutenant Carl Tierney, provided general comments and frequent updates on the progress of the Law of the Sea Convention as it made its way through the Executive Branch to the Senate. Ms. Maureen Walker, Department of State, supplied extensive background on the law of the sea and invaluable insight. Finally, Dr. Lee Ann Otto, Chairman of the Department of Political Science at the University of San Diego, and Mr. William Aceves, a doctoral candidate at Harvard University who has conducted extensive research in the field, reviewed early drafts and provided essential commentary.

For the assistance of these and many others, we express our deepest thanks.

BEYOND THE LAW
OF THE SEA

Chapter One

INTRODUCTION

The long-awaited adoption of the 1982 United Nations Convention on the Law of the Sea by the community of nations represents a watershed for the maritime interests of the international community. This Convention, the final result of the largest single international negotiating process ever undertaken, has enormous implications for the conduct of maritime affairs among nations. As the world's leading maritime state, the United States has a huge stake in the Convention.

For the United States, the Convention represents much more than simply another international treaty. There are vital, immediate, national interests that hinge on continuing U.S. involvement with this Convention. Our core strategic interests—political, economic, and security—are critically dependent on the free access to, and unhampered use of, the 70 percent of the globe covered by water. A universally ratified Convention supports these interests. The Convention is not a panacea. Its rules are not perfect. But widespread acceptance is likely to guide the behavior of nations, promote stability of expectations, enhance adaptation to new circumstances, narrow the scope of disputes to more manageable proportions, and provide a workable framework for issue resolution.[1]

Over a decade and a half ago, in April 1982, the Reagan administration voted against the 1982 United Nations Convention on the Law of the Sea, becoming one of only four nations to vote against the final Convention.[2] Eight months later, in December 1982, the United States stood on the sidelines as 117 other nations and two entities signed the Convention on the first day it was opened for signature.[3] In every sense, the United States made a major policy statement by not signing a treaty that had taken nearly a decade of exhaustive work to produce.[4]

Throughout the preceding decade of detailed dialogue, the United States was deeply involved in the negotiations of the Third United Nations Conference of the Law of the Sea (UNCLOS III).[5] The final product codified existing practice and established new norms of international law in many areas of oceans policy. Coastal jurisdiction and management in territorial seas, contiguous zones, and a 200-mile exclusive economic zone; marine passage and overflight through straits and archipelagos used for international navigation; a special status for archipelagic States; management of fisheries in the high seas and in exclusive economic zones, coastal and flag State jurisdiction over vessels for the purpose of preventing environmental disasters, the general ocean environmental obligations of States, the right to conduct ocean science research; the creation of a system for managing the exploitation of deep seabed minerals; and dozens of other issues were addressed in the comprehensive, 320-article, nine-annex, final document.[6]

By the end of the 1970s, the Carter administration appeared ready to sign the treaty, which contained several fundamental compromises between the Western powers and the developing world, including maintaining an acceptable transit passage regime through international straits to offset extension of the territorial sea to a maximum breadth of twelve nautical miles.[7] The treaty also applied the principles of the "common heritage of mankind" as the guiding philosophy in regard to exploitation of the deep seabed's mineral resources.[8] As Ambassador James Malone, one of the Reagan administration's special representatives at UNCLOS III would say, "After the close of the ninth session of UNCLOS III, the United States was clearly on the verge of signing the treaty."[9] As the principal other blue-water naval power, the Soviet Union was also prepared to sign the treaty and indeed had been on the same side of many critical negotiating positions with the United States in the course of UNCLOS III, particularly on all navigational issues.[10]

By late 1982, as UNCLOS III drew to a close, the treaty had become much more than a piece of paper—it was an international state of mind. It created new international law, codified much of what was customary law in the law of the sea, and established new norms in the negotiation of multi-State agreements.[11] It came as a great disappointment to large segments of the international community when the newly inaugurated Reagan administration, dissatisfied with the seabed mining provisions of the Convention, decided not to sign the final accord.[12] To much of the world, it appeared that the United States wanted to select among the benefits of the treaty, principally the articles relating to navigation and overflight rights, without accepting the negotiated compromise positions in the document relating to deep seabed mining.[13] On a more fundamental scale, in the view of some commentators, the failure of the United States to sign the treaty may have called into question the leadership of the United States with respect to the promotion of international law and order.[14]

Momentous changes to the political, economic, and security environment occurred in the period since the United States elected to vote against the treaty. Significantly, the international community labored mightily, primarily behind the scenes, to make the treaty more acceptable to western nations in general and the United States in particular. For the first time in over five decades, the United

States has an unprecedented window of opportunity to realize a long-standing strategic objective of U.S. oceans policy—the entry into force of a widely accepted and comprehensive treaty on the law of the sea, which, among its more important provisions, preserves traditional freedoms of navigation and overflight essential to our national security and economic well being. Modifications to the objectionable Part XI, deep seabed mining portions of the Convention, spearheaded by the United States, and supported by the other industrialized nations, have opened the way for the United States and other maritime powers to become parties to this important instrument that promotes the maritime interests of the international community as a whole.

The United States has crossed the Rubicon. On 7 October 1994, President Clinton submitted the Convention, along with the Agreement modifying Part XI of the Convention, to the United States Senate for its advice and consent. The Senate may choose to act on the treaty in the near term, or delay acting on it, perhaps indefinitely. Should the Senate act favorably on the treaty and give its advice and consent, what does accession to this Convention portend for United States maritime policy? As the international community continues to adapt to the rules of the Convention—in areas ranging from freedom of navigation and overflight, to deep seabed mining, to environmental protection, to the prevention of piracy, and others—how should United States oceans policy adapt to complying with the rule of law as outlined by the Convention, while at the same time securing the advantages of this comprehensive oceans regime? Does the United States have the mechanisms in place at the federal, state, and even local levels, to craft a comprehensive oceans policy that supports our diverse political, economic, and security imperatives?

The following chapters will address these matters. To provide context on the "law" of the sea, the next chapter examines some fundamental concepts in international law. Next, the processes and interests involved in negotiating the Convention will be examined, including consideration of why the United States found the Convention unacceptable in 1982. Developments since 1982 are then viewed, including those critical events that have successfully modified previous deficiencies in the Convention's provisions.

Later chapters will review why the Convention's provisions and their wide international acceptance are essential to United States security. The final chapters examine the importance of "oceans policy," the fundamentally constitutive nature of the Convention, and the continuing policy challenges for the United States as we face new directions in the law of the sea.

NOTES

1.   William Schachte, Jr., "National Security: Customary International Law and the LOS Convention" (address at the Georgetown International Law Symposium, *Implementing the United Nations Convention on the Law of the Sea*, Washington, D.C., January 1995). Rear Admiral Schachte, Judge Advocate

General's Corps, U.S. Navy (Retired) is a noted expert on the law of the sea, having served as Department of Defense representative for Oceans Policy Affairs, Judge Advocate General, and a long-time architect of U.S. oceans policy positions.

2.   Statement of Ambassador James Malone, special representative of the president for the Third Law of the Sea Conference, before the House Foreign Affairs Subcommittee on 12 August 1982 in Department of State, "Law of the Sea and Oceans Policy," *Current Policy* no. 416 (Washington, D.C.: United States Department of State, Bureau of Public Affairs, 1982), 2. Ambassador Malone's comments followed President Reagan's 9 July 1982 statement in which the president explained the United States' objections to the Part XI deep seabed mining provisions of the 1982 LOS Convention. The other three countries voting against the treaty's adoption were Israel, Turkey, and Venezuela. Nations abstaining were the United Kingdom, the Federal Republic of Germany, Belgium, Netherlands, Luxembourg, Italy, Spain, Thailand, and the entire Soviet Bloc, except for Romania.

3.   James Malone, "Who Needs the Sea Treaty?" *Foreign Policy* 54 (1984): 44. Ambassador Malone served in a number of capacities as a Reagan administration expert on the law of the sea, first as special representative for the Third United Nations Conference on the Law of the Sea, later as assistant secretary of state for Oceans, International Environmental and Scientific Affairs, and finally, as chairman of the United States Delegation to the Law of the Sea Conference.

4.   R. R. Churchill and A. V. Lowe, *The Law of the Sea* (Manchester, U.K.: Manchester University Press, 1983), 14. A second edition of this respected work, with an added section on maritime boundaries, was published in 1988. The entire UNCLOS process continued virtually unabated for a quarter of a century. UNCLOS I, attended by fifty-eight States, convened in Geneva in 1958. It drafted four conventions. UNCLOS II convened in 1960 but failed to adopt any Conventions. Dissatisfaction with the results of these two conferences caused the United Nations General Assembly to convene a Sea Bed Committee in 1967. Based on the Sea Bed Committee's report, General Assembly Resolution 2570 authorized the convening of a Third United Nations Conference (UNCLOS III). The first meeting of this conference was held in 1973 and the various committees met at least semiannually until 1982. In a press release dated 13 December 1991, retiring U.N. Secretary-General Perez de Cuellar emphasized the extent of the efforts that went into negotiating the law of the sea. According to the secretary-general, "The international community has invested some twenty-two years of effort and substantial resources in negotiating it—three years of preparatory work, ten years of negotiations and a further nine years preparing for its entry into force." This statement is reprinted in Council on Oceans Law, *Oceans Policy News* (February 1992).

5.   John Stevenson and Bernard Oxman, "The Future of the United Nations Convention on the Law of the Sea," *American Journal of International Law* 88

(1994): 494. See also Malone, "Who Needs the Sea Treaty?" 48. Ambassador Malone's 1984 *Foreign Policy* article is still widely quoted, over a decade later, in fora ranging from academic publications to congressional testimony.

6.   United Nations, *1982 United Nations Convention on the Law of the Sea*, United Nations Publication, 1261 (New York: United Nations, 1982), reproduced from U.N. Document A/CONF.62/122 of 7 October 1982. The text also incorporates the two English corrections contained in U.N. Documents A/CONF.62/122/CORR.3 of 23 November 1982, and A/CONF.62/122/CORR.8 of 26 November 1982. The final Convention was the most comprehensive codification of maritime law ever assembled by the international community. The 320 articles and nine annexes (containing over 300 more articles) contained in the Convention constitute a guide for behavior by States in the world's oceans, defining maritime zones, laying down rules for drawing sea boundaries, assigning legal rights, duties and responsibilities to States, and providing machinery for the settlement of disputes. See generally Robert Friedheim, *Negotiating the New Ocean Regime* (Columbia, South Carolina: University of South Carolina Press, 1993).

7.   Churchill and Lowe, *Law of the Sea*, 61. The width of the territorial sea has always been a contentious issue. The 1982 Law of the Sea Convention set the limit of territorial waters at twelve nautical miles in accordance with the clearly dominant trend in State practice.

8.   Martin Harry, "The Deep Seabed: The Common Heritage of Mankind or Arena for Unilateral Exploitation?" *Naval Law Review* 40 (1992): 210.

9.   Malone, "Who Needs the Sea Treaty?" 48. See William Schachte, Jr., interview with George Galdorisi, 14 June 1995, Washington, D.C. (on file with author). Rear Admiral Schachte emphasized the prominent role that Ambassador Malone played in the Reagan administration's law of the sea policy making process.

10.   Mark Janis and Donald Daniel, *The USSR: Ocean Use and Ocean Law* (Kingston, Rhode Island: University of Rhode Island Press, 1974). The United States' position on straits passage has been well known for some time. The forcefulness of the Soviet position on this issue at UNCLOS III is less well known. For example, the Soviet draft articles on Straits Used for International Navigation stated that "No State shall be entitled to interrupt or suspend the transit of ships through straits or engage therein in any acts which interfere with the transit of ships, or require ships in transit to stop or communicate information of any kind."

11.   Churchill and Lowe, *Law of the Sea*, 16. Between 1973 and 1980, numerous negotiating drafts evolved that allowed UNCLOS III committee members to voice their opinions. As the process continued with semiannual meetings, an increasing level of consensus was reached among UNCLOS III delegates. See also United Nations, *The Law of the Sea: Annual Review of Ocean Affairs, Law and Policy, Main Documents* (New York: United Nations, 1993), 3-28.

12.   Statement of the president before the House Merchant Marine and Fisheries Committee on 29 January 1982, reprinted in Department of State, "Law of the Sea," *Current Policy* no. 371 (Washington, D.C.: Department of State, 1982), 2. In articulating U.S. objections to the draft articles, the president noted that "Our review has concluded that while most provisions of the Draft Convention are acceptable and consistent with U.S. interests, some major elements of the deep seabed mining regime are not acceptable." See also Elliot Richardson, "The Politics of the Law of the Sea," *Ocean Development and International Law* 11 (1982): 10. Ambassador Richardson, the chairman of the United States law-of-the-sea delegation from 1977 to 1980, describes the uncertainty created by the U.S. decision and notes that: "delegates were stunned by the announcement of the United States government."

13.   Report of the president of the conference, U.N. Document A/Conf. 62/C. 141 (1982), reproduced in M. H. Nordquist and C. H. Park, eds., *Report of the U.S. Delegation to the Third U.N. Conference on the Law of the Sea* (Honolulu: Law of the Sea Institute Press, 1983).

14.   James B. Morell, *The Law of the Sea: An Historical Analysis of the 1982 Treaty and Its Rejection by the United States* (Jefferson, North Carolina: McFarland and Company, 1992), xiv.

Chapter Two

THE LAW OF THE SEA AND INTERNATIONAL LAW

HISTORICAL DEVELOPMENT OF THE LAW OF THE SEA

"International Law" can be described as "that body of rules or norms that are considered legally binding by States in their intercourse with each other."[1] As Rear Admiral (retired) and former Judge Advocate General of the Navy, Horace B. Robertson, Jr., has observed, several portions of this description warrant further comment:[2]

- The description refers to "rules or norms." The term "rules" connotes greater specificity than "norms," but each refers to the creation and existence of rights and obligations.
- These rules or norms are considered legally binding. States comply with international law because they feel legally obligated to do so, not just because they want to or are merely morally obligated to do so.
- The rules, generally, apply specifically to countries—sovereign, independent States.

These tenets of international law are particularly germane with respect to the specific body of international law regarding the law of the sea. The development of the law of the sea is inseparably intertwined with the development of international law. It is not at all surprising that the law of the sea enjoys such a prominent place in the deliberations of nations. Efforts to effect order for users of the 70 percent of the earth covered by water represent some of the earliest activities of the international community and grew up in parallel with the first truly international relations coincident with the emergence of independent States.

In the second century, the Roman jurist Marcianus advanced the proposition that the sea was common to all as a part of the natural law, and this position was codified in Roman law. While the Roman Empire accepted the legal status of the sea as common property for all, nonetheless it declared in the "Theory of Glassators" that it exercised effective control over the Mediterranean Sea. The principle of common use of the sea and its products was not formal international law—because there were no States in the Mediterranean basin independent of the Roman Empire—but rather basic public policy of the Roman State. Because the Mediterranean was a "Roman lake," completely controlled by the Roman Navy, there was no need to assert explicit dominion. Nor was there any need to restrict access to living resources, for the problems of overfishing and depletion of sea resources had not yet emerged. In the final analysis, this exercise of Roman jurisdiction over the adjacent sea was made for two limited purposes: to extend Rome's power onto the sea and to suppress piracy.[3]

With the collapse of the Roman Empire, and the ensuing fragmentation of Western Europe into basically insecure small States, conflicting claims for supremacy over various parts of the seas emerged as States attempted to obtain exclusive control over trade routes and rich fishing grounds.[4] Thus, the continuing tension between coastal State jurisdictional claims and the contradictory claims to "freedom of the seas" is of venerable origin.

The attempted extension of State sovereignty from land to sea was continued as an accepted practice during the Middle Ages as commerce and trade began to develop in the Mediterranean. Early rules were drawn partly from the canons of Roman law, which underwent a revival in Western Europe beginning in the late eleventh century, and partly from State practice, which gave rise to customary rules concerning such things as the exchange of legations and the conduct of war. By the twelfth and thirteenth centuries, the Italian city-states, particularly Venice and Genoa, competed with each other for domination over the Mediterranean and Adriatic waters that provided the connecting link with trade routes to the Far East.

The trend of States to attempt to exercise sovereignty over the oceans also took place beyond the Mediterranean. The Scandinavian countries imposed their control over adjacent waters: Denmark over the Baltic, Norway over the sea routes to Iceland and Greenland, and Sweden over the Gulf of Bothnia. The English claimed the channel between England and France and parts of the North Sea. The exploits of Prince Henry the Navigator in the fifteenth century enabled Portugal to explore the coast of West Africa and significantly, through a Papal Bull, Pope Nicholas V granted Portugal the "exclusive and permanent rights" to that part of Africa.[5]

The historical trend of attempting to place ocean areas under State control culminated in 1494 in the Treaty of Tordesillas, later approved by Pope Alexander VI, in which Spain and Portugal agreed to a division of the world's oceans between themselves, the former claiming exclusive navigation rights in the western part of the Mediterranean, the Gulf of Mexico, and the Pacific, and the latter claiming such rights in the Atlantic south of Morocco and in the Indian Ocean. The demarcation line between the possessions of Spain and those of

Portugal was 370 leagues west of the Cape Verde Islands and ran from the North Pole to the South Pole. Understandably, the major opponents of this move were the two most important maritime rivals of Spain and Portugal, Britain and Holland.[6]

The Treaty of Tordesillas was a landmark event in that it was a formal treaty drawn up by two powerful European maritime powers for the specific purpose of dividing the ownership of the oceans and the land possessions lying beyond into exclusive jurisdictions. The treaty granted to Spain and Portugal exclusive navigational rights and trade privileges covering an enormous span of ocean space. Each nation was to enjoy navigational rights in the other's jurisdiction, but other States did not enjoy these rights. The Papal Bull was a powerful document and prohibited everyone else, under pain of excommunication, from traveling west of the demarcation line, "for the purpose of trade or any other reason to the islands or mainlands, found or to be found," without prior permission.[7]

The articulation of rules of international relations under Roman law and custom fell largely upon jurists who reflected the influence of the Renaissance and Reformation. For example, the Italian, Alverico Gentili, published *De Jure Belli* in 1598, which advanced the proposition that a sovereign could legitimately treat waters adjacent to his State in the same way he treated his land territory. The genesis of this concept appears to have been based on the need to prevent piracy and other acts that might threaten the security of a sovereign. In a similar fashion, but for the opposite purpose of establishing non-exclusive use of the high seas, the Dutchman, Hugo Grotius, commonly considered the father of modern international maritime law, regarded reason and natural law as the bases for his statements of the law; State practice constituted only a lesser source of law. This was a definitive break with the past, for it was Grotius who is generally acknowledged as establishing an international regime whose rules remained consistent to the principles and rules he articulated, so that the expectations of States would converge.[8] In *The International Law of the Sea*, author, D. P. O'Connell, amplifies the point made by Grotius:

The history of the law of the sea has been dominated by a central and persistent theme: the competition between the exercise of governmental authority over the sea and the idea of freedom of the seas. The tension between these has waxed and waned through the centuries, and has reflected the political, strategic, and economic circumstances of each particular age. When one or two great commercial powers have been dominant or have achieved parity of power, the emphasis in practice has lain upon the liberty of navigation and the immunity of shipping from local control; in such ages the seas have been viewed more as strategic than as economic areas of competition. When, on the other hand, great powers have been in decline or have been unable to impose their wills upon smaller States, or when an equilibrium of power has been attained between a multiplicity of States, the emphasis has lain upon the protection and preservation of maritime resources, and consequently upon the assertion of local authority over the sea.[9]

Early treatises on the law of the sea were often written in the context of particular disputes, as were tracts on other subjects of international law. For instance, Grotius's great work, *Mare Liberum*, published in 1608, was written to corroborate the claims of the Dutch East India Company to trade in the Far East, in contradiction to the monopoly on trade in the area claimed by the Portuguese, as well to dispute the claims of Spain and Portugal for exclusive rights to the seas. *Mare Liberum* upheld the doctrine of the freedom of the seas and was seen as threatening contemporary British claims to control the seas around Great Britain.[10] Grotius defended the freedom of the seas by arguing that the sea cannot be owned, that "the sea is one of those things which is not an article of merchandise, and which cannot become private property. Hence it follows, to speak strictly, that no part of the sea can be considered as territory of any people whatsoever".[11]

Grotius's assertions were met by contrary argument from such writers as William Welwood in his *Abridgment of All Sea Lawes*, published in 1613, and John Selden in his *Mare Clausum*, published in 1635.[12] While Welwood accepted Grotius's argument that the high seas were open to free use by all, he contended that the depletion of fishery stocks off the coast of Britain justified a claim of sovereign authority to exclude foreigners from coastal waters. Similarly, Selden maintained that marine resources "may through a promiscuous and common use of the sea, be diminished in any sea whatever," and therefore concluded that any such sea is susceptible to national appropriation. These literary exchanges helped to highlight and clarify understanding of the issues involved in the law of the sea and to refine the concepts upon which it was based.[13]

In the ensuing centuries, exclusive coastal State claims began to recede in the face of emerging Dutch, English, French, and other colonial power interests in free and unencumbered trade and commerce the world over. Eventually, only a relatively narrow band of waters, nominally within cannon shot of a coast (three nautical miles), the so-called territorial sea, was generally recognized as subject to coastal State sovereignty. In his work *De Dominio Maris*, published in 1702, the Dutch publicist Cornelis van Bynkershoek provided a rationale for that limit:

Wherefore on the whole it seems a better rule that the control of the land over the sea extend as far as cannon will carry, for that is as far as we seem to have both command and possession. I should have to say in general terms that the control from the land ends where the power of man's weapons ends.[14]

Remarkably, this concept of the territorial sea being three miles in width endured until the middle of the twentieth century.

During the eighteenth century, the natural-law traditions of an earlier age began to be displaced by political theories based upon the notion of consensus government such as Rousseau's "social contract." In the realm of international law, this change was reflected in the opinion that the voluntary assumption of obligations by States, as evidenced by their practice and contained in the rules of customary and treaty law, was of greater importance than natural law. This trend continued and gained strength during the early eighteenth century and was reinforced by both the American and French Revolutions. Modern international law in general, and the law of the sea specifically, have developed through a continuing process of modification and refinement from those early foundations.

Thus, through the end of the nineteenth century, the "twin pillars" of the freedom of the seas and the coastal jurisdiction over a narrow band of territorial waters became well established in State practice. While the ocean regime was viewed primarily by maritime States as an open ocean system, the prevailing concern of coastal States was in seeking means to expand their control of ocean spaces and to resolve problems that arose from disputes over extension of maritime boundaries from the coast. By the end of the nineteenth century, the stage was set for the development of the law of the sea as we know it today.

THE SOURCES OF INTERNATIONAL LAW

The sources of the modern law of the sea have paralleled developments in general international law. Since the turn of the century, international law has been seen as the product of the voluntary subscription of States to rules of law, rather than as principles of natural law binding upon States regardless of their will. As Professor Robertson has remarked: "[Because] the subjects of international law are States, which are sovereign, independent, and equal, it is obvious that the law's ultimate source (practically as well as philosophically) must be the consent of the States to be governed by it."[15] This foundation in consent of nations is reflected in the Statute of the International Court of Justice, which sets forth two primary sources and three secondary sources of international law to which the Court should refer to determine the law. Explicit consent is found in the treaties to which a State is a party. Implicit or tacit consent is reflected in customary practices so regular and widespread as to have become, in effect, legally binding.[16] The secondary sources of law are the general principles of law recognized by civilized nations, judicial decisions, and the teachings of highly qualified international lawyers.[17]

International agreements between States establish rights and obligations expressly recognized by those States. Formal international agreements are the clearest expression of legal undertakings made by States.[18] Thus, the existence of a treaty relating to any particular matter will usually provide the clearest statement of the rights of the States party to it in their relations with each other. Treaties are binding only upon the States party to them; their relations to nonparty States continuing to be regulated by customary law. The provisions of treaties, however, may become binding upon other States if they achieve acceptance as expressions of customary law.

Before they enter into force, treaties often require, in addition to signatures, both ratification by the parties and, in the case of multilateral treaties, ratification by a prescribed minimum number of States. International conventions relating to the law of the sea of the late nineteenth century will be discussed in the next chapter.

The second source of international law and of the modern law of the sea is customary international law. The Intentional Court's Statute refers to "international custom, as evidence of a general practice accepted as law," as a source of international law. Orthodox legal theory requires proof of two elements in order to establish the existence of a rule of customary international law. The first element is a general and consistent practice adopted by States. The practice need not be universally adopted, and in assessing its generality, special weight will be given to the practice of States most directly concerned—for example the practice of coastal States in the case of claims to maritime zones or of the major shipping States in claims to jurisdiction over merchant ships. The second element is evidence of the conviction by States that the practice is one that is followed out of the same legal obligation.[19]

The combination of these two elements in the formation of customary law can be seen, for instance, in the emergence of the "continental shelf" as a legal concept. In 1945 President Truman claimed for the United States ownership of the resources of the seabed adjacent to the American coast, and this was followed by similar claims by many other States. These claims, coupled with the belief that they were permissible in international law, provided the basis of a customary rule, recognizing coastal States' ownership of continental shelf resources, which emerged in the late 1950s.[20]

In principle, customary international law is binding upon all States. The essential role of consent in the development of customary law has two important consequences. First, if a State persistently objects to an emerging rule of customary law, that State will not be bound by that rule. Such objections, however, must be persistent; States will not be permitted to acquiesce in rules of law and later claim not to be bound. This point arose in the Anglo-Norwegian Fisheries Case in 1951; in that case, before the International Court, the United Kingdom sought to demonstrate that State practice had established a customary rule imposing a ten-mile limit on lines drawn across the mouth of bays to serve as the baselines from which the territorial sea is measured. In denying this claim, the court found that the United Kingdom had failed to prove sufficient generality in the practice of adopting a ten-mile limit to establish it as a rule of customary law. Moreover, the United Kingdom was specifically precluded from enforcing any such limit against Norway because Norway had consistently opposed any attempt to apply this rule to the Norwegian coast. Second, because consent is the basis of obligation in customary law, it is not necessary to view the general practice of States in order to create a presumption that an individual State has consented to some rule; a state is bound if it has in fact so consented, even if the majority of States have not adopted that rule.[21]

Customary international law, particularly as it applies to the law of the sea, is not a monolithic body of general rules uniformly binding upon all States alike, but rather, the existence of customary law obligations between particular States is ultimately a question of the extent to which other States either acquiesce in or object to a claim. Thus, customary law may develop by shifts in the pattern of State practice. For instance, at a time when most States claimed only three- or twelve-mile fishery zones, but a few Latin American States claimed 200-mile zones that included fishery rights, it could be said that the "general" rule was that international law admitted fishery jurisdiction only up to three or twelve miles from shore, and that, as an exception, 200-mile claims may have been assertable against the Latin American States alone. As more and more States have claimed 200-mile zones of resource jurisdiction, the balance has shifted, so that the "general" rule now admits the legality of such claims, even though they may not be applicable to any States that have persistently objected to such claims.[22]

A third source of international law and the modern law of the sea comes under the category of general principles of international law. Although this category is not used extensively in law of the sea analysis, it does have relevance in the modern maritime law. Such rules as the freedom of the high seas and the exclusiveness of jurisdiction over ships on the high seas by the State whose flag is flown by that ship are sometimes described as general principles of law, in the sense that in the absence of clear proof of, for example, a treaty obligation by the flag State to permit exercise jurisdiction by others over its ships on the high seas, no such right will exist. Therefore, any doubt over the existence of the nonflag State's jurisdiction would be settled in favor of the exclusiveness of the flag State's jurisdiction by referring to the general principle. Thus the general principle functions as a legal presumption for the resolution of doubtful claims.[23]

A final "source" of international law and the modern law of the sea is the combination of judicial decisions and the writings of publicists. These sources are a subsidiary means for the determination of rules of law. They cannot create law; only States can do that, through the formation of treaties and customary rules and general principles of law. However, judicial decisions and writings aid in the identification of rules created by States and often contain valuable collections and analyses of State practice and treaty law. In the realm of the modern law of the sea, the work of writers such as C. J. Columbus, M. S. McDougal, W. T. Burke, and Gilbert Gidel are illustrative. The latter's monumental work *Le Droit International Public de la Mer*, published in 1934, remains of great value today in understanding the genesis of the modern law of the sea; this work presented some of the strongest arguments for international regulation of the high seas.[24]

This centuries-long intertwining of international law and its constituent law of the sea provide the international community a flexible set of principles by which to continue development of a comprehensive maritime regime. History has demonstrated a compelling need to make these rules generally accepted international law. The continuum leading ultimately to the 1982 United Nations Convention on the Law of the Sea was noted by Philip Allott in the *American*

Journal of International Law in 1990:

The U.N. Convention on the Law of the Sea of 1982 is the product of a total international social process extending back, philosophically and historically, to the sixteenth century and far beyond....In the history of international diplomacy, there has been nothing to equal the 1982 Convention in scope, sophistication and universality.[25]

Contemporary efforts of the community of nations to develop and apply the rule of law for the world's oceans, and the role of the United States in these extensive deliberations, will be examined in the next chapter.

NOTES

1.   Horace B. Robertson, "Contemporary International Law: Relevant to Today's World?" *Naval War College Review* 45 (Summer 1992): 89.

2.   Ibid. Rear Admiral Robertson's article provides an excellent, succinct look at the nature, origins, trends, and sources of international law.

3.   Thomas Clingan, *The Law of the Sea: Ocean Law and Policy* (San Francisco: Austin and Winfield, 1994), 11.

4.   Ibid.

5.   James Wang, *Handbook on Ocean Politics and Law* (Westport, Connecticut: Greenwood Press, 1992), 41-42.

6.   R. R. Churchill and A. V. Lowe, *The Law of the Sea* (Manchester, U.K.: Manchester University Press, 1983), 22.   See Mark Zacher and James McConnell, "Down to the Sea with Stakes: The Evolving Law of the Sea and the Future of the Deep Seabed Regime," *Ocean Development and International Law* 21 (1990): 76. For additional background, see Hugo Grotius, *Mare Liberum: The Freedom of the Seas or The Right Which Belongs to the Dutch to Take Part in the East Indian Trade*, 1608, trans. Ralph Magoffin and J. B. Scott, ed. (New York: Oxford University Press, 1916), vii. The text of the Treaty of Tordesillas, as well as other key documents in the law-of-the-sea development process, are reprinted in John Norton Moore, ed., *International and United States Documents on Oceans Law and Policy* vol. 1. (Buffalo, New York: William Hein and Company, 1986).

7.   Clingan, *Ocean Law and Policy*, 11. The author notes that the language of the treaty strongly implied that the two sovereigns owned the seas within their respective spheres; however, because Spanish ships had to cross Portuguese waters to reach the Americas, the Spaniards had the limited permission: "to sail...freely, securely, and peacefully, over the said seas of the said King of Portugal, and within the said line....They shall take their courses direct to the desired region...and shall not leave their course, unless compelled to do so by contrary weather." These phrases are remarkably similar to those now used to define innocent passage in the territorial sea.

8.   Robert Friedheim, *Negotiating the New Ocean Regime* (Columbia, South Carolina: University of South Carolina Press, 1993). See also Churchill and

Lowe, *Law of the Sea*, 5.   The authors note that earlier publicists, such as Victoria (1480-1546), Suarez (1548-1617), and Gentilis (1552-1608), wrote on similar subjects, but none had the lasting impact of Grotius. Friedheim notes that the ocean regime credited to Grotius lasted for almost four centuries. See also Burdick Brittin, *International Law for Seagoing Officers*, 5th ed. (Annapolis, Maryland: Naval Institute Press, 1986) and Grotius, *Mare Liberum*. Although he emphasized the importance of the rule of law, Grotius recognized the fact that the law is not the only determinant of the way in which the seas were used, noting that: "There are times when maritime powers want freedom of navigation, and there are times when coastal States wish to claim exclusive ownership over parts or the whole of the oceans. The legal outcome depends upon who dominates whom."

9.   D. P. O'Connell, *The International Law of the Sea*, vol. 1 (Oxford, U.K.: Clarendon Press, 1987), 1.

10.   Grotius, *Mare Liberum*, 24. See also, Edward Dumbauld, *The Life and Legal Writings of Hugo Grotius* (Norman, Oklahoma: University of Oklahoma Press, 1969); Hedley Bull, Benedict Kingsbury, and Adam Roberts, eds., *Hugo Grotius and International Relations* (Oxford, U.K.: Clarendon Press, 1990); Scott Allen, "Mare Liberum," *Naval Institute Proceedings*, 109 (July 1983): 45-49; and Department of the Navy, *The Commander's Handbook on the Law of Naval Operations*, NWP-9A/FMFM 1-10 (Washington, D.C.: Naval Warfare Publications Library, 1989). Significantly, writers such as Grotius were not engaged in purely philosophic exercises. Grotius, for example, was retained by the Dutch East India Company to justify the capture by one of its ships of a Portuguese galleon in the Straits of Malacca in the year 1602. The treatise on the law of prize, of which the *Mare Liberum* is a chapter, was in the nature of a brief. Further, the first systematic treatise on the law of nations—the Law of War and Peace—was not merely a philosophical discourse, but rather the direct outgrowth of an actual case and of professional employment. A short excerpt from Grotius's eighty-page treatise provides some indication of the forcefulness of his position:

My intention is to demonstrate briefly and clearly that the Dutch—that is to say, the subjects of the United Netherlands—have the right to sail to the East Indies, as they are now doing, and to engage in trade with the people there. I shall base my argument on the following most specific and unimpeachable axiom of the Law of Nations, called a primary rule or first principle, the spirit of which is self-evident and immutable, to wit: every nation is free to travel to every other nation, and to trade with it. God Himself says this speaking through the voice of nature; and inasmuch as it is not His will to have Nature supply every place with all the necessities of life, He ordains that some nations excel in one art and others in another.

For an abbreviated text containing key excerpts of Grotius's *The Freedom of the Seas or the Right Which Belongs to the Dutch to Take Part in the East Indian Trade*, see Clingan, *Ocean Law and Policy*, 13-18.

11.   Grotius, *Mare Liberum*, 34. For further discussion, see William Aceves, "The Freedom of Navigation Program: A Study of the Relationship Between Law and Politics," *Hastings International and Comparative Law Review* 19 (1996): 261.

12.   Churchill and Lowe, *Law of the Sea*, 5.

13.   James B. Morell, *The Law of the Sea: An Historical Analysis of the 1982 Treaty and Its Rejection by the United States* (Jefferson, North Carolina: McFarland and Company, 1992), 174, referring to John Selden, *Mare Clausum: Seu De Dominio Maris Libri Duo* (London, 1635), 65. *Mare Clausum* was actually written in 1617 and 1618, but was not published until 1635. *Mare Clausum* was written specifically to refute *Mare Liberum*. In the dedication to King Charles I, Selden said:

There are among foreign writers, who rashly attribute your Majesty's more southern and eastern sea to their princes. Nor are there a few, who following chiefly some of the ancient Caesarian lawyers, endeavor to affirm, or beyond reason too easily admit, that all seas are common to the universality of mankind.

Selden made two key points: (1) "That the sea, by the law of nature or nations, is not common to all men, but capable of private dominion or property as well as the land," and (2) "That the King of Great Britain is lord of the sea flowing about, as an inseparable and perpetual appendant of the British Empire."

Selden's position was perhaps best summarized by two contemporary writers, Steven David and Peter Digeser, *The United States and the Law of the Sea Treaty* (Washington, D.C.: The Johns Hopkins University, 1990), 3. They noted: "As advocated by John Selden in *Mare Clausum*, this alternative divided the seas in much the same way that land would be divided: the jurisdiction of a state would extend across the ocean until it met the jurisdiction of another state."

United Nations negotiators who were displeased over the difficulty of gaining consensus during the UNCLOS debates would have done well to recall how far apart the camps represented by Grotius and Selden were in the early part of the seventeenth century.

14.   Brittin, *International Law for the Seagoing Officer*, 72. Brittin goes into some detail regarding the three-mile territorial sea. Many experts believe that the three-mile rule was predicated on Bynkershoek's idea. There is alternative evidence, however, that it may not have had anything to do with the range of cannon shot, but originated from the line of sight from the shoreline, which, at sea level, is approximately three miles. The two theories supported each other, perhaps by coincidence, to produce the same result: the three-mile limit. The international community accepted this limit for centuries largely because it had been found practical and acceptable. Importantly, the three-mile breadth of territorial seas was a product of the collective thinking of important maritime States; other countries either had concerns of more importance to them or had no interest in the use of the oceans. The United States, a growing maritime

power, adopted the three-mile limit on 8 November 1793, when United States' secretary of state, Thomas Jefferson, informed the British minister, Mr. Hammond, of that decision. By an act of 5 June 1794, the United States gave its unqualified support to the three-mile limit and became the first State to make the limit a part of its domestic law. For a text of Jefferson's letter, see Clingan, *Ocean Law and Policy*, 84.

15.   Robertson, "Contemporary International Law," 92.

16.   Ibid., 92-93. See also, Churchill and Lowe, *Law of the Sea*, 6, for further explanation of these sources of contemporary international law and the modern law of the sea.

17.   "Statute of the International Court of Justice," Article 38, 26 June 1945. All members of the United Nations are automatically parties to the Statute of the International Court of Justice. See Robertson, "Contemporary International Law," 103, note 5.

18.   Brittin, *International Law for the Seagoing Officer*, 13-17. According to Brittin, the words "convention" and "treaty," as well as "State," "nation," and "country," require some amplification. A convention is a pact or agreement between several States in the nature of a treaty: the term is usually applied to agreements for the regulation of matters of common interest, such as the law of the sea, international fisheries, or the protection of war victims. A treaty is an international agreement embodied in a single formal instrument made between entities that are subject to international law, possessed of international status and treaty-making capacity, intended to create rights and obligations, or to establish relationships governed by international law. In view of their similar usage, the two terms are used interchangeably. In a similar fashion, the word "State" stresses the authority of the government of a geographical entity, the word "nation" places emphasis on people and their cultural ties, common language, customs and religion, and the word "country" brings to mind territory and physical boundaries as we see them on the map. The three words have essentially synonymous meaning and are used interchangeably herein.

19.   Churchill and Lowe, *Law of the Sea*, 7. See Ian Brownlie, *Principles of Public International Law*, 3d ed. (Oxford, U.K.: Clarendon Press, 1979), 5-12.

20.   Department of the Navy, *The Commander's Handbook on the Law of Naval Operations*, AS1-1-2. See also Presidential Proclamation No. 2667, "Policy of the United States with Respect to the Natural Resources of the Subsoil and Sea-Bed of the Continental Shelf," 10 Fed. Reg. 12303 (28 September 1945); Presidential Proclamation No. 2668, "Policy of the United States with Respect to Coastal Fisheries in Certain Areas of the High Seas," 10 Fed. Reg. 12304 (28 September 1945). These proclamations, generally referred to collectively as the "Truman Proclamation," were viewed as the first important assertion of exclusive jurisdiction beyond the territorial sea.

21.   Churchill and Lowe, *Law of the Sea*, 9.

22.   Ibid., 10. This is one of the earlier cases of what would later become known as the "persistent objector" viewpoint which has now become a key tenet

of customary international law.

23.   Ibid., 11.

24.   For a discussion of these authors and their works, see Morell, *The Law of the Sea: Historical Analysis*, 175; R. P. Anand, *Origin and Development of the Law of the Sea* (Boston: Martinus Nijhoff, 1983), 233, referring to Gilbert Gidel, *Le Droit International Public de la Mer* (1934). Gidel was one of the earliest publicists who made the distinction between the essentially inexhaustible use of the high seas for navigation and the depletion of marine resources resulting from unregulated exploitation of the seas as a source of wealth.

25.   Philip Allott, "Mare Nostrum: A New International Law of the Sea," *American Journal of International Law* 86 (1990): 764-787. Allott reviews the historical and philosophical underpinnings of the law of the sea debate and evolves a contemporary, compromise position, "Mare Nostrum:"

For all these reasons, it is right to propose that a new international law of the sea be founded on a concept of the sea that is not only a profound intuition but also an evident fact....The sea is neither *mare liberum* (Grotius) nor *mare clausum* (Selden) but *mare nostrum* (our sea).

Chapter Three

THE UNITED STATES AND THE LAW OF THE SEA NEGOTIATIONS

NEGOTIATIONS PRIOR TO WORLD WAR II

For over a century, the United States has been at the forefront of international deliberations on rules regarding the use of the oceans. Beginning with various law associations in the late 1800s, continuing with the League of Nations immediately after World War I, and especially with the United Nations during the last half-century, the United States has been a leading participant in the movement toward development of an orderly regime of international law for the world's oceans.

Initial efforts to codify the rules of customary international law began in the 1870s. The International Law Association, Institute for International Law, and Harvard Law School were all involved in parallel efforts to achieve an orderly codification of maritime rules and regulations. The United States government was an active and involved participant in these deliberations. The principal output of these early efforts included resolutions on such matters as international waterways, the high seas, submarine cables, marine resources, the territorial sea and international waters and marine pollution.[1]

By the late 1800s, various conventions began to appear codifying different aspects of the use of the oceans, and principally, the transit of ships through straits used for international navigation. The first such treaty was the 1884 Paris Convention on the Protection of Submarine Cables. In 1888, the Constantinople Convention was signed by nine major powers guaranteeing free and open passage through the Suez Canal in time of peace and of war to every ship without distinction of flag. At the western end of the Mediterranean, freedom of navigation in the Strait of Gibraltar was acknowledged in the Anglo-French Declaration of 1904, which Spain later adhered to in the Franco-Spanish Treaty of 1912. A decade later, in 1923, the Treaty of Lausanne, later the Montreux Convention of 1936, established a navigation regime for the Turkish Strait of the Dardenelles. In the years between the 1884 Paris Convention and the beginning of World War II, a total of thirty-six conventions or protocols governing various aspects of the law of the sea were negotiated.[2]

The interwar years saw additional attempts at codification of the peacetime rules of the law of the sea. The League of Nations took the lead in efforts to codify general principles of peacetime maritime law. As these efforts intensified, so did the United States participation in these deliberations. These actions seemed particularly necessary because of the tension that had built up between those nations that adhered to the concept of free use of the sea and those that wanted to expand further the enclosure or division of the ocean. As both a coastal State and a growing maritime power, the United States believed that it had a great deal to contribute as an "honest broker" and was particularly active in these deliberations. Significantly, the United States facilitated the assistance of the Harvard Law School, which developed a comprehensive research program, known as the Harvard Research, on State practice; this ultimately grew into a draft document, "Basis of Discussion," for a conference called by the League of Nations.

The League's efforts to codify international law, including the law of the sea, culminated in the first conference on "the Progressive Codification of International Law," which met at the Hague in 1930. Delegates from forty-eight states met for one month. The conference was unable to agree on any treaty relating to the law of the sea, as it encountered difficulties in reaching a consensus related to two areas: (1) the breadth of the territorial seas, with twenty States supporting three miles, four Scandinavian States backing four miles, and twelve nations advocating six miles; and (2) the right of a State in a contiguous zone, extending up to twelve miles from its coast, to take measures to prevent infringement of its customs and sanitary regulations, a right that was opposed by the maritime powers of Great Britain, Japan, and the United States.[3]

The conference was successful, however, in preparing a draft on "The Legal Status of the Territorial Sea," which, even though only a draft, constituted an important document in the history of codification of the law of the sea; this draft heavily influenced the subsequent work of the First United Nations Conference on the Law of the Sea. The draft explicitly recognized the right of innocent passage of foreign merchant vessels through a coastal State's territorial sea, provided that "no acts were done prejudicial to the security, public policy, or fiscal interests of the State." With respect to warships, the draft provided: "As a general rule, a coastal State will not forbid the passage of foreign warships in its territorial sea, and will not require a previous authorization or notification. The coastal State has the right to regulate the conditions of such passage. Submarines shall navigate on the surface."[4]

In spite of the positive aspects of the Hague Codification Conference, the width of the territorial sea remained an unresolved issue. Up through the outbreak of World War II, however, most nations, including the United States, recognized a three-nautical-mile territorial sea.

POST-WORLD WAR II DEVELOPMENTS

Immediately after the end of World War II, as the League of Nations gave way to the United Nations, both coastal and maritime nations continued to seek an orderly codification of the law of the sea. In the decade immediately following the end of the war, over two dozen international agreements were concluded by multilateral negotiations in areas such as fishery conservation and management, seamen's welfare, sanitary regulations, stowaways, and oil pollution at sea.[5] The piecemeal nature of these treaties ultimately led to renewed efforts to provide for the establishment of a body charged with the progressive codification of international law. Towards this end, the United Nations General Assembly established the International Law Commission (ILC). The ILC conducted painstaking research and analysis and produced the documentation that would ultimately form the basis of the work of the first United Nations Conference on the Law of the Sea (UNCLOS I). Concurrently, the ILC recommended that an international conference be convened specifically to address the issue of the breadth of the territorial sea.[6]

Part of the impetus for UNCLOS I was directly attributable to the unilateral actions of the United States. The 1945 Truman Proclamations and subsequent legislation, such as the 1953 Submerged Lands Act and Outer Continental Shelf Lands Act, claimed U.S. sovereign rights over a large portion of the continental shelf. The two Truman Proclamations of 28 September 1945 claimed control over marine resources and coastal fisheries well beyond the seaward reach of the U.S. territorial sea. In the first Truman Proclamation, the United States declared:

Having concern for the urgency of conserving and prudently utilizing its natural resources, the Government of the United States regards the natural resources of the subsoil and the sea-bed of the continental shelf beneath the high seas, but contiguous to the coasts of the U. S., subject to its jurisdiction and control.

In the second Truman Proclamation the United States declared:

In view of the pressing need for conservation and protection of fishery resources, the Government of the United States regards it as proper to establish conservation zones in those areas of the high seas contiguous to the coasts of the United States wherein fishing activities have been or in the future may be developed and maintained on a substantial scale. Where such activities have been or shall hereafter be developed and maintained by its nationals alone, the United States regards it as proper to establish explicitly bounded conservation zones in which fishing activities shall be subject to the regulation and control of the United States.[7]

Although the Truman Proclamations explicitly preserved the status of superjacent waters as high seas, they nonetheless impelled "creeping jurisdiction" claims—attempts to garner an exclusive share of the ocean's riches—by many other nations over the resources in the water column itself. In many ways, the genie now was out of the bottle. The race was one, not just to match the United States, but to surpass it in unilateral claims. Clearly, as pointed out by James Wang, the Truman Proclamation was central in providing impetus to this "creeping jurisdiction."

The single most significant event that affected both the direction and the scope of the law of the sea in the aftermath of World War II was the Truman Proclamation of 1945, which triggered a chain reaction of unilateral claims by coastal States to enclose the oceans. Certainly, one of the motivating forces for calling a new international conference on the law of the sea was to address the mounting controversy among nations on the meaning, limits, and legal status of the continental shelf doctrine embodied in the Truman Proclamation.[8]

Some of these claims received international notoriety, the most well known of which was the Albanian claim which ultimately led to the celebrated *Corfu Channel Case* in 1949. The case was one of the most noteworthy international law cases in the years immediately following World War II, and was a direct result of the attempts at ocean closure associated with the "creeping jurisdiction" movement.

Albania attempted in 1946 to close the Corfu Channel, part of which lay within Albanian territorial seas and part of which lay within Greek territorial seas. In May 1946, two British warships were fired upon by Albanian coastal batteries while the ships were transiting the Albanian part of the strait. Subsequent diplomatic negotiations failed to resolve the matter and the United Kingdom elected to test the Albanian attitude by sending warships through the strait again. During the attempted transit, two British destroyers struck mines, which resulted in considerable damage to the vessels and loss of life. The United Kingdom subsequently invoked the compulsory jurisdiction of the International Court of Justice. After lengthy deliberations, the Court rendered a decision in 1949 in the *Corfu Channel Case*, finding Albania internationally responsible for the deaths of seamen and damage to the British warships. Albania was bound to pay due compensation to the United Kingdom for having failed to warn the British warships of the existence of the minefield in its waters.

Having resolved the British damage claim, the Court then proceeded to address the Albanian claim that the British warships in transiting the Corfu Channel violated Albanian sovereignty. The Court rejected the Albanian contention, finding instead that the strait was an international highway through which States could send their warships in peacetime without the previous authorization of the coastal State, so long as the passage was innocent. The clear import of this case was that coastal State authority over passage of warships through contiguous international straits was limited to the exclusion of noninnocent passage. An underlying premise to the Court's decision was the implicit assumption that the character of the vessel did not necessarily determine whether passage through straits was innocent. Rather, the Court put warships in the same category with merchant vessels with respect to protection of the right of access to international straits.[9]

The change in the international approach to jurisdiction of the oceans that occurred at midcentury cannot be overstated. Up to this time, the traditional pattern of jurisdiction in the ocean was one consisting largely of high seas, free for all States to use, with narrow bands of territorial waters over which coastal States exercised complete sovereignty, subject to the right of innocent passage by foreign vessels. The Truman Proclamation precipitated a desire of coastal States to claim jurisdiction over wider areas of the world ocean adjacent to their shores. This desire was a combination of the need for additional resources such as fish, oil, and minerals by many coastal States—especially newly independent and developing nations—and the existence of emerging technology to exploit these resources. Nations have claimed not only known resources for which they possess current technology to permit exploitation, but have made broad claims to potential resources that they may have the ability to exploit in the future. Thus, these claims have grown spatially extensive, functionally inclusive, and jurisdictionally exclusive, setting the stage for a natural tension between two competing interests; the "exclusive" interests of coastal States and the "inclusive" interests of user States.[10] The haphazard and conflicting nature of these claims made the need for a United Nations Conference to resolve these disputes compelling.[11]

Thus, the Truman Proclamation and subsequent legislation designed to expand State control of the contiguous seabed had a seminal role in beginning the UNCLOS process.[12] Ironically, by the beginning of the conference in 1958, the United States, now adhering to its traditional position as a maritime nation, insisted on maintaining a maximum degree of high-seas freedoms and limiting coastal state jurisdiction that adversely affected navigation and overflight. The United States sought to ensure the continuation of unimpeded transit through international straits in the face of an increased breadth of the territorial sea and treated freedom of transit of international straits as a nonnegotiable right.[13]

UNCLOS I AND II

The First United Nations Conference on the Law of the Sea (UNCLOS I), held at Geneva in 1958, was attended by delegates from eighty-six States. After two months of work, UNCLOS I produced a consensus on many issues, including four Conventions—the Convention on the Territorial Sea and the Contiguous Zone, the Convention on the High Seas, the Convention on the Continental Shelf, and the Convention on Fishing and Conservation of the Living Resources of the High Seas—but left other issues, in particular the width of the territorial sea, unresolved.[14]

The Second United Nations Conference on the Law of the Sea (UNCLOS II), convened in 1960. It was attended by delegates of eighty-eight States and sought to resolve the principal issue left over from UNCLOS I—establishing a maximum breadth for the territorial sea—and to discuss the question of fishery limits. In contrast to the previous UNCLOS I negotiations, UNCLOS II reached no conventions and did not accomplish anything noteworthy, although it did come within one vote of adopting a compromise formula providing for a six-mile territorial sea plus a six-mile fishery zone. The failure of UNCLOS I and II to achieve full international agreement on the questions of the breadth of the territorial sea and the rights of coastal States to living and nonliving resources beyond the outer limits of their territorial sea set the stage for several confrontations and ultimately necessitated renewed international efforts to resolve these problems. A series of major international incidents during the 1960s—perhaps the best known of which was the so-called "cod wars" involving Iceland, the Federal Republic of Germany, and the United Kingdom—vividly demonstrated the potentially serious nature of these international disputes. In addition, through diplomatic activities, in which the Soviet Union and the United States were principal actors, attempts to formulate a universal arrangement for the territorial sea and related matters continued with little publicity.[15]

Significantly, in the aftermath of UNCLOS I and II, the world community's interest in the oceans increased as the growing need to obtain food and energy resources from the sea and mounting concern over marine pollution began to receive increased international attention. Many States wondered whether the four Conventions adopted at UNCLOS I were up to the task of managing the oceans through the latter half of the century. In addition to the continued deterioration of fish stocks and uncertainty about jurisdiction on the seabed, evidence was mounting that the ocean environment was being degraded.[16]

The United States and the Soviet Union shared in this skepticism regarding the ability of what had already been negotiated to suffice for the rule of law in the oceans. Both superpowers were quick to recognize the need to continue to refine the law of the sea. In 1965, informal U.S. and Soviet discussions were held in Washington, D.C., for the purpose of exchanging views on whether it would be possible to resolve the question of the breadth of the territorial sea if a new U.N. Conference should be called. The discussions reaffirmed the fact that it was not possible to do so without simultaneously solving the problems of fisheries and straits. In the summer of 1967, the Soviet Union formally approached the United States and proposed reopening a number of oceans issues, most notably the twelve-mile territorial sea. Discussions between the United States, the Soviet Union, and several other countries were held during the next few years and showed general acknowledgment of the interrelationship between territorial seas, straits, and fisheries.[17]

PREPARATIONS FOR UNCLOS III

In late 1967, in response to growing concern over the possible militarization of the seabed, and amid calls for the designation of resources of the deep seabed as the common heritage of mankind, the General Assembly established the Ad Hoc Committee to Study the Peaceful Uses of the Seabed and the Ocean Floor Beyond the Limits of National Jurisdiction. It is difficult to overstate the importance of this "common heritage of mankind" concept as a galvanizing force for third world aspirations. Ironically, although the concept is generally credited to Malta's Arvid Pardo, it was President Lyndon Johnson who articulated this idea well before UNCLOS III. In a brief, but widely quoted, speech at the commissioning of the research ship *Oceanographer* in 1966, President Johnson noted:

Under no circumstances, we believe, must we ever allow the prospect of a rich harvest of mineral wealth to create a new form of colonial competition among the maritime nations. We must be careful to avoid a race to grab and hold the lands under the high seas. We must ensure that the deep seas and the ocean bottom are, and remain, the legacy of all human beings.[18]

However, Pardo's name remains most closely associated with this principle, primarily because of his delegation's clearly articulated definition of the problem and proposed solution. In August 1967, Pardo stated:

In view of the rapid progress in the development of new techniques by technologically advanced countries, it is feared that the sea-bed and the ocean floor will become progressively and competitively subject to national appropriation and use. This is likely to result in the militarization of the accessible ocean floor through the establishment of fixed military installations and in the exploitation and depletion of resources of immense potential benefit to the world, for the national advantage of technologically developed countries.

It is, therefore, considered that the time has come to declare the sea-bed and the ocean floor a common heritage of mankind and that immediate steps should be taken to draft a treaty embodying the following principles: (a) the sea-bed and the ocean floor are not subject to national appropriation in any manner whatsoever, (b) the use of the sea-bed and of the ocean floor shall be undertaken with the aim of safeguarding the interests of mankind. The net financial benefits derived from the use and exploitation of the sea-bed and of the ocean floor shall be used primarily to promote the development of poor countries and (c) the sea-bed and the ocean floor shall be reserved exclusively for peaceful purposes in perpetuity.

An international agency should be established: (a) to assume jurisdiction, as a trustee for all countries, over the sea-bed and the ocean floor, (b) to regulate, supervise and control all activities thereon, and (c) to ensure that the activities undertaken are consistent with the principles and provisions of the proposed treaty.[19]

After reviewing the ad hoc committee's initial report, the General Assembly established the Committee on the Peaceful Uses of the Seabed and the Ocean

Floor Beyond the Limits of National Jurisdiction. This committee, under the chairmanship of Ambassador Hamilton Amerasinghe of Sri Lanka, was charged to begin work on a statement of legal principles to govern the uses of the seabed and its resources. Concurrently, the Seabed Arms Control Treaty, negotiated in 1969, permanently prohibited nuclear weapons and other weapons of mass destruction from the ocean floor. This Treaty, signed by nearly one hundred countries, served as a preliminary model for the Third United Nations Conference on the Law of the Sea.[20]

In 1970, the General Assembly unanimously adopted the committee's Declaration of Principles which stated:

The seabed and ocean floor, and the subsoil thereof, beyond the limits of national jurisdiction (hereinafter referred to as the area), as well as the resources of the area are the common heritage of mankind....

No State or person...shall claim, exercise or acquire rights with respect to the area or to its resources incompatible with the international regime to be established....

The area shall be used exclusively for peaceful purposes....

The exploration of the area and the exploitation of its resources shall be carried out for the benefit of mankind as a whole....[21]

Additionally, the General Assembly, emphasizing that the problems of ocean space are interrelated and need to be considered as a whole, proposed convening a new Conference on the Law of the Sea to prepare a single, comprehensive treaty.[22]

The issue of mining the deep seabed was of enormous importance to the many newly independent nations of Africa and Asia. To the vast majority of the developing third-world nations, the seabed was the last frontier for mankind. But these nations also were keenly aware that without the advanced undersea technology for deep seabed exploration and exploitation, or sharing of such technology, they would be deprived of any economic benefits. The concern of the developing world about the uses and ownership of the sea was in many ways motivated by the view that technology would be a panacea for their economic ills. These nations were also very much aware the combined numerical strength of the African-Asian-Latin American nations totaled more than the two-thirds voting majority needed for decision making in the United Nations proceedings.[23]

As discussions on the law of the sea continued in the U.N. forum, the United States was one of the nations that was most involved in keeping the United Nations committed to ongoing negotiations. The United States pressed hard for negotiation of a new conference. In 1970, President Richard Nixon stated that, in the absence of multilateral regulation of ocean uses, "unilateral action and international conflict are inevitable."[24] Two years later, he reiterated the urgency of the situation, noting that, "competition among nations for control of the ocean's resources, and the growing divergence of national claims, could constitute serious threats to world peace."[25] The United States' position regarding the importance of keeping negotiations moving was forcefully articulated by Ambassador Elliot Richardson, chief U.S. delegate to the Law of the Sea negotiations from 1977 to 1980. Ambassador Richardson noted that if we do not have "sea law" we will have "jungle law," but "rarely has any generation had so clear a choice between order and anarchy."[26]

UNCLOS III

Throughout the early 1970s, the international community continued to recognize that the breadth of the territorial sea was one of the most important unresolved issues. UNCLOS II had failed, by a single vote, to adopt a compromise formula providing for a six-mile territorial sea plus a six-mile fishery zone. Agreement on the breadth of the territorial sea had to await the preparation of the convention drawn up by the Third United Nations Conference on the Law of the Sea (UNCLOS III) more than half a century after the first attempt at the Hague.[27] Additionally, a new issue, seabed mining—which was tied to Pardo's now-popular concept that the resources of the seabed are the "common heritage of mankind"—became a highly visible and oftentimes emotional issue.[28] Thus, the need for a third conference crystallized, and UNCLOS III was convened in New York in December 1973. The first session of the Conference was attended by approximately 5000 delegates, representing 148 States, ten United Nations agencies, ten intergovernmental organizations, and thirty-three nongovernmental organizations.[29]

The United States entered UNCLOS III with clear-cut goals and priorities. In 1973 the paramount concern was preserving navigation and overflight freedoms against creeping jurisdiction of coastal states. The next priority was the conservation of fishery resources, which had been threatened by the destructive practices of distant water factory ships. The third priority was protection of the marine environment and control over the hydrocarbon potential in the American outer continental shelf. Deep seabed mining was not considered a compelling issue and was deemed an interest that could be sacrificed to achieve other interests.[30] This was not necessarily due to any overt act by U.S. policy makers, but primarily a result of the fact that, at that time, United States mineral and mining interests were not well represented in the interagency process.

The United States' position entering the UNCLOS III negotiations was influenced by the Report of the Stratton Commission. This widely circulated report on national maritime policy termed pollution in U.S. coastal waters "a growing national disgrace" and called for greater regulatory control of potentially harmful and conflicting ocean uses. While acknowledging a general lack of sufficient knowledge to permit hard decisions on alternative courses of action for the development of ocean resources, the commission emphasized the need for a U.S. Navy capable of carrying out its national defense missions anywhere in the oceans, at any desired depth, at any time. It called for "new international frameworks" to promote efficient development of deep-sea mineral resources, and it urged that the benefits of ocean use be shared with developing states in order to promote greater international stability.[31]

As the United Nations Conference opened, the United States and other Western nations recognized that the pressure for a twelve nautical mile territorial sea was probably overwhelming.[32] As a consequence, United States and other Western nation negotiators indicated they would be willing to accept this expanded territorial sea width if it was tied to an acceptable regime for transit passage of straits, retaining in straits used for international navigation freedoms nearly equivalent to high-seas freedoms.[33] This was particularly important to the United States since well over 100 straits important to international navigation would have been closed if the territorial sea limit were expanded to twelve miles without a concomitant acceptance of a regime of transit passage.[34] This approach received general approval within the Second Committee of UNCLOS III, which was charged with dealing with the issues of the territorial sea and contiguous zone.[35]

As UNCLOS III continued through the 1970s, world events helped to solidify and validate the initial U.S. position. The 1973 war in the Middle East was soon followed by an oil embargo. One "lesson" of the Middle East conflict was the unwillingness of NATO allies and others to provide refueling and overflight rights to the United States for a conflict they did not support. The right of transit through and over the Strait of Gibraltar, for example, was crucial to U.S. support of Israel. The Administration concluded that an internationally guaranteed right of access through international straits was indispensable to the projection of U.S. force and the protection of U.S. interests.[36] The "lesson" of the subsequent 1973 energy crisis was the need to protect transport of vital commodities by keeping the sea lanes open.[37]

This real concern with keeping sea lines of communication open in general, and maintaining guaranteed access through international straits worldwide specifically, was exacerbated by a shift in international attitudes regarding the width of the territorial sea. The previous decade witnessed a significant shift in territorial sea claims, with an increasing number of countries claiming wider territorial seas. Burdick Brittin noted the shift in claimed territorial seas in the decade between 1968 and 1978.[38] See Table 3.1. Furthermore, Brittin's 1978 analysis also counted a total of sixty-nine states claiming a 200-mile fishing or exclusive economic zone.

At mid-decade, the United States was still one of the prime movers in the UNCLOS III negotiations. Like the Nixon administration, the Ford administration felt a sense of urgency in effecting a completed negotiating process. Secretary of State Henry Kissinger noted that "the extension of legal order is a boon to humanity and a necessity," further describing the UNCLOS III negotiations as "the world's last chance to avoid unrestrained military and commercial rivalry and mounting political turmoil."[39] Like its two Republican predecessors, in 1977 the Carter administration was firmly behind the convention as a means to stabilize the order of the world's oceans.

Table 3.1
Shift in Claimed Territorial Seas

Territorial Sea Claims	1968	1978
3 Miles	31 States	20 States
4-10 Miles	16 States	9 States
12 Miles	46 States	70 States
12-200 Miles	12 States	12 States
200 Miles	15 States	15 States

In the late 1970s, however, the United States began to review its priorities at UNCLOS III and attempted to take a broader view of U.S. oceans interests. With the decrease in the size of the United States Navy and the rise in the size of the Soviet Navy, some within the United States began to view naval power in relative, rather than absolute, terms. The United States had free and unhampered access to both the Atlantic and Pacific, and, while ensuring freedom of transit of international straits was still of great importance to the United States, the straits issue was now viewed by some in the context of its impact on both the United States and its principal adversary, the Soviet Union.[40] Concurrently, other pressure groups within the United States, most notably hard mineral conglomerates, began to lobby for the United States to take a stronger position with respect to protecting deep seabed mining interests. They urged U.S. negotiators to ensure recognition of an adequate jurisdictional basis for unilateral claims in order to maximize areas of U.S. exploitation and to resist schemes for sharing technology and profits in common ventures with other nations.[41] These forces coalesced under the Reagan administration in early 1981.[42] By 1981, the majority of developing nations represented at UNCLOS III recognized superpower desires to decouple straits transit and resource related issues.[43] These developing States, loosely organized as the so-called Group of 77 (G-77), decided to work together to ensure that straits issues would remain linked to resource issues such as deep seabed mining, because that afforded the G-77 the better bargaining position. These G-77 nations were firm in their demands because they were particularly wary of the existing international legal and economic order established prior to their independence which, in their view, systematically suppressed indigenous rights and national aspirations. During the negotiations, the Group of 77 openly attacked the traditional freedom of the seas concept, a doctrine, in their view, "long perceived as no more than a code word for the protection of the naval requirements of the great powers."[44]

As the law-of-the-sea "endgame" began to take shape, clear-cut divisions solidified: the United States, the Soviet Union, and other developed States seeking maximum freedom of navigation and overflight; and the developing States, led by the G-77, seeking to extract the greatest degree of concessions from economically developed States, especially in the area of seabed mining, an area where a large number of third-world nations faced significant economic challenges.[45] One of the unique factors in these negotiations was the degree of cooperation and congruence of interests between the United States and the Soviet Union, still bitter Cold War rivals, throughout the negotiations. The links between these two nations during the UNCLOS process are examined in the next section.

SUPERPOWER RELATIONS AND THE LAW OF THE SEA

The United States and the Soviet Union were the world's principal maritime powers during the latter half of the twentieth century. Although they entered the law of the sea codification process as bitter ideological enemies, the United States and the Soviet Union often found themselves in agreement in the UNCLOS negotiations, especially as the lengthy Third Conference neared its conclusion in the late 1970s and the early 1980s. While the United States' negotiating position remained essentially unchanged until the conclusion of the UNCLOS III negotiations, it was the substantial swing in Soviet policy that finally brought the two great powers together on the major law of the sea issues.

A study of the Soviet Union's approach to the law of the sea negotiations provides an illustrative analysis regarding the interaction between maritime capabilities, interests, and attitudes towards the law of the sea. Unlike the case of the United States, where multiple actors influenced the foreign policy decision-making process, in the Soviet Union, law-of-the-sea policy marched virtually exclusively to a naval drummer.[46] As a minor naval power throughout most of its history, Tsarist and Soviet Russia were preoccupied with considerations of coastal defense and with the protection of economic resources in developing a regime for territorial waters. Concurrently, Tsarist and Soviet practice and legal doctrine emphasized freedom of navigation as an essential principle underlying freedom of the seas. Because of Russia's heavy dependence upon foreign shipping to carry her seaborne commerce, it has been important from the Russian point of view that all States must be assured equal access to, and usage of, international sea lanes and that major naval powers should have minimal rights to place restraints upon, or otherwise hamper the flow of, international maritime commerce. Thus, the principle of freedom of the seas was treated in Soviet legal documents and in Soviet diplomacy as a politicolegal principle to be characterized and applied so that the rights of smaller maritime powers received maximum protection and the undue exercise of naval predominance by adversary powers would become tainted by its allegedly inherent unlawfulness.[47]

In the postwar years, the Soviet Union saw itself as especially vulnerable, and the prevailing law of the sea especially helpful, to its powerful naval adversaries. Commencing in 1948, Soviet diplomats and jurists, without exception, and in striking contrast to the legal doctrine of the prewar world, sought to create a legal basis for broad claims over coastal waters and expanded jurisdiction on the high seas.[48] Those Soviet jurists who prior to 1940 had interpreted Soviet legislation as creating contiguous zones in addition to territorial seas were criticized for their harmful and mistaken views. It was now insisted that the Soviet Union had always claimed a twelve-mile limit, supposedly fixed by Tsarist Russia in 1909. Some jurists went so far as to question the existence in international law of a "right" of innocent passage.[49] The United States watched this development with alarm, viewing the Soviet Bloc insistence on a twelve-mile or greater territorial sea as threatening the security of the United States by reducing the mobility of naval and air forces. The Soviet positions entering the UNCLOS I negotiations were a substantive departure from customary international law and from previous Soviet attitudes, all reflected in an obsession with encirclement and national security. Thus, the Soviet Union sought increased coastal state control as what W. E. Butler has described a "sand-in-the-gearbox" technique to restrict Western maritime mobility. The strenuous efforts of the Soviet delegation to UNCLOS I to incorporate their ideas into the four Conventions adopted by the 1958 conference were unsuccessful.[50]

The major change in the Soviet Union's position during the UNCLOS negotiating process occurred between UNCLOS I and UNCLOS III and is directly linked to the substantial changes in the Soviet Navy between 1958 and 1973. This period saw the Soviet Navy transition from a reactive coastal fleet designed to counter U.S. nuclear-armed aircraft carriers to a proactive, expansionist, blue-water navy. Although large in numbers, the Soviet fleet of the 1950s was optimized for defense of the Soviet homeland. It was still assigned a primary role of coastal defense consistent with its mission and capabilities and was treated largely as an adjunct to land-based forces.[51] The large numbers of submarines, short-range cruisers and destroyers, as well as Badger, Bear and Bison aircraft, with their antiship cruise missiles, were primarily designed to thwart attempts by U.S. carriers to launch attacks on the Soviet Union.

By the 1970s, however, the emphasis had shifted. Large "antisubmarine cruisers" like the *Kiev* were operating, and a full-size aircraft carrier was on the drawing board. The Soviets began to build a U.S.-type navy capable of projecting power at some distance from their shores, thereby supporting a foreign policy designed to take advantage of new political opportunities in the international arena offered by the breaking away of newly independent States from their former colonial masters as well as new economic opportunities offered by the rapidly growing Soviet merchant, fishing, and research fleets. This vigorous maritime expansion is consistent with the Soviet Union's position in the early 1970s as an ascendant world power. This ascendancy was highlighted by Anthony Allison who points out that: "By the early 1970s the Soviet Union possessed one of the two most powerful navies, the largest (in gross tonnage) fishing fleet, one of the ten largest (in deadweight tonnage) merchant marines, and the largest (in gross tonnage and number of vessels) research fleet in the world."[52]

Political and national security concerns that encouraged the growth of the Soviet Navy caused the transition from the protective, security-oriented maritime jurisprudence of the immediate postwar era to a greater interest in freedom of navigation on the high seas. Soviet jurists revised their previous view that a State may fix the limits of its territorial waters in accordance with its historical, economic, or security interests by stipulating a maximum breadth of twelve miles. The right of passage for vessels was reaffirmed in law and practice. The closed-sea doctrine was diluted to a less-restrictive notion, and the list of Soviet historic waters was significantly abbreviated. In the UNCLOS III negotiations, Soviet diplomats insisted upon adequate guarantees for observance of the freedoms of the seas.[53]

The Soviet Union's position on navigational rights through international straits changed dramatically during the first half of the 1960s, but then remained relatively consistent from the beginning of the seabed debate in 1967. Significantly, in 1960, the Soviets were advocating the widest limit for the breadth of the territorial sea that could command widespread support. By 1966, however, the Soviet Union was advocating agreement on the narrowest limit for the breadth of the territorial sea that could command widespread support.[54] The Soviet Union now wanted a maximum limit of twelve miles for the territorial sea and guaranteed transit passage through straits used for international navigation. These desires were articulated in proposed draft articles submitted in 1972. Soviet delegate Khlestov described the surface navigational regime of innocent passage, which required submarines to steam on the surface and denied aircraft the right of overflight, as "totally inadequate" for international straits. In a particularly strongly worded statement, delegate Khlestov noted:

It was hardly possible to claim that a regime of innocent passage would suffice for international straits. Experience in recent years has shown that the regime was sometimes interpreted in different ways. It might result in attempts by States to regulate the passage of ships unilaterally and to obstruct freedom of navigation. In practice, control of these straits would be in the hands of a small group of States, which would be prejudicial not only to international navigation but to the entire international community.[55]

Recognizing that restrictions on navigation of any kind could limit the mobility of Soviet submarines and also impair the ability of the Soviet surface fleet to maneuver close to foreign shores to support friends or to deter enemies, the Soviet Union appended an additional clause to its basic "Draft Articles on Straits Used for International Navigation" which sought to guarantee unhampered transit through international straits.[56] This represented a significant departure from the rules of innocent passage because the determination of wrongdoing would lie with the flag, not the coastal State, and the coastal State would have no power under any circumstances to prevent or delay passage.

The Soviet Union worked diligently to make their draft articles on straits used for international navigation as palatable as possible to other nations, particularly straits States. In their second draft article, they articulated a number of duties for ships in transit such as observance of rules of the prevention of collisions, observance of pollution precautions, and restrictions on naval exercises of virtually any kind, particularly the launching of naval aircraft, a clear attempt to restrict U.S. aircraft-carrier flexibility. In addition, by crafting the draft articles in such a way as to make no distinction between straits overlapped by territorial seas, and thereby already governed by the regime of innocent passage, and those with high seas corridors within them, the Soviet Union sought to improve upon its position with respect to both the Danish and Turkish straits.[57]

The Soviet Union agreed to accept a 200-mile economic zone but noted that this was strictly contingent upon the preservation of high seas freedoms in the zone for nonresource use. Delegate Kolosovsky clearly articulated the Soviet Union's stance on decoupling resource and nonresource use of the oceans: "The delegation wishes to point out that the granting of sovereign rights in the economic zone was not equivalent to the granting of territorial sovereignty and must in no way interfere with the other lawful activities of States on the high seas, especially with international navigation."[58]

The caveats that the Soviet Union attached to accepting a 200-mile economic zone in exchange for transit rights must be seen as an example of the priority of naval interests over fishing interests and is indicative of the actual and perceived naval strength of the Soviet Union. The Soviet Union clearly linked foreign and defense policies in the statements made by the father of the modern Soviet Navy, Admiral of the Fleet, S. G. Gorshkov. Admiral Gorshkov frequently and forcefully articulated the Soviet Union's insistence on a regime of unhampered use of international straits.[59]

The basic political, ideological, and military orientation of the United States and the Soviet Union had been one of mutual rivalry since the end of World War II. This was never forgotten during the UNCLOS negotiations. The question was never whether cooperation in the law of the sea negotiations would overcome this basic rivalry, but whether the two governments could work together in pursuit of common interests despite that rivalry and narrow the extent to which it made all cooperative endeavor difficult.[60] Thus, while the Soviet Union entered the UNCLOS process with a negotiating philosophy primarily designed to impede the United States, and particularly the United States Navy, from using the high-seas to pursue policies seen as inimical to the interests of the Soviet Union, its position changed substantially as it found mutual interests with the United States in the law of the sea.

As the UNCLOS process evolved and the Soviet Union built a superpower navy, it changed its position to focus on the predominance of high seas freedoms and absolute guarantees regarding transit of international straits, a position closely paralleling that of the United States.[61] As major powers in a world of almost 200 States, the two governments clearly shared some similar perspectives.

Each was concerned with the potential problems of challenges to its interests by unilateral actions of smaller coastal States and by the organized influence of the G-77 or other developing countries—occasionally described as the "tyranny of the weak." The essence of cooperation between the two superpowers was freedom of the seas, the same type of accommodation that had been reached centuries earlier by other maritime powers: no maritime power would seek to tie up the peacetime mobility of another, and none would force another to pay for its navigation rights with either carrots or sticks.[62]

As the UNCLOS process entered its endgame, the Soviet Union continued to press vigorously for unhampered use of the seas while the United States began to consider naval mobility in relative rather than absolute terms. Some interests within the United States, principally free-market advocates and those concerned with mining and mineral access rights, began to question the viability of the UNCLOS process itself as a vehicle for protecting and preserving U.S. interests in the oceans. Ultimately, the Soviet Union found the treaty to be one it could live with, although the United States developed serious reservations regarding the convention.[63] The United States would soon find that its position was open to greater criticism than that of the Soviet Union. In the end, though, as the world's two leading maritime powers, the United States and the Soviet Union shared a deep concern over the continuing creep of coastal-state jurisdiction, with concomitant restrictions on freedom of the seas. With their joint support, the Third United Nations Convention on the Law of the Sea convened in 1973.[64]

NOTES

1.   R. R. Churchill and A. V. Lowe, *The Law of the Sea* (Manchester, U.K.: Manchester University Press, 1983), 17. Churchill and Lowe trace significant attempts at codification of the law of the sea back at least a century and demonstrate that the United States has been an active participant for most of that period.

2.   James Wang, *Handbook on Ocean Politics and Law* (New York: Greenwood Press, 1992), 483. Wang provides a comprehensive, chronological listing of protocols and treaties on the law of the sea, listing a total of 162 multilateral conventions and protocols beginning with the Paris Convention in 1884. See also Giuilo Pontecorvo, ed., *The New Order of the Oceans: The Advent of a Managed Environment* (New York: Columbia University Press, 1986).

3.   Panel on the Law of Ocean Uses, "U.S. Interests and the United Nations Convention on the Law of the Sea," *Ocean Development and International Law* 21 (1990): 385. The Panel on the Law of Ocean Uses was created by the Council on Ocean Law in 1983. All its members were ocean experts, with many of them having served as members of the U.S. delegation to the Law of the Sea negotiations. The panel was brought together to advise the council and the public on issues relating to UNCLOS. Professor Louis Henkin was chosen

chairman, thus the panel is frequently referred to as the "Henkin Panel." From 1983 to 1988 the panel published many reports in support of UNCLOS III and United States participation. See also Wang, *Handbook on Ocean Law and Politics*, 23–24. Wang points out that of the forty-eight States attending the conference, thirty-seven elected not to vote on any proposals, a remarkable lack of consensus in view of the good intentions and idealism that was associated with the conference. See also Clyde Sanger, *Ordering the Oceans: The Making of the Law of the Sea* (Toronto: University of Toronto Press, 1987), 13-14. Sanger makes the point that what the Hague Conference did not accomplish was, in some ways, more important than what it did accomplish:

The Codification Conference was useful in other ways....By failing to agree on a single limit for all purposes, it repudiated the argument of the British delegate that the three mile limit was the rule of international law because the maritime powers which owned most of the world's shipping had so decided. The conference's most important act may have been to disregard this imperial assertion.

4.   See Richard Grunawalt, "United States Policy on International Straits," *Ocean Development and International Law*, 18 (1987): 448. In this article, Professor Grunawalt, a retired Navy Judge Advocate General Corps Captain and director of the Oceans Law and Policy Department in the Center for Naval Warfare Studies at the Naval War College, traces the U.S. position on straits used for international navigation throughout the law-of-the-sea process.

5.   See Wang, *Handbook on Ocean Politics and Law*, 487–489.

6.   Churchill and Lowe, *Law of the Sea*, 14. The authors outline the efforts of the ILC in preparing draft articles that ultimately formed the basis for the first United Nations Conference of the Law of the Sea. They also develop substantially the entire UNCLOS negotiating process. See also Burdick Brittin, *International Law for Seagoing Officers*, 5th ed. (Annapolis: Naval Institute Press, 1986), 75-78. The ILC, providing a critical service in framing the issues for UNCLOS I and II, identified the following:

1. The Commission recognizes that international practice is not uniform as regards the delimitation of the territorial sea.
2. The Commission considers that international law does not permit an extension of the territorial sea beyond twelve miles.
3. The Commission, without taking any decision as to the breadth of the territorial sea up to that limit, notes on the one hand, that many States have fixed a breadth greater than three miles and, on the other hand, that many States do not recognize such a breadth when that of their own territorial sea is less.
4. The Commission considers that the breadth of the territorial sea should be fixed by an international conference.

See also Wang, *Handbook on Ocean Politics and Law*, 21-22. The author notes that between the end of World War II and the convening of UNCLOS I in 1958 the three key international concerns in the area of the law of the sea included regional fishery organization, seaman's welfare, and shipping concerns.

7.   See Chapter 2, note 20. The 1945 Truman Proclamations and the 1953 Submerged Lands Act and Outer Continental Shelf Lands Act were critically important milestones in the development of the law of the sea.

8.   Wang, *Handbook on Ocean Politics and Law*, 25–26.

9.   For further discussion of the Corfu Channel case, see Thomas Clingan, *The Law of the Sea: Ocean Law and Policy* (San Francisco: Austin and Winfield, 1994), 110-111. See also Department of the Navy, *The Commander's Handbook on the Law of Naval Operations* NWP-9A/FMFM 1-10 (Washington, D.C.: Naval Warfare Publications Library, 1989),   AS 1-1-3. This publication has been revised and reissued as Department of the Navy, *The Commander's Handbook on the Law of Naval Operations*, NWP 1-14M/MCWP 5-2.1 (Washington, D.C.: Naval Warfare Publications Library, 1995).

10.   See Dalchoong Kim and Jin-Hyun Paik, "The Relation Between User States and Coastal States with Respect to International Navigation" in *The Law of the Sea in the 1990s: A Framework for Further International Cooperation*, Tadao Kuribayashi and Edward Miles, eds. (Honolulu: Law of the Sea Institute Press, 1992), 51. This volume is a recapitulation of the *Proceedings of the Law of the Sea Institute Twenty-fourth Annual Conference*, co-sponsored by the Ocean Association of Japan, held in Tokyo in July 1990.

11.   A. L. Hollick, *U.S. Foreign Policy and the Law of the Sea*, (Princeton: Princeton University Press, 1981), 13. The Truman Proclamation represented the culmination of a policy process begun by individuals such as President Franklin Delano Roosevelt, Secretary of the Interior Harold Ickes and others who wanted to protect United States interests in a postwar world.

12.   See Churchill and Lowe, *Law of the Sea*, 3, 7.

13.   R. E. Osgood and A. L. Hollick, *Toward a National Ocean Policy, 1976 and Beyond* (Washington, D.C.: The Johns Hopkins Press, 1977), 46. Robert Osgood believed that the United States put itself in a poor position at the negotiations and noted that: "The United States was locked into an excessively rigid position on free transit of straits that may have jeopardized the achievement of minimal ocean order that is essential to broader U.S. interests."

14.   Churchill and Lowe, *The Law of the Sea*, 14. UNCLOS I adopted four conventions: the Convention on the Territorial Sea and the Contiguous Zone, reprinted in *United Nations Treaty Series*, vol. 516, no. 7477; the Convention on the High Seas, reprinted in *United Nations Treaty Series*, vol. 450, no. 6465; the Convention on the Continental Shelf, reprinted in *United Nations Treaty Series*, vol. 499, no. 7302; and the Convention on Fishing and Conservation of the Living Resources of the High Seas, reprinted in *United Nations Treaty Series*, vol. 559, no. 8164. See also James B. Morell, *The Law of the Sea: An Historical Analysis of the 1982 Treaty and Its Rejection by the United States* (Jefferson, North Carolina: McFarland and Company, 1992), 6–8, for a fuller presentation of the details of each Convention. Morell notes that the Convention on the

Continental Shelf constituted international affirmation of the Truman Proclamation, as formulated in the draft articles of the International Law Commission. Additionally, the Convention on the High Seas expressly identified four protected "freedoms of the seas" of particular importance to the United States—navigation, overflight, laying of submarine cables and pipelines, and fishing—as well as "other freedoms recognized by the general principles of international law."

15.   Myron H. Nordquist, Satya Nandan, and Shabtai Rosenne, eds., *United Nations Convention on the Law of the Sea 1982: A Commentary*, vol. 2 (Boston: Martinus Nijhoff, 1993), 2. The "Cod War" led to major international litigation in the *Fisheries Jurisdiction* cases occupying the International Court of Justice between 1972 and 1974.

16.   See Wang, *Handbook on Ocean Politics and Law*, 28.

17.   Robert Friedheim, *Negotiating the New Ocean Regime*, (Columbia, South Carolina: University of South Carolina Press, 1993), 26. See also Brittin, *International Law for Seagoing Officers*, 81, wherein John Stevenson, legal advisor to the Department of State, is quoted summarizing the problem in an address on 18 February 1970:

While no State in our view is obliged to recognize territorial seas exceeding three miles, there is nothing like uniform agreement on this figure. About 30 States claim three miles, another 15 between four and ten miles, and about 40 claim 12 miles. Approximately 11 States claim some sort of jurisdiction, but in some cases full territorial jurisdiction as far out as 200 miles. Given this state of affairs, it can readily be seen, as the President pointed out in his foreign policy message to Congress today, that it is urgent that international agreement be reached on the breadth of the territorial sea to head off the threat of escalating national claims over the ocean.

18.   See Martin Harry, "The Deep Seabed: The Common Heritage of Mankind or Arena for Unilateral Exploitation?" *Naval Law Review* 40 (1992): 210. See also Morell, *Law of the Sea: Historical Analysis*, 18.

19.   See Clingan, *The Law of the Sea: Ocean Law and Policy*; and Friedheim, *Negotiating the New Ocean Regime* for extensive treatment of the Pardo, "common heritage of mankind" concept and its impact on the UNCLOS III negotiations throughout the 1960s and 1970s.

20.   See David Larson, "Foreword," *Ocean Development and International Law* 11 (1982): 2. See also *The Commander's Handbook on the Law of Naval Operations*, AS 1-1-3.

21.   See Morell, *Law of the Sea: Historical Analysis*, 32, referring to United Nations General Assembly, 25th Session, Resolution 2749, December 1970.

22.   Ibid., 33.

23.   Wang, *Handbook on Ocean Politics and Law*, 27-30.

24.   President Richard M. Nixon, "United States Policy for the Seabed," *U.S. Department of State Bulletin 62* (Washington, D.C.: USGPO, 1970).

25.   President Richard M. Nixon, "Report to the Congress: U.S. Foreign

Policy for the 1970s—A New Strategy for Peace," *Department of State Bulletin 62* (Washington, D.C.: USGPO, 1970), 273. President Nixon further stipulated that the need to reach agreement on the breadth of the territorial sea was the most pressing issue facing the law of the sea. See also Morell, *Law of the Sea: Historical Analysis*, 203. Morell traces U.S. efforts to keep negotiations on track through the Nixon, Ford, and Carter administrations.

26.   Mumba Kapumpa, "Reflections on Institutional Aspects and How to Facilitate Universal Acceptance of the Convention," in *Law of the Sea in the 1990s*, Kuribayashi and Miles, eds., 330.

27.   Churchill and Lowe, *Law of the Sea*, 15.

28.   Morell, *Law of the Sea: Historical Analysis*, 18–20, 31–32.

29.   James Malone, "Who Needs the Sea Treaty?" *Foreign Policy* 54 (1984): 48. Ambassador Malone served in a number of capacities as a Reagan administration expert on the law of the sea, first as the Special Representative for the Third United Nations Conference on the Law of the Sea (UNCLOS III), later as assistant secretary of state for Oceans, International Environmental and Scientific Affairs and, finally, as chairman of the United States Delegation to UNCLOS III. See also Morell, *Law of the Sea: Historical Analysis*, 52.

30.   Elliot Richardson, "Law of the Sea: A Reassessment of U.S. Interests," *Mediterranean Quarterly* 1 (1990): 4. See also Morell, *Law of the Sea: Historical Analysis*, 43.

31.   See Morell, *Law of the Sea: Historical Analysis*, 43, referring to Commission on Marine Science, Engineering, and Resources, *Our Nation and the Sea* (Washington, D.C.: USGPO, 1969).

32.   Churchill and Lowe, *Law of the Sea*, 61. By 1973, the twelve-mile territorial sea was clearly the dominant trend in State practice.

33.   John R. Stevenson, "International Law and the Oceans," *Department of State Bulletin 62* (Washington, D.C.: USGPO, 1970), 273. Stevenson, who was legal advisor to the State Department, articulated the administration's position in a speech before the Philadelphia World Affairs Council in February 1970. He noted, in particular, that the United States had consulted with a large number of nations regarding the desirability of fixing the breadth of the territorial sea at twelve miles. Additionally, he maintained that the treaty fixing the twelve-mile territorial sea should provide for freedom of transit through and over international straits. His speech was followed by a 25 February 1970 announcement by the State Department:

The United States supports the 12-mile limit as the most widely accepted one, but only if a treaty can be negotiated which will achieve widespread international acceptance and will provide for freedom of navigation through and over international straits. At the same time, the United States will attempt to accommodate the interests of coastal states in the fishery resources off their coasts.

Ibid., 343. See also Shigeru Oda, "Proposals Regarding a Twelve-Mile Limit for the Territorial Sea by the United States in 1970 and Japan in 1971: Implications and Consequences" in *Law of the Sea in the 1990s*, Kuribayashi and Miles, eds., 162-163. This article revisits the period of the early 1970s and emphasizes the connectivity between the expanded territorial sea and the straits passage regime:

It cannot be over-emphasized that the proposal for the twelve mile territorial sea could not have been conceivable without the adoption, together with it, of its inseparable corollary; that is, the free passage of warships or military aircraft through international straits to be included within he extended twelve mile territorial sea. The U.S. and some other major powers would not otherwise have agreed, in 1973, to hold UNCLOS III which finally led to the conclusion of the U.N. Convention on the Law of the Sea in 1982.

34.   Department of Defense, *National Security and the Convention on the Law of the Sea* (Washington, D.C: Department of Defense, 1994), 10.

35.   Myron H. Nordquist, Satya Nandan, and Shabtai Rosenne, *United Nations Convention on the Law of the Sea 1982: A Commentary*, vol. 2 (Boston: Martinus Nijhoff, 1993), 11. The Chairman of the Second Committee, Ambassador Andres Aguilar of Venezuela, noted:

The idea of a territorial sea of 12 miles and an exclusive economic zone beyond the territorial sea up to a total maximum distance of 200 miles is, at least at this time, the keystone of the compromise solution favored by the majority of the States participating in the Conference, as is apparent from the general debate in the plenary meetings and the discussions held in our Committee.

Acceptance of this idea is, of course, dependent on the satisfactory solution of other issues, especially the issue of passage through straits used for international navigation, the outermost limit of the continental shelf and the actual retention of this concept and, last but not least, the aspirations of the land-locked countries and of other countries which, for one reason or another, consider themselves geographically disadvantaged.

36.   Mark Janis, *Sea Power and the Law of the Sea* (Lexington, Massachusetts: Lexington Books, 1976), 7.

37.   Osgood and Hollick, *Toward a National Ocean Policy*, 46.

38.   Brittin, *International Law for Seagoing Officers*, 82–83. The author cites statistics generated by the United Nations Food and Agriculture Organization and the International Law Association.

39.   Morell, *Law of the Sea: Historical Analysis*, 203. Kissinger's address, before the American Bar Association, represented a powerful commitment by the administration to effect international cooperation on this issue.

40.   Janis, *Sea Power*, 7. Janis makes the point that with the exception of transit of Gibraltar and the Indonesian Straits, unhampered straits passage is not vital for the United States Navy since it has free access to both the Atlantic and Pacific, a luxury not enjoyed by the Soviet Union. See also Michael Reisman, "The Regime of Straits and National Security: An Appraisal of International Law Making," *American Journal of International Law* 74 (1980): 48-76.

41.   Churchill and Lowe, *Law of the Sea*, 156. See also Morell, *The Law of the Sea: Historical Analysis*, xiii. Although petroleum and other mineral resources have been recovered from the continental shelf, deep-sea mineral exploitation has, to date, been regarded as technologically feasible only with respect to the millions of ferromanganese nodules which were discovered more than a century ago at the bottom of the world's largest ocean basins. Clustered at depths of 400 to 3400 fathoms, these nodules vary in composition but have been found to contain as much as 40 percent manganese, 4.6 percent nickel, 4.5 percent copper, and 0.9 percent cobalt, as well as trace amounts of other metals such as zinc and molybdenum.

42.   David Larson, "The Reagan Administration and the Law of the Sea," *Ocean Development and International Law* 11 (1982): 298. The author points out that the position of the administration on the law of the sea in general, and deep seabed mining in particular, should not have been a surprise. The July 1980, Republican Party platform plank made the following commentary on the law of the sea:

Multilateral negotiations have thus far insufficiently focused attention on U.S. long-term security requirements. A pertinent example of this phenomenon is the Law of the Sea Conference, where negotiations have served to inhibit U.S. exploitation of the sea-bed for its abundant mineral resources. Too much concern has been lavished on nations unable to carry out sea-bed mining with insufficient attention paid to gaining early American access to it. A Republican Administration will conduct multilateral negotiations in a manner that reflects America's abilities and long-term interest in access to raw material and energy resources.

43.   Finn Laursen, *Superpower at Sea: U.S. Ocean Policy* (New York: Praeger Publishers, 1983), 20. Laursen captured the consensus view that the most important linkage at UNCLOS III was between navigation rights, particularly transit through international straits and deep seabed mining.

44.   Morell, *Law of the Sea: Historical Analysis*, 47. The Group of 77 was founded in 1964, in the context of the first U.N. Conference on Trade and Development (UNCTAD), as an instrument for the political mobilization and coordination of developing States—most of them former colonial territories—in international organizations. As an organ of the General Assembly, UNCTAD was convened specifically to develop ways to address the growing economic gap between developed States and the newly independent, developing States. The Group of 77 as a whole was naturally enticed by Pardo's vision of an international mechanism to redress the historical imbalances between developed and developing countries which remained following decolonization; the common heritage of mankind principle was readily adopted as an important symbol of the struggle against economic domination by the developed nations, who were often former colonial powers. See also Euripides Evriviades, "The Third World's Approach to the Deep Seabed," *Ocean Development and International Law* 11 (1982): 207. For a contradictory view, see Lewis Alexander, *The Law of the*

Sea: A New Geneva Conference (Kingston, Rhode Island: Rhode Island University Press, 1972), 91–93. Alexander quotes Leigh Ratiner, chairman of the Department of Defense Advisory Group on the Law of the Sea, as Ratiner perhaps best summed up the position of the United States: "The fact of the matter is that a desire to keep the military away from the coasts is a bogeyman. Where are the countries that are damaged by a United States or a Soviet military presence in the oceans?" Alexander, "A New Geneva Conference," 93.

45.   Wang, *Ocean Law and Politics*, 187–188. The author points out that the issue of deep seabed mining was not one solely of third-world nations attempting to register gains at the expense of the Western industrialized countries, but rather of attempts to redress what were potentially severe economic dislocations that would occur if those nations with the technology to do so mined the deep seabed at will. The chairman of the First Committee at UNCLOS III noted:

The impact of sea-bed production would be most evident in the drastic redistribution of production and production revenues which would result if compared with current patterns of production and trade. Gross revenues presently accruing to developing countries from cobalt production amount to approximately $95 million annually in terms of 1970 prices. By 1980, if there were no production from the sea-bed, this latter amount is projected to increase to $240 million at 1970 prices. In the event of sea-bed production, however, developing countries' revenues would be less, between $120-$220 million for 1980, depending on the level of sea-bed production assumed.

46.   W. E. Butler, *The Soviet Union and the Law of the Sea* (Baltimore, Maryland: The Johns Hopkins Press, 1971), 182.

47.   Butler, *The Soviet Union and the Law of the Sea*, 184. See also W. E. Butler, *The USSR, Eastern Europe and the Development of the Law of the Sea* (Dobbs Ferry, New York: Oceana Publications, 1987). Taken together, these two books, produced by the same author a decade-and-a-half apart, present a revealing look at the change in the Soviet position on the law of the sea. The latter publication catalogues then-recent Soviet statutes on the various aspects of oceans law.

48.   M. W. Janis, *The Influence of Naval Interests on the Development of the Law of the Sea* (Newport, Rhode Island: Naval War College Press, 1975), 8.

49.   Butler, *The Soviet Union and the Law of the Sea*, 199.

50.   Ibid., 200.

51.   Anthony Allison, "The Soviet Union and UNCLOS III: Pragmatism and Policy Evolution," *Ocean Development and International Law* 16 (1986): 110.

52.   Ibid., 112. Additionally, there are a plethora of publications dealing with the history, structure, doctrine, procedures and other aspects of the Soviet Navy. Among the more well known sources are R. B. Bathurst, *Understanding the Soviet Navy: A Handbook* (Newport, Rhode Island: Naval War College Press, 1979); K. R. McGruther *The Evolving Soviet Navy* (Newport, Rhode Island: Naval War College Press, 1978); Department of Defense, *Soviet Military Power 1983* (Washington, D.C.: USGPO, 1983); Department of the Navy,

Understanding Soviet Naval Developments (Washington, D.C.: USGPO, 1985). See also Admiral J. L. Holloway, "Victory and an Uncertain Future," *U.S. Naval Institute Proceedings* 121 (1995): 51-53.

53.   Butler, *The Soviet Union and the Law of the Sea*, 201.

54.   Bernard Oxman, *From Cooperation to Conflict: The Soviet Union and the United States at the Third U.N. Conference on the Law of the Sea* (Seattle: University of Washington Press, 1985), 5.

55.   Janis, "Influence of Naval Interests," 10.

56.   Ibid., 55. Illustrative of the Soviet Union's forcefulness was its position on straits in the draft articles: "No State shall be entitled to interrupt or suspend the transit of ships through straits or engage therein in any acts which interfere with the transit of ships, or require ships in transit to stop or communicate information of any kind." For a full text of this draft article, see John Norton Moore, ed., *International and United States Documents on Oceans Law and Policy*, vol. 1. (Buffalo, New York: William Hein and Company, 1986), 162–163.

57.   Butler, *The Soviet Union and the Law of the Sea*, 33.

58.   Janis, "Influence of Naval Interests," 33. For a full text of this statement, see John Norton Moore, ed., *International and United States Documents on Oceans Law and Policy*, vol. 1.

59.   S. G. Gorshkov, *The Sea Power and the State* (Annapolis, Maryland: Naval Institute Press, 1976), 53. Admiral Gorshkov strongly pressed the Soviet Union's position. Some key excerpts of his comments sum up the Soviet stance on this issue:

For straits linking individual seas and oceans and intensively used for international shipping, by virtue of historically-established norms of ordinary maritime law in such straits, there has always existed and must exist freedom of passage for ships and flight of aircraft on the basis of equality of all flags, since the States of the world are interested in normal functioning of international sea routes.

However, some countries whose shores are washed by the international straits, on the pretext of protecting their sovereignty and ensuring security, act against the freedom by seeking to bring under their control all international shipping and in some cases damage the legitimate vitally important interests of individual States.

The Soviet Union is anxious to see that in the straits used for international shipping, freedom of passage of ships and flight of aircraft of all countries is ensured, with the observance of guarantees of the security of coastal states. Unless such freedom is ensured, it is inconceivable and practically impossible to implement the generally recognized principle of freedom of the open sea promoting the normal development of mutual relations between States.

60.   Oxman, *From Cooperation to Conflict*, 3.

61.   Janis, "Influence of Naval Interests," 35. The author reemphasizes that Soviet ocean policy is a direct reflection of Soviet naval interest in all areas in which the Soviet Navy has a stake. He notes that there did not seem to be the

same sort of policy struggles among various maritime interests in the Soviet Union as in the United States. This is consistent with the nature of Soviet maritime interests and is reflected in the development of public Soviet law of the sea positions (many of which are articulated in Butler, *The USSR, Eastern Europe and the Development of the Law of the Sea*). Thus, the Soviet Navy's law of the sea preferences are consistently supported in Soviet ocean policy.

62.   Oxman, *From Cooperation to Conflict*, 8. The author concisely spells out the common objectives that lay at the heart of the U.S.-U.S.S.R. cooperation in planning and negotiating at the Conference. They were a widely accepted treaty that established the following:

- a 12-mile maximum breadth for the territorial sea
- free transit of straits used for international navigation
- freedom for navigation, overflight, and military activities beyond 12 miles
- an accommodation of coastal state interests in fisheries beyond 12 miles

63.   Butler, *The USSR, Eastern Europe and the Development of the Law of the Sea*, 1. Butler notes that the completeness of the transition of Russia and the Soviet Union from a land power with limited coastal concerns to a sea power of the first rank is illustrated by the fact that, in 1983, the Soviet Union was the largest maritime power to sign the 1982 United Nations Convention on the Law of the Sea.

64.   National Intelligence Council, *The Law of the Sea: The End Game* (Washington, D.C.: National Intelligence Council, 1996). The Russian government continues to share interests with the United States in preservation of maritime freedoms. See Captain First Rank Andrey Y. E. Druganov, "Regimentation of Naval Activity as a Way to Assure Stability and Security of the World Seas" (address at the *Tenth Annual U.S. Pacific Command International Military Operations and Law Conference*, Honolulu, April 1997). Captain Druganov serves in the office of International Legal Service, Main Russian Navy Staff. He advocated expansion of safety and confidence building measures, by way of international agreements, to ensure safety of operations when navies interact.

Chapter Four

THE LAW OF THE SEA
NEGOTIATING PROCESS
ENDGAME: TREATY REJECTION
BY THE UNITED STATES

THE THIRD UNITED NATIONS CONVENTION ON THE
LAW OF THE SEA

The Third United Nations Law of the Sea Conference (UNCLOS III) lasted throughout the 1970s, and while consensus was achieved on some issues, other issues remained contentious. As the 1980s began, the UNCLOS III process entered its "endgame" and divisions within the community of nations became clear. The United States, the Soviet Union, and the overwhelming majority of the Western industrialized nations were on one side, while the developing States, and particularly the loosely organized Group of 77 (G-77), were on the other.[1]

A major issue dividing the two sides was straits transit, specifically the transit of straits used for international navigation that threatened to be restricted by an expanding territorial sea regime. The G-77 nations recognized the desire of the West to have transit of international straits remain unencumbered and used this negotiating leverage to attempt to extract concessions from the developed maritime powers. Additionally, the issue of deep seabed mining caused polarization between the two sides. Significantly, the United States increasingly became identified as the leader of the opposition to the final draft of the Law of the Sea Convention.

Much of the change in United States' attitude coincided with the ascendancy of the Reagan administration in early 1981. The draft treaty produced at UNCLOS III appeared a bad bargain to many in the Reagan administration who claimed that the United States "was paying dear with seabeds for something cheap like navigation rights." In contrast to previous U.S. thinking, the Reagan negotiators judged their alternatives to a law of the sea treaty, in the realm of both mining and mobility, as being reasonably attractive.[2] These shifts, over time, in the perception of U.S. interests and alternatives, culminated in the 1982 decision first to vote against, and then not sign, the treaty.[3]   This extraordinary move by the United States did not result from a cavalier decision by the Reagan administration, but was impelled by the structure of the United Nations Conference in general, and in particular by the negotiating endgame that led to the final draft of the treaty.

The Third United Nations Conference on the Law of the Sea began in 1973 and conducted its business through three distinct committees, which were divided along functional lines. Committee One, led by delegate Paul Engo of Cameroon, dealt with the problem of the legal regime of the seabed beyond national jurisdiction; Committee Two, led by delegate Andres Anguilar of Venezuela, dealt with the regimes of the territorial sea and contiguous zone, the continental shelf, exclusive economic zone, the high seas, and fishing and conservation of the living resources of the high seas, as well as with specific aspects of these topics, such as the questions of straits and archipelagic states; Committee Three, led by delegate Alexander Yankov of Bulgaria, dealt with the question of the preservation of the marine environment and scientific research.[4]

At the outset of the UNCLOS III process, the participating nations were so far apart on most issues that, while voting procedures could be agreed upon, there was little likelihood of agreement on substantive measures. Consequently, and also in the interest of accommodating the broadest interest in a treaty, it was agreed to proceed by way of "consensus," looking for areas of maximum agreement without formal votes. The conference worked for the entirety of the deliberations on this basis, producing a series of negotiating texts containing draft articles on all of the topics under consideration by the conference.   This consensus approach to decision making proved unwieldy and led to the establishment of various networks of special interests.[5]

The United Nations Conference encompassed a series of seventeen sessions (consisting of eleven numbered sessions and six "resumed" sessions), meeting roughly semiannually between December 1973 and December 1982.   At the conclusion of each session, the committees published a draft negotiating text that summarized deliberations and provided a starting point for negotiations in the next session. Armed with these negotiating texts, individual States were able to determine their positions for the next session.[6]

As the conference drew to a close and the negotiating texts and draft articles began to take their final form, the Western industrialized nations, led by the United States, focused on those portions of the convention with which they did not fully agree, and pushed through a resolution that called for a vote on the final treaty, in accordance with the voting procedures established in 1974. Intense lobbying efforts continued through the early 1980s as the impending final vote drew closer. The United States' negotiators and political decision makers recognized that the completed convention could contain provisions, specifically regarding deep seabed mining, that it could not support; thus, the U.S. negotiators became the most visible and prominent lobbyist in opposition to the

Convention in its existing form.

UNITED STATES POLICY IN TRANSITION: CARTER TO REAGAN

The change in attitude regarding the viability of the Convention between the Carter and Reagan administrations reflected the confluence of many factors as the United States entered the 1980s. A primary consideration was U.S. naval strength, particularly our strength as it compared to the only other superpower navy of the day, the Soviet Navy. The United States was no longer the only "super navy." The retirement of older ships and the long lead times required to build new ones had a dramatic affect on the size of the United States Navy; this caused increasing operating tempo of existing ships to the point where resignations of naval personal had reached epidemic proportions. Additionally, due partly to the lack of deployable naval units, the trend of increasing jurisdictional assertions by sending ships and aircraft through and over waters that were nominally restricted by coastal States (the United States Freedom of Navigation Program) slowed considerably. The advent of the U.S. *Trident* ballistic missile submarine, with its increased ballistic missile range, improved the U.S. Navy's options regarding deployment patterns for these submarines and relegated submerged passage of international straits to a less compelling issue from the U.S. standpoint. Conversely, the rapid growth in the size of the Soviet Navy and its transition to a blue-water fleet caused the United States to revisit the need for naval mobility and view it in relative, rather than absolute, terms. Thus, within the newly inaugurated Reagan administration, U.S. naval mobility concerns may have become less of a determining issue than they had been a decade earlier.[7]

While the need for naval mobility was perceived as less compelling, mineral and energy interests within the United States were gaining ascendancy and were presenting a valid case for ensuring that the United States had virtually guaranteed access to natural resources under the sea. The "energy shocks" of the 1970s and the unprecedented strength of the Organization of Petroleum Exporting Countries (OPEC) cartel were still a vivid memory. The Cold War continued unabated, and the need for continuing, unimpeded access to strategic minerals, particularly cobalt, manganese, copper, iron, nickel, platinum, zinc, and sulfur, became a significant national concern. Discoveries of large amounts of both polymetallic nodules and polymetallic sulfides on the deep-ocean floor promised to provide a rich harvest of vital resources for decades, if not centuries.[8]

By 1980, in the wake of further oil price increases initiated by the OPEC cartel, assured access to seabed nodules had emerged as a primary goal of the United States in the UNCLOS III negotiations. Many within the U.S. government believed that mining the ocean floor could provide this assured access for critical minerals such as cobalt and manganese, which were imported primarily from third-world countries at an annual cost of over $2 billion, and could insulate the United States from being blackmailed and subjected to price extortion by producers of these strategic minerals.[9] Deep seabed mining became, in many ways, a symbolic "last straw" issue at a time when U.S. interests were perceived as being under attack throughout the world. The United States now believed that it, more than any other nation, had the most to lose from a restricted deep seabed mining regime; it wanted assured access to critical strategic materials in an environment where there was concern that nodule mining operations might be monopolized.[10]

These concerns were voiced by Ambassador James Malone, chief U.S. negotiator at the Law of the Sea Conference, in testimony before a House of Representatives committee. Ambassador Malone articulated nine specific concerns regarding deep seabed mining that were raised during the newly inaugurated Reagan administration's oceans policy review. Ambassador Malone noted that this mining regime in the draft convention was unsatisfactory in that it:

- placed burdensome international regulations on seabed mining;
- established a supranational mining entity;
- compelled the sale of technology on deep seabed mining from private companies;
- limited manganese nodule production from deep seabed mining sites;
- created a one-man, one-vote procedure in the Assembly, disregarding disparate levels of interest and making the Assembly a supreme organ;
- provided uncertainty by the review process in deep seabed mining provisions;
- imposed revenue-sharing obligations for deep seabed mining on the continental shelf;
- lacked provisions for protecting investment made in deep seabed mining; and
- made it possible for "national liberation" movements to share revenue generated.[11]

By now, deep seabed mining was an important issue for the United States. Extensive analyses were conducted to attempt to determine the amount of strategic minerals available from the deep ocean floor. Sophisticated models were built that quantified the amount of each material that could be harvested, and some estimates promised a rich mining bonanza. For example, one estimate indicated that recovery of only 1 percent of deep-sea nodules would satisfy world demand for nickel, copper, cobalt, and manganese for fifty years.[12] Much of this analysis was supported, and much of it funded, by United States mineral interests, particularly by large, U.S.-based multinational consortia.[13]

Pressure by U.S. hard mineral interests was substantial. In 1980 Congress responded with the Deep Seabed Hard Mineral Resources Act (Public Law 96-283) for continued development in deep seabed mining. One section of this act expressed the need for guarantees for investment already made by the mining industry if a seabed mining regime were established. Pursuant to this act, licenses were granted for four deep ocean mine sites to begin seabed mining operations as early as 1984.[14] Thus, a confluence of factors—a need for assured access to strategic materials, the perceived lack of reliability of foreign sources of these materials, the apparent existence of necessary technologies to harvest seabed minerals, and the formation of aggressive American corporations determined to harvest this mineral bonanza—provided natural resource interests with more prominence as the Reagan administration grappled with the treaty.

THE REAGAN ADMINISTRATION'S APPROACH TO THE LAW OF THE SEA

The Reagan administration's dissatisfaction with the deep seabed mining provisions of the United Nations Convention reflected much more than just support for the commercial desires of U.S. deep seabed mining pioneers. Perhaps more so than any other two recent administration's, the Carter and Reagan administrations were ideologically opposed. Some believed the Reagan administration's approach to government had its roots in social Darwinism, reflected in a program of deregulation on the part of the federal government and a deliberate effort to dismantle much of the advisory and policy-making machinery of government.[15] With respect to the convention, the objections of the Reagan administration were, in large part, grounded in a concern that the convention might set other undesirable precedents for international organizations and would be perceived as a sign of American weakness. Many within the administration were particularly concerned that the precedent set by the "common heritage of mankind principle" as it applied to deep seabed mining might be extrapolated to the development of other resources including outer space, the moon, geosynchronous satellite orbits, and Antarctica.   The powers vested in the International Seabed Authority were particularly bothersome to the administration. During the military and ideological escalation of the early 1980s, treaty opponents within the Reagan administration felt that the Law of the Sea Convention would have "enormous adverse consequences as a precedent by conceding virtually unrestrained control over a major new international organization to the developing countries and Warsaw Pact States."[16] Nor was the administration alone in its objections. Congressional critics of the treaty claimed that it would set a "highly adverse precedent," that its provisions for collective ownership would constitute a "subterfuge for despotism," and that the International Seabed Authority would be an overly ambitious extension in international organizations, with full operational as well as regulatory powers—competencies regarded in some quarters as dangerous and as having a potentially "sweeping impact" on future international negotiations.[17]

Transcending these specific concerns, and beyond any possible damage that might befall U.S. mining companies, the Reagan administration opposed the elaborate mechanisms and significant bureaucracy of the proposed International Seabed Authority on philosophical grounds. The requirement to share profits and technology and to subject virtually all decisions on seabed mining to approval of the International Sea Bed Authority was in conflict with the free-market and free-enterprise approach of the Reagan administration. One view of the ideological basis for the administration's decision was offered by Lee Kimball of the Council on Ocean Law, who noted:

Mining company opposition to the LOS Convention mining regime was in the end less important to the Administration's decision to oppose the 1982 Convention than more fundamental ideological concerns. These concerns centered around the establishment of an international bureaucracy to regulate deep sea mining with decision-making procedures that did not adequately reflect the political and economic influence and financial contributions of the United States....These institutional arrangements were viewed as unfavorable precedents for other international discussions and agreements. Moreover, they were inimical to free enterprise.[18]

Nevertheless, the United States did not want to lose the significant benefits derived by other provisions of the treaty; therefore, as the UNCLOS III negotiations neared completion, the Reagan administration began a series of actions and policy pronouncements designed to influence the final form of the Convention. These actions were ultimately unsuccessful and may have led to a belief among some nations that the United States was trying to mold the treaty to its own use.

THE REAGAN ADMINISTRATION IN THE FINAL NEGOTIATIONS

In late 1981 it was announced that the final vote on the UNCLOS III Treaty would be held in April of the next year. The Reagan administration wasted no time in making a statement, a statement designed to influence the UNCLOS III delegates to make the Treaty more acceptable to the United States, particularly with respect to Part XI, the deep seabed mining section. On 29 January 1982, prepared presidential remarks before the House Merchant Marine and Fisheries (MM&F) Committee declared that a review by the United States had concluded that while most provisions of the draft Convention were acceptable and consistent with United States interests, some major elements of the deep seabed mining regime were not acceptable. The presidential statement elaborated on the reasons for this lack of acceptability and declared that U.S. representatives were "prepared to return to those negotiations and work with other countries to achieve an acceptable Treaty."[19]

One month later, on 23 February 1982, Ambassador James Malone, special representative of the president for UNCLOS III, appeared before the House MM&F Committee. Ambassador Malone reiterated the administration's dissatisfaction with Part XI of the treaty—the seabed mining provisions. He went into much greater detail than the president regarding specific ways in which Part XI needed to be amended for it to be acceptable to the United States. Ambassador Malone laid out six objectives that the United States sought to achieve in Part XI of the treaty:

First, the Treaty must not deter development of any deep seabed mineral resources to meet national and world demand. Second, the Treaty must assure national access to those resources by current and future qualified entities to enhance U.S. security of supply, avoid monopolization of the resources by the operating arm of the International Authority and promote the economic development of the resources. Third, the Treaty must provide a decision making role in the deep seabed regime that fairly reflects and effectively protects the political and economic interests and financial contributions of participating States. Fourth, the Treaty must not allow for amendments to come into force without approval of the participating states, including, in our case, the advice and consent of the Senate. Fifth, the Treaty must not set other undesirable precedents for international organizations. Sixth, the Treaty must be likely to receive the advice and consent of the Senate. In this regard, the Convention should not contain provisions for the mandatory transfer of private technology and participation by and funding for national liberation movements.[20]

Ambassador Malone then elaborated U.S. expectations for the community of nations as they reviewed the Part XI draft during intercessional negotiations during March of that year. Additionally, he made special mention of the fact that the United States was consulting with the Soviet Union on these potential changes to the treaty, a remarkable concession given the Cold War polarization of the two nations on almost all other global issues. The timing and the specificity of Ambassador Malone's remarks left little to the imagination: the United States expected that Part XI of the treaty would be changed to reflect and protect U.S. interests.

In spite of this pressure by the United States, Part XI of the treaty remained substantially unchanged when the final UNCLOS III treaty was voted on at the eleventh session in New York on 30 April 1982. On this date, the United States became one of only four countries to vote against the treaty. One hundred and thirty nations voted in favor of the treaty and there were a total of seventeen abstentions.[21] This first attempt by the United States to change the makeup of the treaty was unsuccessful.

Undaunted, the Reagan administration attempted to use the time between the vote on the treaty and its opening for signature to change Part XI in a way that would protect U.S. interests. Again, it was the president himself, followed by Ambassador Malone, who spoke strongly for the need for these changes. Speaking from the White House on 9 July 1982, the president expressed U.S. dissatisfaction with the results of the final vote. He noted the extensive work by the United States throughout the entire UNCLOS III negotiating process and reviewed his 29 January statement stipulating that the United States would return to the negotiations to try to make Part XI meet the six basic objectives that had been articulated in Ambassador Malone's statement before the House MM&F Committee the prior February. The president went on to point out that although 130 nations voted for the treaty, the nations voting "no" and "abstaining" produced more than 60 percent of the world's gross national product and provided more than 60 percent of the contributions to the United Nations.[22] This pointed reminder of the potential consequences of failing to change Part XI to meet U.S. desires represented enormous pressure by the United States to effect revisions to the treaty.

President Reagan's statement was followed a month later by Ambassador Malone's. Speaking to the MM&F Committee on 12 August, Ambassador Malone repeated the president's concerns in even more forceful and explicit terms. The Ambassador reported that:

No meaningful negotiations took place on the U.S. proposed changes to Part XI of the Treaty. The attitude of many was actively resistant to change that might have made it possible to alleviate our concerns....The negotiations on the seabed mining provisions represent a major failure of international diplomacy, in that important concerns of those countries most closely related to seabed mining were not taken into account. Furthermore, the deep seabed mining provisions do not even minimally meet U.S. objectives.[23]

The United States was still seeking to influence the work of the UNCLOS III Drafting Committee scheduled to meet in Geneva the following month, as well as the Plenary Session, scheduled to meet in New York after that. Additionally, in evaluating its ability to change Part XI as increasingly remote, the Reagan administration was also preparing the nation and the international community for its forthcoming oceans policy pronouncements.

On 10 December 1982, the United Nations Convention on the Law of the Sea was opened for signature in Montego Bay, Jamaica. It was immediately signed by 117 States and two other entities, representing the largest number of signatures ever affixed to a treaty on its first day.[24] The Convention remained open for signature until December 1984, by which time 158 countries had signed. The nation of Fiji claimed the honor of being the first nation to ratify the Convention. Eight more States ratified the Convention by the end of 1983.[25] The final treaty retained all of the unacceptable Part XI provisions regarding seabed mining that the Reagan administration had vigorously opposed.

Faced with this failure to make the treaty fully acceptable to the interests of the United States, the president sought, nevertheless, to preserve the progress and consensus in the non-deep-seabed mining portions of the Convention. In an address before the Mentor Group in Washington, D.C. on 10 March 1983, President Reagan outlined both the reasons why the United States did not sign the treaty and the ways in which the United States now intended to move unilaterally in the area of oceans policy.[26]

This presidential statement was a bold policy pronouncement. President Reagan noted that although the convention contained seabed mining provisions that were contrary to the interests and principles of all industrialized nations, there were also provisions with respect to traditional uses of the oceans that generally confirmed existing maritime law and practice and that fairly balanced the interests of all States. The president went further and announced three decisions to promote and protect the oceans interests of the United States.

First, he noted, the United States was prepared to accept and act in accordance with the balance of interests relating to traditional uses of the oceans—such as navigation and overflight. Second, the United States would exercise and assert its navigation and overflight rights and freedoms on a worldwide basis in a manner consistent with the balance of interests reflected in the Convention. Third, the United States would claim a 200-nautical mile exclusive economic zone (EEZ) in which it would exercise sovereign rights with respect to living and nonliving resources. Finally, the president noted that the United States would continue to work with other countries to develop a regime, free of unnecessary political and economic restraints, for mining deep seabed minerals that are beyond national jurisdiction. The president firmly stated his administration's views on the seabeds issue: "Deep seabed mining remains a lawful exercise of the freedom of the high seas open to all nations. The United States will continue to allow its firms to explore for and, when the market permits, exploit these resources."[27]

Later, Ambassador Malone elaborated on the president's statement. He went into some detail regarding the rationale for the 200-nautical mile EEZ also noting that fifty-six nations currently claimed a 200-nautical mile EEZ and that an additional twenty-three claimed a 200-nautical mile fisheries zone.[28] Although the president's remarks, Ambassador Malone's more lengthy comments, and the concurrent Presidential Proclamation 5030, focused primarily on the EEZ, the true watershed was the president's assertion that the United States was prepared to act in accordance with the "balance of interests relating to traditional uses of the oceans—such as navigation and overflight."[29]

The Reagan administration had charted a course outside of the mainstream view of the 1982 United Nations Convention on the Law of the Sea. The United States was now firmly against the treaty. Ambassador Malone summarized this strong opposition:

Let me state very emphatically that the United States cannot and will not sign the United Nations Convention on the Law of the Sea. The Treaty is fatally flawed and cannot be cured. In its present form it presents a serious threat to U.S. vital national interests and, in fact, to global security. Once more, it is inimical to the fundamental principles of political liberty, private property, and free enterprise. The Administration firmly believes that those very principles are the key to economic well-being for all countries—developing as well as developed.[30]

To much of the world, it appeared that the United States wanted to select among the benefits of the treaty without accepting the negotiated compromise portions of the document. Nevertheless, the Reagan administration appeared to genuinely believe that it could shape the treaty in a way that it would make it satisfactory to its needs. In testifying before the Senate Foreign Relations Committee on 15 September 1982, Theodore Kronmiller, deputy assistant secretary of state for Oceans and Fisheries Affairs, commented:

It has been suggested that we have thrown out the baby with the bath water—that is, that we will not be able to exercise the navigation and overflight rights and freedoms recognized by the Convention without taking on the obligations of its deep seabed mining provisions. This is a distorted view of the rights of the United States under international law. The exercise by the United States of rights and freedoms under international law can be limited only with our consent. This point holds true with regard to both our right to mine the deep seabed and to our right to navigate under, on and over the world's oceans, including international straits. We have those rights today, we are proceeding with their exercise and we intend to maintain them.[31]

The following chapter examines some of the consequences of the U.S. action and, ultimately, the efforts of the international community to achieve a broad consensus on the treaty.

NOTES

1.   James Wang, *Handbook on Ocean Politics and Law* (New York: Greenwood Press, 1992), 452–457. The author provides a detailed analysis of the rationale behind the voting position of the G-77 nations. He notes that the G-77 was by no means monolithic, but through the group's ability to compromise across regional boundaries, it was able to exert enormous influence on the UNCLOS III negotiations.

2.   J. K. Sebenius, *Negotiating the Law of the Sea* (Cambridge, Massachusetts: Harvard University Press, 1984), 84.

3.   Department of State, "Law of the Sea," *Current Policy* no. 371, (Washington, D.C.: Department of State, Bureau of Public Affairs, 1982), 2. Ambassador James Malone, special representative of the president for UNCLOS III, made the following statement before the House Merchant Marine and Fisheries Committee in February 1982:

It is important that the Law of the Sea Treaty be fashioned so that the United States can join in and support it. Major elements of the deep seabed mining regime are not acceptable to the United States. We have six broad objectives with regard to the deep seabed mining regime, and we will be seeking changes in the draft treaty to achieve them. The United States remains committed to the multilateral treaty process and will support ratification if our six objectives are fulfilled.

Ambassador Malone's statement conveys the impression that the United States expected the UNCLOS III parties to change the treaty to more closely accommodate U.S. desires. See also Senate, *Treaty Document 103-39, United Nations Convention on the Law of the Sea, with Annexes, and the Agreement Relating to the Implementation of Part XI of the United Nations Convention on the Law of the Sea of 10 December 1982, with Annex*, 103d Cong., 2d sess., 1994. This document outlines principal U.S. objections to Part XI:

[I]t established a structure for administering the seabed mining regime that did not accord industrialized States influence in the regime commensurate with their interests. [I]t incorporated economic principles inconsistent with free market philosophy. [I]ts specific provisions created numerous problems from an economic and commercial policy perspective that would have impeded access by the United States and other industrialized countries to the resources of the deep seabed beyond national jurisdiction.

Ibid., 59.

4.   R. R. Churchill and A. V. Lowe, *The Law of the Sea* (Manchester, U.K.: Manchester University Press, 1983), 15. See also Euripides Evriviades, "The Third World's Approach to the Deep Seabed," *Ocean Development and International Law* 11 (1982): 213.

5.   John Craven, "The Evolution of Ocean Policy," in *The Law of the Sea in the 1990s: A Framework for Further International Cooperation*, Tadao Kuribayashi and Edward Miles, eds. (Honolulu: Law of the Sea Institute Press, 1992), 386–387.

6.   Myron H. Nordquist, Satya Nandan, and Shabtai Rosenne, eds., *United Nations Convention on the Law of the Sea 1982: A Commentary*, vol. 2 (Boston: Martinus Nijhoff, 1993), xlvii. The seventeen conference sessions alternated principally between New York and Geneva, with one session in Caracas and the final session in Montego Bay. This publication is part of a comprehensive multivolume analysis of the 1982 United Nations Convention on the Law of the Sea sponsored by the Center for Oceans Law and Policy at the University of Virginia. See also Wang, *Ocean Law and Politics*, 30. Significant benchmarks in the ten years of negotiations were marked by various comprehensive negotiating texts; the initial Draft Negotiating Text in 1974, the Informal Single Negotiating Text (ISNT) in 1975; the Revised Single Negotiating Text (RSNT) in 1976; the Informal Composite Negotiating Text (ICNT) for 1977 to 1979; and the Draft Convention on the Law of the Sea (Informal Text) in 1980.

7.   Finn Laursen, *Superpower at Sea: U.S. Ocean Policy* (New York: Praeger Publishers, 1983), 171.

8.   Ted McDorman, "Will Canada Ratify the Law of the Sea Convention?" *Ocean Development and International Law* 25 (1988): 559. See also Robert Knecht, Biliana Cicin-Sain, and Jack Archer, "National Ocean Policy: A Window of Opportunity" *Ocean Development and International Law* 19 (1988): 119; Bernard Oxman, "United States Interests in the Law of the Sea Convention," *American Journal of International Law* 88 (1994): 488.

9.   Wang, *Ocean Politics and Law*, 187. The author focuses on the "strategic" nature of these minerals, pointing out the nickel is used as a high-temperature steel alloy for jet engines, manganese is vital in high-technology steel manufacture, copper is used as an electrical conductor in all electrical instruments, and cobalt is used in jet engine blades and as an alloy to toughen steel to provide it with high-temperature resistance in missiles and jet engines. As one example of the U.S. need for these minerals, he offers the example that the building and deployment of 200 land-based intercontinental ballistic missiles would need more than 10,000 tons of aluminum; 2,500 tons of chromium; 150 tons of titanium; and twenty-four tons of beryllium.

10.   James Morell, *The Law of the Sea: An Historical Analysis of the 1982 Treaty and its Rejection by the United States* (Jefferson, North Carolina: McFarland and Company, 1992), 47. Clearly, the U.S. position was not universally shared and in many ways opened up the United States to further international criticism. Morell cites a particularly strong statement by Jack

Barkenbus in *Deep Seabed Resources: Politics and Technology* (New York: Free Press, 1979), 152:

What is in dispute is not only deep seabed mining, but more importantly, alternative visions of a future economic and political international order....The preferred U.S. vision of the future, not surprisingly, is one that retains U.S., or at least Western, hegemony over global economic transactions...often cloaked in more technical terms like "economic efficiency" and "free market assurances."

11.   Wang, *Ocean Politics and Law*, 35-36.

12.   Professor J. Daniel Nyhart, interview by George Galdorisi, MIT Sloan School of Management, 12 November 1991. Dr. Nyhart, a charter member of the Panel on the Law of Ocean Uses, was an active participant in the law-of-the-sea process and led the team that developed some of the first mathematical models for estimating the amount of various minerals that would be garnered by deep seabed mining. Dr. Nyhart notes that there was speculation at the time of virtually unlimited amounts of some minerals on the deep seabed floor. See also Burdick Brittin, *International Law for Seagoing Officers* 5th ed., (Annapolis, Maryland: Naval Institute Press, 1986), 170–176. Brittin quantifies the extent of this mineral bonanza:

With respect to manganese nodules (composed primarily of cobalt, nickel, copper and manganese), while the potential of all the world's oceans is vast, those in the Clarion-Clipperton Zone of the Pacific Ocean have attracted most attention because of their high concentrations of nickel, copper, and cobalt. A single mine in this area would produce annually an estimated 4,000 tons of cobalt, 42,000 tons of nickel, 37,000 tons of copper, and 750,000 tons of manganese.

13.   Lee Kimball, "Turning Points in the Future of Deep Seabed Mining," *Ocean Development and International Law* 17 (1986): 389. The four principal consortia with long-term interest in deep seabed mining were Kennecott Group, Ocean Mining Associates, Ocean Management Incorporated, and Ocean Minerals Company.

14.   Morell, *Law of the Sea: Historical Analysis*, 155. See also U.S. House Committee on Foreign Affairs, Subcommittee on International Organizations and Movements, *Law of the Sea and Peaceful Uses of the Seabed*, 92d Cong., 2d sess., 1972; Wang, *Ocean Politics and Law*, chap. 7, for a comprehensive analysis of the deep seabed mining issue.

15.   Craven, "The Evolution of Ocean Policy," 390–391. The author details many of the ways in which the Reagan administration curtailed support for various agencies involved in oceans policy formulation.

16.   David Larson, "Deep Seabed Mining: A Definition of the Problem," *Ocean Development and International Law* 17 (1986): 289. See also Morell, *Law of the Sea: Historical Analysis*, 149.

17.   Statement of Representative Ronald Paul, 28 April 1982, reprinted in

Congressional Digest, 62 (1983): 25.

18.   Brittin, *International Law for Seagoing Officers*, 86.

19.   *Current Policy*, no. 371, 1.   See also Lewis Alexander, "The Cooperative Approach to Ocean Affairs: Twenty Years Later," *Ocean Development and International Law* 21 (1990): 107; Myron Nordquist and C. H. Park, eds., *Reports of the U.S. Delegation to the Third U.N. Conference on the Law of the Sea*, (Honolulu: Law of the Sea Institute Press, 1983), 665-666. At the Final Session of UNCLOS III, acting chief of the U.S. delegation, Ambassador Thomas Clingan presented the U.S. position:

The United States recognizes that certain aspects of the Convention represent positive accomplishments. Indeed, those parts of the Convention dealing with navigation and overflight and most other provisions of the Convention serve the interests of the international community....Unfortunately, the deep seabed mining regime that would be established by the Convention is unacceptable and would not serve the interests of the international community.

20.   Department of State, "Law of the Sea," *Current Policy*, no. 371, 3.

21.   Churchill and Lowe, *Law of the Sea*, 16. See also Brittin, *International Law for Seagoing Officers*, 84-85. Following the U.S. "no" vote, there was worldwide discussion in academia; the press, journals, and legislative bodies; and by heads of state; ocean-oriented industries and their trade associations; public-interest groups; and individuals with particular ocean interests. The U.S. Congress responded, reflecting the fact that the administration's decision did not necessarily reflect the consensus view within the Congress. The chairman of the House Committee on Foreign Affairs, with eighty-three supporting congressmen of both parties, sent a letter to the White House on 23 June 1982 saying, in part,

The United States "no" vote on the Treaty package raises critical issues concerning our nation's ability to promote and protect effectively our foreign policy and national security interests in ocean matters. Thus, we strongly believe a thorough Congressional review of these issues is imperative and that every effort should be made to improve the Treaty prior to its final, official acceptance by the Conference.

22.   Department of State, "Law of the Sea and Oceans Policy," *Current Policy*, no. 416 (Washington, D.C.: Department of State, Bureau of Public Affairs, 1982), 2.

23.   Ibid., 4.   Ambassador Malone fit well into the role of the administration's "point man" for oceans matters. Intimately involved in the entire UNCLOS III process, he would articulate the administration's views primarily in official State Department public affairs organs. Additionally, he had significant success publishing his, and the administration's, views in several respected journals. See, for example, James Malone, "Who Needs the Sea Treaty?" *Foreign Policy* 54 (1984): 44.

24.   Churchill and Lowe, *Law of the Sea*, 7.

25.   Department of State Publication 112, *Limits in the Seas: United States Responses to Excessive Maritime Claims* (Washington, D.C.: Department of State, Bureau of Oceans and International Environmental and Scientific Affairs, 1992), 82.

26.   *Presidential Documents*, vol. 19, no. 10 (Washington, D.C.: USGPO, 1983),   383–385.

27.   Department of State, *Limits in the Seas*, 80.   The presidential statement strongly reaffirmed the U.S. position on seabed mining.

28.   Department of State, "Ocean Policy and the Exclusive Economic Zone," *Current Policy* No. 471 (Washington, D.C.: Department of State, Bureau of Public Affairs, 1983), 2.

29.   Department of State, *Limits in the Seas*, 77.

30.   Malone, "Who Needs the Sea Treaty?" 63.   Ambassador Malone's article was a most pointed attack on the treaty.

31.   Brittin, *International Law for Seagoing Officers*, 87.   Outside of the administration, the view of the ability of the United States to shape international policy on the law of the sea was less sanguine.   In the spring of 1984, the Panel on the Law of Ocean Uses, a group of independent international lawyers expert in ocean law, chaired by Professor Louis Henkin of Columbia University, reviewed the law-of-the-sea policy of the United States.   One of its findings was as follows:

It is of paramount importance that the United States scrupulously conform its behavior to the provisions of the Convention. Our rejection of the deep seabed mining portion of the Convention in itself inevitably tempts other States to think in terms of rejecting or making exceptions to other provisions. However, the deep seabed mining system is not relevant as such to the fundamental issues of coastal areas, nor is substantial mining beyond the economic zone and continental shelf likely in the near future. But virtually all of the other provisions of the Convention deal directly or indirectly with those fundamental issues.

Chapter Five

THE INTERVENING YEARS
AND TREATY RATIFICATION

The decade following the last session of the Law of the Sea Conference in December 1982 was a tumultuous one for the international community in general and the United States in particular. By not signing the treaty, for what it perceived as good and sufficient reasons, the Reagan administration hoped, nevertheless, to establish the benefits reflected in the negotiated navigation and overflight provisions of the text without having to recognize the seabed mining provisions of a treaty that it found philosophically, politically, and economically flawed. Unfortunately for the United States, the international community did not uniformly "fall in line." Rather, many criticized the United States for rejection of what was regarded as a "package deal."

The decision by the United States to vote against and subsequently not sign the Convention was based on dissatisfaction with the restrictions imposed by the deep seabed mining sections of Part XI of the treaty.[1] Shortly after the treaty was opened for signature in Jamaica, the United States publicly articulated the position that the navigation and overflight provisions were, in fact, part of customary law, making several specific points. In its first point, the United States made specific reference to the fact that these navigation and overflight rights are "reflected in the Convention," making it clear that it would build its oceans policy by complying with the non-seabed-mining provisions of the treaty:

First, the United States is prepared to accept and act in accordance with the balance of interests relating to traditional uses of the oceans—such as navigation and overflight. In this respect, the United States will recognize the rights of other States in the waters off their coasts, as reflected in the Convention, so long as the rights and freedoms of the United States and others under international law are recognized by coastal States.[2]

The United States went even further in serving notice to the community of nations that it would not tolerate any restrictions on its rights and freedoms by any nation. President Reagan gave renewed credibility to the Freedom of Navigation (FON) Program, initiated by the Carter administration, by serving notice, in his second point:

The United States will exercise and assert its navigation and overflight rights and freedoms on a worldwide basis in a manner that is consistent with the balance of interests reflected in the Convention. The United States will not, however, acquiesce in unilateral acts of other States designed to restrict the rights and freedoms of the international community in navigation and overflight and other related high seas uses.[3]

This was a U.S. call for other nations to recognize that the non-seabed-mining provisions of the treaty had the force of customary international law. The Reagan administration believed that maintaining this staunch approach would eventually cause other nations to change their positions and accept the U.S. position.

Throughout the early 1980s the reaction of some in the international community seemed to indicate that the U.S. approach had backfired and that the United States was in a position outside of the mainstream of ocean law as it was evolving in the community of nations. However, the tenor and substance of both the president's and Ambassador Malone's oceans policy statements on 10 March 1983 indicated that they expected most countries to follow the U.S. lead. The administration was unequivocal in its policy statement:

Deep seabed mining remains a lawful exercise of the freedom of the high seas open to all nations. The exclusive economic zone is a lawful claim of sovereign rights and jurisdiction under customary international law and brings within U.S. jurisdiction and control those natural resources which are rightfully ours.[4]

Unfortunately, such bold statements may well have been perceived as indicative of a policy of unilateralism by the United States and also indicative of a lack of sensitivity to the aspirations of the other United Nations Conference on the Law of the Sea (UNCLOS) III participants.

The timing of the U.S. ocean policy statements was an attempt to influence the treaty-ratification process. This delivery, which occurred exactly three months after the treaty was opened for ratification, conveyed to the world that signing the treaty was not required because the United States had presented a concise policy that neatly tied together navigation and overflight, seabed mining, and the use of the exclusive economic zone.[5]

The administration had also decided to increase budgetary pressure on the United Nations treaty principals and perhaps undermine the deep seabed mining regime embodied in the new Convention. In a presidential statement issued in January 1983, President Reagan stipulated that the United States would withhold funding for the Law of the Sea Preparatory Commission, the entity created to develop rules and regulations pursuant to the deep seabed portions of the treaty. Using particularly strong language, the president observed:

The Preparatory Commission is not a proper expense of the United Nations within the meaning of its own Charter, as the Law of the Sea Preparatory Commission is legally independent of and distinct from the United Nations....Moreover, these funds are destined to finance the very aspects of the Law of the Sea Treaty that are unacceptable to the United States....Our review of this financing scheme has confirmed that it is an improper assessment under the United Nations Charter....The United States is opposed to improper assessments and is determined to resist such abuses of the United Nations budget....In this light, I have decided that the United States will withhold its pro rata share of the cost to the United Nation's budget of funding the Preparatory Commission.[6]

Such a strongly worded statement was viewed by some as an attempt by the Reagan administration to preserve its interests by dictating the terms of the United States participation in, and support for, the Law of the Sea Convention. Apparently, the administration believed that such a strong stance would make the community of nations more agreeable with respect to amending the treaty to more closely match U.S. interests.

This approach seemed like a win-win situation. The president committed the United States to follow what seemed like a practical path. We would be entitled to full navigation and overflight rights articulated in the treaty based upon their status as codification of existing and emerging customary international law.[7] In cases where a State failed to accord to the United States those rights, the U.S. Navy and Air Force would exercise maritime strength in full accord with the navigation articles of the treaty via the Freedom of Navigation Program.[8] Concurrently, U.S. mineral interests would remain free to conduct an ambitious seabed mining program under traditional freedom of the high seas (and seabed), independent of the troublesome deep seabed mining regime and its extensive bureaucracy. Many predicted that this mining bonanza would provide a significant percentage of our manganese, nickel, copper and cobalt requirements as early as the turn of the century.[9]

At this juncture, it appeared that the administration had made a very beneficial tradeoff, having discarded the necessity of binding itself to the undesirable deep seabed mining provisions of the treaty while embracing the careful balance of rights and duties contained in the nonseabed articles. All that was required, it seemed, was to maintain course and wait for other nations to fall in line. Unfortunately for the United States, the international community did not react accordingly.

The immediate effect of the failure to sign the 1982 United Nations Convention on the Law of the Sea was a loss of political capital by the United States. Had the United States been only a peripheral player in the UNCLOS III process, or had it objected earlier and more vigorously to certain proposals, the refusal to sign would not have been so conspicuous. Unfortunately, twenty-five years of active participation in the process, and less-than-adamant initial objections when deep seabed mining provisions were first discussed and negotiated, gave the community of nations reason to expect that the United States was going to sign and support the treaty. Refusal to sign at the very end of the process was thus viewed as a significant, and to many, a capricious policy reversal, resulting in significant political costs.[10] The situation was exacerbated by the 1983 Reagan Proclamation,[11] which appeared to some segments of the international community as a U.S. attempt to mold the treaty for its own use.

This action touched off a torrent of criticism in the wake of the Presidential statement. The viewpoint of Ambassador Satya Nandan of Fiji is typical of Group of Seventy-seven (G-77) reaction to the U.S. position on the issue:

To attempt to rationalize parts of the Convention as being simply customary international law is to ignore the fact that what was customary law has been clarified and modified and if parts have been preserved, it was done as a quid pro quo for other provisions. This selected use of the Convention, therefore, will be unacceptable.[12]

A large number of nations in the international community refused to accept the U.S. contention that the nonseabed provisions of the treaty reflected customary law and, therefore, were applicable to all States whether or not they were parties to it. As one of the most influential UNCLOS III negotiators, Tommy Koh of Singapore, expressed it:

The provisions of the Convention are closely interrelated and form an integral package. Thus, it is not possible for a State to pick what it likes and disregard what it does not like....It was also said that rights and obligations go hand in hand and it is not permissible to claim rights under the Convention without being willing to shoulder corresponding obligations.[13]

These criticisms of the United States' position were not limited to third-world representatives. Allen Maceachen, Canadian prime minister, stated:

The Convention sets out a broad range of new rights and responsibilities. If States may arbitrarily select those they will recognize or deny, we will see not only the end of our dreams of a universal comprehensive Convention on the Law of the Sea but perhaps the end of any prospect for global cooperation on issues that touch the lives of all mankind.[14]

This criticism should not have come as a surprise to the United States. Throughout the entire course of the UNCLOS III negotiations, as a direct result of the consensus approach to the drafting process, the "package deal" aspects of the Convention, designed to promote maximum participation by the community of nations, were emphasized recurringly. At the December 1982 signing ceremony, many States emphasized that the treaty was indeed a package deal and that they would oppose U.S. efforts to claim the selective benefits of its nonseabed provisions. Some nations were direct and specific in spelling out their intentions and directing their remarks at the U.S. delegation. Indonesian delegate

Hasjim Dajal reminded the U.S. delegation that: "Indonesia is not legally obligated to grant rights of transit passage through the Straits of Malacca to non-ratifying nations."[15] Many of the over 150 nations that signed the Law of the Sea Convention have maintained essentially the same position over the past decade. In the 1990 meeting of the Preparatory Commission, the commission's chairman noted the shortcomings of the United States' position, specifically with regard to U.S. desire to take advantage of the navigation and overflight provisions of the Convention while failing to support the seabed mining provisions and not signing and ratifying the treaty, noting, in part:

While many legal concepts and legal institutions found in the 1982 Convention, such as the archipelagic state concept, the twelve mile territorial sea principle, and the two hundred mile exclusive economic zone rule, among others, are considered by many of us as general international law today, the same cannot be said in respect of the detailed provisions in which these legal concepts and institutions are translated in the Convention.[16]

As the United States continued throughout the 1980s to base its oceans policy on the Reagan Proclamation, the results of Reagan administration's refusal to sign the 1982 Convention began to manifest themselves. These went beyond those associated with the international political fallout resulting from the United States dropping out of the UNCLOS III process and the negative international reaction to the Reagan Proclamation and began to indicate that the provisions of the Convention were in some danger of unraveling. In 1992, a widely circulated position paper prepared by the Panel on the Law of Ocean Uses summed up the difficulties with the U.S. position:

U.S. policy during the last decade has been based on the assumption that, notwithstanding the absence of widespread ratification of the Convention and of compulsory arbitration, the United States can achieve equivalent restraints on national behavior by treating the provisions of the Convention (except for the deep seabed provisions) as declaratory of customary international law. The assumption has already been proved incorrect by the erosion of important terms of the Convention that has already taken place, and further erosions are likely to accelerate with time.[17]

Thus, by the end of the 1980s the United States was still outside the treaty process.   Fortunately, the international community recognized that the participation of the United States and other Western industrialized nations was essential if the Convention was to function as it was originally conceived, a watershed document for the governance of the oceans[18] and that actions such as the formation of an alternative seabed mining regime by the United States and seven European nations, as well as Japan, under the 1984 Provisional Understanding Regarding Deep Seabed Matters, might cause the Convention to unravel.[19]

It became increasingly clear that a universally acceptable regime could be achieved only by effecting changes to the Convention that would remove, or at least minimize, the fundamental objections—philosophical, commercial, and operational—of the United States and the other nations which shared these objections. But it was also vital that any modifications to the Convention should safeguard the principal concerns of the developing countries, in particular the basic principle that the resources of the deep seabed beyond the limits of national jurisdiction are the "common heritage of mankind." Therefore, as the 1990s began, actions were initiated under the United Nations auspices to address the objections of the United States and other Western nations and make the Convention more universally acceptable.

In an effort to gain consensus on the Convention among both developing and developed States, the secretary-general of the United Nations, Javier Perez de Cuellar, initiated informal negotiations in July 1990 between representatives of some of the major participants in the UNCLOS-negotiation process. Secretary-General Perez de Cuellar acknowledged that there were problems with aspects of the deep seabed mining provisions that had prevented some States from ratifying or acceding to the Convention. Additionally, it was becoming increasingly apparent that the deep seabed mining regime of the Convention, which was intended to contribute to the economic strengthening of developing countries, could not fulfill its purpose in its present form. Therefore, it was necessary to amend these provisions to make the Convention a more useful and workable regime for both developing and developed nations.[20]

Contributing to a conservative approach on deep seabed mining were emerging concerns regarding the environmental impact of mining the ocean floor. These concerns fit generally into three categories: concerns over the impact on the deep seabed, concerns regarding the discharge of waste water from mining ships, and concerns relating to onshore processing. The majority of these concerns stemmed primarily from a lack of detailed knowledge of the impact of a type of enterprise never before conducted. Additionally, concerns were raised regarding the structure of Part XI, especially the potential for a conflict of interest for the Authority, the entity charged both with directing profitable deep seabed mining industrial activities and with elaborating and enforcing environmental rules and regulations against itself and others engaged in mining activities. The net result was both a slowdown of the urgency to move ahead with deep seabed mining and a willingness on the part of developing nations to revisit Part XI.[21]

Consultations convened by Secretary-General Perez de Cuellar and continued by his successor, Boutros Boutros Ghali, were held from 1990 to 1994, during which fifteen meetings took place. The first phase of the consultations included the identification of issues, the approach to be taken in examining them, and the search for solutions. During the second phase, more precision and definition was given to the consensus reached during the first phase and additional points were raised for consideration. There was general agreement that any modifications had to be put into place before the 1982 Convention entered into force in order to avoid the complex constitutional and treaty law problems that would need to be resolved in amending it through the procedures set forth in the Convention.[22]

The United States was an active participant throughout the course of these consultations, and the U.S. delegation signaled strongly that the United States approved of the direction in which the negotiations were moving. In December 1990, during the annual General Assembly review of the Law of the Sea Convention, the United States' U.N. ambassador, Thomas Pickering, made positive commentary regarding the progress of consultations on the Convention, pledged continued U.S. support, but noted that, reluctantly, the United States still could not support the treaty in its current form due to the unsatisfactory provisions of Part XI. Two years later, sufficient progress had been made in the secretary-general's consultations that U.S. Ambassador Pickering was able to announce that, while the United States could not yet register full support for the Treaty, it recognized that great progress had been made, and the United States would abstain, rather than vote against the Treaty.[23]

As the secretary-general's consultations continued, with the United States playing an increasingly proactive role under the leadership of Ambassador Pickering, a consensus gradually emerged. A group of developing and developed nations cobbled together an anonymous compromise proposal, the so-called "Boat Paper," and successive versions of this "Boat Paper," which first appeared in August 1993, contained substantive changes that would make Part XI of the Convention acceptable to the nations that had reservations regarding it. This compromise proposal also dealt with the provisions to be adopted in order to satisfy the very complicated procedural requirements of international treaty law and national constitutions. The consensus was finally embodied in the "Agreement" which was adopted by the General Assembly at a Special Resumed Session on 28 July 1994.

This "Agreement Relating to the Implementation of Part XI of the United Nations Convention on the Law of the Sea of 10 December 1982" is a treaty instrument that introduces significant changes to the seabed mining regime of Part XI of the Convention. Although the Agreement does not use the term "amendment," its clear intent and unmistakable effect is to amend substantially the regime in Part XI of the Convention. Article 2 of the Agreement, for example, states that the Agreement and Part XI shall be interpreted and applied as a single instrument, but, in case of inconsistency, the provisions of the Agreement shall prevail.

Through this innovative treaty-law device, an unbreakable link is established between the Agreement and the 1982 Convention, such that there would be no possibility of competing treaty regimes on seabed mining. In essence, this made it impossible for a State to become a party to the Agreement without also becoming a party to the Convention. The States that had ratified the Convention before the adoption of the Agreement are enabled to express their consent to be bound by the Agreement through a simplified procedure which thus makes it possible for them to overcome domestic constitutional constraints.[24]

This well-crafted solution to what had been a previously impossible impasse led to rapid and positive response on the part of developed nations in general and the United States in particular. The Agreement was opened for signature on 29 July 1994 and was quickly signed by over sixty-nine States, including all of the world's major industrial powers—the United States, Germany, Japan, France, Italy, and the United Kingdom, among others—as well as the European Community. Officials from the U.S. Department of State and Department of Commerce have gone on record as saying that the Agreement "more than meets" originally stated U.S. requirements for the deep seabed mining regime. Additionally, noted law-of-the-sea expert Rear Admiral William Schachte, Judge Advocate General's Corps, U.S. Navy (retired), has opined that "The Part XI Implementing Agreement eliminates the U.S. objections to the deep seabed mining regime and paves the way for Senate action on the Convention."[25] Finally, indicating administration opinion on the salutary effects of the Agreement, Karen Davidson of the Office of the General Consul for the National Oceanic and Atmospheric Administration (NOAA), stated:

The Agreement modifying Part XI addresses the specific objections to Part XI raised by the United States in 1982. It also goes further than those specific concerns. The Agreement does eliminate the most onerous and economically unworkable provisions of Part XI. It also significantly changes the basic orientation of that Part. The Agreement incorporates free market principles, including considerations of cost-effectiveness and efficiency, and provides for the functioning of institutions of the regime—and development of regime requirements—on an incremental, as-needed basis, taking into account the existing economic circumstances.[26]

This position was echoed by the Department of State. Wesley Scholz, director of the Office of International Commodities in the Bureau of Economic and Business Affairs recapped the department's position on the Agreement:

In 1982, after failed effort to renegotiate the [seabed mining] regime, President Reagan decided that notwithstanding the general acceptability of its other parts, the United States would not sign the Convention. History has proven him right. The principled stand taken by the United States, coupled with the dramatic changes in the international political and economic environment in the intervening years, created the opportunity to secure an agreement modifying the Convention's seabed mining regime to better reflect free market principles.
    In response to these objections (articulated by the United States in 1983) the new Agreement (to amend Part XI of the Convention) substantially increases the influence of the U.S. and other industrialized countries in the area of governance. It streamlines the operation of the Seabed Authority and promotes efficient administration. It reorients the regime to better reflect free market principles in relation to economic and commercial issues. It ensures recognition of the claims to sea-bed mine sites established on the basis of exploration work already conducted by U.S. and other countries. Finally, it improves provisions to promote protection of the marine environment.[27]

In the wake of the signing of the Agreement, ratifications and accessions to the Convention have accelerated. By January 1995, Australia, Germany, and Italy had become parties to the Convention and the majority of Western nations were preparing for ratification or accession, including the European Union and the adhering States of Austria, Finland, and Sweden, as well as India, Japan, New Zealand, and the Republic of Korea.[28]   In a February 1995 address, Maureen O'C. Walker, head of the Department of State's Division of Maritime Law and Policy, indicated that the combination of States that had already ratified the Convention and those who had signaled their intent to do so represented 70 percent of world population and 83 percent of world gross national product, clearly signaling a virtually universal commitment on the part of the world community to be bound by the Convention.[29]   Ratifications accelerated throughout 1995 and 1996, and by April 1997, a total of 116 States had become parties to the Convention.[30]

This response to the Agreement from the United States and the rest of the developed world represented a major commitment to the Convention. Although the Agreement was the major factor that removed the objectionable portions of Part XI and enabled the United States to move towards acceding to the Convention, there were a number of other factors at work throughout the late 1980s and early 1990s that coalesced to move the Convention from a treaty the United States could not live with, to a pact that it should not live without. These factors set the stage for the U.S. accession to the Convention; they will frame U.S. oceans policy as we move into the next century.

NOTES

1.   Department of State, "Law of the Sea and Oceans Policy," *Current Policy* no. 416 (Washington, D.C.: Department of State, Bureau of Public Affairs, 1982), 2.

2.   Department of State, "Oceans Policy and the Exclusive Economic Zone," *Current Policy*, no. 471 (Washington, D.C.: Department of State, Bureau of Public Affairs, 1983), 3.

3.   *Presidential Documents*, vol. 19, no. 10 (14 March 1983), 383.

4.   Department of State, "Oceans Policy and the Exclusive Economic Zone," *Current Policy*, no. 471, 3.

5.   Department of State, *Limits in the Seas, no. 112: United States Responses to Excessive Maritime Claims* (Washington, D.C.: United States Department of State, Bureau of Oceans and International Environmental and Scientific Affairs, 1992), 82.

6.   "Law of the Sea and Oceans Policy," *Current Policy*, no. 471, attachment. The Presidential Statement was made on 30 December 1982, exactly twenty days after the opening of the treaty for signature. It was issued in a 3 January 1983 press release at United Nations Headquarters and was accompanied by an even more strongly worded Fact Sheet entitled "U.N. Assessments for the Seabed Authority and Law of the Sea Preparatory Commission."   Among the

statements on this Fact Sheet:

The United States has consistently opposed this improper financing scheme....The expenses of the Law of the Sea Preparatory Commission are not expenses of the Organization since that commission is legally independent of and distinct from the U.N. organization....The LOS Preparatory Commission is established pursuant to a treaty regime separate from the U.N. Charter. It was created neither by the U.N. General Assembly under Article 22 of the U.N. Charter nor by the Security Council under Article 29, and is not a subsidiary organ of the U.N. It is not answerable to the United Nations. Membership in the U.N. does not obligate any member to finance or to otherwise support any other organization....The deep seabed part (Part XI) contains major provisions that are unacceptable and damaging to the United States and other countries interests....The Administration's review of the financing scheme in the recent resolution has confirmed that it is an improper assessment within the meaning of the U.N. Charter....It is in this light that President Reagan has decided to withhold the United States pro rata share of the cost to the U.N. budget of funding for the Preparatory Commission. This is estimated to be between $500,000 and $700,000 of the Preparatory Commission's funding for 1983.

7.   J. K. Sebenius, *Negotiating the Law of the Sea* (Cambridge, Massachusetts: Harvard University Press, 1984), 94.

8.   Department of State, "Navigation Rights and the Gulf of Sidra," *GIST* (Washington D.C.: Department of State, Bureau of Public Affairs, 1986), 1. See generally *Limits in the Seas*.

9.   For example, see R. R. Churchill and A. V. Lowe, *The Law of the Sea* (Manchester, U.K.: Manchester University Press, 1983), 155.

10.   Panel on the Law of Ocean Uses, "U.S. Interests and the United Nations Convention on the Law of the Sea," *Ocean Development and International Law* 21 (1990): 382.

11.   "Law of the Sea and Oceans Policy," *Current Policy*, no. 471, 2.

12.   Sebenius, *Negotiating the Law of the Sea*, 93.

13.   Ibid., 93. See also Bernardo Zuleta, "The Law of the Sea After Montego Bay," *San Diego Law Review* 20 (1983): 478; David Larson, "When Will the U.N. Convention on the Law of the Sea Come Into Effect?" *Ocean Development and International Law* 20 (1989): 176; Edward Miles, "Preparations for UNCLOS IV?" *Ocean Development and International Law* 19 (1988): 424. Miles is even more critical of the United States' position:

It must be said bluntly that the U.S. claim that all of the non-seabed portion of the treaty represents customary international law simply cannot be supported and therefore costs the U.S. credibility. Concepts like transit passage, archipelagic sealanes passage, the regime of archipelagoes, the exclusive economic zone and the like did not exist prior to the Third United Nations Conference on the Law of the Sea and are indistinguishable from it. These could not have become customary international law prior to the 1980s.

14.   Luke T. Lee, "The Law of the Sea Convention and Third States," *American Journal of International Law* 77 (1983): 548.

15. J. M. Van Dyke, ed., *Consensus and Confrontation: The United States and the Law of the Sea Convention* (Honolulu: Law of the Sea Institute Press, 1985), 282.

16. James B. Morell, *The Law of the Sea: An Historical Analysis of the 1982 Treaty and Its Rejection by the United States* (Jefferson, North Carolina: McFarland and Company, 1992), 190.

17. Panel on the Law of Ocean Uses, "United States Interests in the Law of the Sea Convention," *Ocean Development and International Law* 21 (1992): 410.

18. Satya Nandan, "The 1982 U.N. Convention on the Law of the Sea: At a Crossroad," *Ocean Development and International Law* 20 (1989): 516. In remarks at the 23d Annual Conference of the Law of the Sea Institute in June 1989, United Nations Under Secretary General Nandan highlighted the necessity of bringing the United States and other Western nations onboard with the Convention:

It would be an absurd situation if the Convention should come into force on the strength of small States while larger States sit back and use the Convention as a reference point for their protests against the actions or omissions of others. They will have neither the legal or moral authority to ask others to respect an instrument to which they themselves are not prepared to become parties.

19. James Wang, *Handbook on Ocean Politics and Law* (New York: Greenwood Press, 1992), 205. The author points out that the Provisional Understanding Regarding Deep Seabed Matters was interpreted as a strong signal that the Western industrialized countries would never be satisfied with the deep seabed mining regime as it existed in Part XI of the 1982 Convention.

20. See Motoo Ogiso, "International Cooperation in the New Sea Regime" in *The Law of the Sea in the 1990s: A Framework for Further International Cooperation*, Tadao Kuribayashi and Edward Miles, eds. (Honolulu: Law of the Sea Institute Press, 1992), 15. This volume is a recapitulation of the *Proceedings of the Law of the Sea Institute Twenty-fourth Annual Conference* (co-sponsored by the Ocean Association of Japan), held in Tokyo in July 1990. The authors point out that, although the United States was most closely associated with pressing for a revised seabed mining regime, other industrialized nations, most notably Japan, also presented very strong arguments for amending Part XI of the Convention.

21. See generally Stig Berge, Jan Markussen, and Gudmund Vigerust, *Environmental Consequences of Deep Seabed Mining—Problem Areas and Regulations* (Oslo, Norway: Fridtjof Nassen Institute Press, 1991), 1-183. See generally Levan Imnadze, "Common Heritage of Mankind: a Concept of Cooperation," and Jan Markussen, "Commentaries" in *The Law of the Sea in the 1990s*, Kuribayashi and Miles, eds. The issue of the environmental impact of deep seabed mining was addressed by numerous speakers and was, arguably, one of the more important issues discussed at the Twenty-fourth Annual Conference

of the Law of the Sea Institute.

22.   See Doug Bandow, George Galdorisi, and M. Casey Jarman, *The United Nations Convention on the Law of the Sea: The Cases Pro and Con*, Occasional Paper no. 38 (Honolulu: Law of the Sea Institute Press, 1995), 2.

23.   United Nations, *The Law of the Sea: Annual Review of Ocean Affairs, Law and Policy, Main Documents* (New York: United Nations Press, 1993), 64. Ambassador Pickering's statement was made at the forty-fifth session of the U.N. General Assembly in December 1990, on Agenda Item 33.

24.   Bandow, Galdorisi, and Jarman, *The Cases Pro and Con*, 4.

25.   William Schachte, Jr., "National Security: Customary International Law and the LOS Convention" (address at the Georgetown University Law Center symposium, *Implementing the United Nations Convention on the Law of the Sea*, Washington, D.C., January 1995).

26.   Senate Committee on Foreign Relations, "Current Status of the Convention on the Law of the Sea," 103d Cong., 2d sess., 1994, 17. See also Schachte, "National Security: Customary International Law and the LOS Convention"; Karen Davidson, "Law of the Sea and Deep Seabed Mining: The Agreement Modifying Part XI of the U.N. Law of the Sea Convention" (address at the Center for Oceans Law and Policy Symposium, *Toward Senate Consideration of the 1982 Law of the Sea Convention*, Washington, D.C., June 1995).

27.   Walter Doran, "An Operational Commander's Perspective on the 1982 LOS Convention," *International Journal of Maritime and Coastal Law* 10 (1995): 335. Rear Admiral Doran was director of the Navy's Office of Plans and Political Military Affairs. In this article, he quotes Wesley Scholz, who stated the State Department's position on the "Agreement."

28.   Moritaka Hayashi, "Prospects for a Universal Acceptance of the Part XI Agreement" (address at the Georgetown University Law Center Symposium, *Implementing the United Nations Convention on the Law of the Sea: An International Symposium*, Washington, D.C., January 1995). In his prepared remarks, Mr. Hayashi, a member of the United Nations Secretariat, reviewed the current status of the Convention and the Agreement, including those States party to the Convention and those who have accepted the Agreement, and those who have established their consent to be bound by the Convention and the Agreement, concluding that the prospects for further acceptance of the Convention and the Agreement are bright and predicting that the Convention/Agreement package soon will be accepted virtually universally.

29.   Maureen O'C. Walker, "Efforts to Obtain Senate Ratification" (address at the U.S. Department of the Navy's Fifth Freedom of Navigation Workshop, Pensacola, Florida, February 1995). Ms. Walker is also a member of the executive branch's Interagency Task Force on the Law of the Sea and is one of the Department of State's principal representatives on law-of-the-sea matters. See also the statements of the Honorable David Colson, deputy assistant secretary for Oceans, Department of State and the statement of Karen Davidson, Senior

Counsel for International Law, National Oceanic and Atmospheric Administration, in Senate Committee on Foreign Relations, *Current Status on the Convention on the Law of the Sea*, 11, 34.

30.   John Norton Moore, "Observations by former Special Representatives of the President for the Law of the Sea" (address at the Center for Oceans Law and Policy Symposium, *Toward Senate Consideration of the 1982 Law of the Sea Convention*, Washington, D.C., June 1995); John Norton Moore, "Remarks" (address at the Twenty-First Annual Seminar of the Center of Oceans Law and Policy, *Security Flashpoints: Oil, Islands, Sea Access and Military Confrontation*, New York, February 1997).

Chapter Six

CHANGES IN THE U.S. POSITION: WHY THE UNITED STATES SAID "YES"

On 7 October 1994 President Clinton submitted the United Nations Convention on the Law of the Sea (UNCLOS) and the Agreement Relating to the Implementation of Part XI of the Convention to the United States Senate for its advice and consent, culminating over two decades of work by Republican and Democratic administrations to secure an oceans regime that will serve U.S. strategic, economic, and environmental interests.[1]   In a strongly worded statement, the president stated:

The United States has basic and enduring national interest in the oceans and has consistently taken the view that the full range of those interests is best protected through a widely accepted international framework governing the uses of the seas. Since the 1960s, the basic U.S. strategy has been to conclude a comprehensive treaty on the law of the sea which will be respected by all countries. Each succeeding Administration has recognized this as the cornerstone of U.S. oceans policy. Following adoption of the Convention in 1982, it has been the policy of the United States to act in a manner consistent with the provisions relating to traditional uses of the oceans and to encourage other countries to do likewise....Early adherence by the United States to the Convention and the Agreement is important to maintain a stable legal regime for all uses of the sea, which covers more than 70 percent of the surface of the globe. Maintenance of such stability is vital to U.S. national security and economic strength.

In his transmittal letter the president outlined six key reasons arguing for the Senate's advice and consent. According to the president:

The Convention advances the interests of the United States as a global maritime power. It preserves the right of the U.S. military to use the world's oceans to meet national security requirements and of commercial vessels to carry sea-going cargoes. It achieves this, inter alia, by stabilizing the breadth of the territorial sea at twelve nautical miles; by setting forth navigation regimes of innocent passage in the territorial sea, transit passage in straits used for international navigation and archipelagic sea lanes passage; and by reaffirming the traditional freedoms of navigation and overflight in the exclusive economic zone and the high seas beyond.

The Convention advances the interests of the United States as a coastal State. It achieves this, inter alia, by providing for an exclusive economic zone out to 200 nautical miles from shore and by securing our rights regarding resources and artificial islands, installations and structures for economic purposes over the full extent of the continental shelf. These revisions fully comport with U.S. oil and gas leasing practices, domestic management of coastal fishery resources, and international fisheries agreements.

As a far-reaching environmental accord addressing vessel pollution, pollution from seabed activities, ocean dumping, and land-based sources of marine pollution, the Convention promotes continuing improvement in the health of the world's oceans.

In light of the essential role of marine scientific research in understanding and managing the oceans, the Convention sets forth criteria and procedures to promote access to marine areas, including coastal waters for research activities.

The Convention facilitates solutions to the increasingly complex problems of the uses of the ocean—solutions that respect the essential balance between our interests as both a coastal and a maritime nation.

Through its dispute settlement provisions, the Convention provides for mechanisms to enhance compliance by Parties with the Convention's provisions.[2]

Understanding how the United States reached the position where the executive branch took such a strong advocacy position in urging Senate advice and consent to the Convention can help frame the opportunities for new directions in U.S. oceans policy. Substantial political, economic, security, and ideological changes all coalesced to impel the administration to come "on board" with the Convention. A number of reasons comprise the rationale for the change in U.S. direction on the law of the sea. Collectively, these reasons help explain why the Clinton administration now says "yes" on the Convention and the Agreement.

THE CONVENTION'S ENTRY INTO FORCE

First, a sense of urgency was engendered by the sixtieth ratification of the Convention by Guyana on 16 November 1993.[3] By its own terms, the treaty would enter into force one year later; Guyana's ratification started the clock that would see the Convention effective for State parties ratifying it. For the United States, this ratification moved the treaty from a futuristic "what might be" to an emergent international protocol that demanded a place on the Clinton administration's agenda. The United States now had to weigh the very real prospects of being an "outsider looking in" at a completed treaty process, a prospect that was particularly unattractive in terms of exercising leverage in moving the Convention through its implementation phase.

The penalties for "jumping in late" with the Convention became very apparent to the United States once the treaty came into force, on 16 November 1994, for

States that had already ratified or acceded to the treaty. The United States recognized that, comprehensive as it is, the 320-article, nine-annex Convention also provides a framework for future negotiation in the international arena. In many ways, the treaty is a "constitution" for the evolution of future ocean law.[4]

One of the fora for these negotiations will be the International Maritime Organization, where supplemental international regulations, particularly those regarding navigation and overflight, will be decided.[5] Another is the International Tribunal for the Law of the Sea to be established in Hamburg, Germany. This is an international judicial agency charged with adjudicating law-of-the-sea issues under the Convention. Only States party to the Convention can nominate or vote on the twenty-one members of the Tribunal. Additionally, some have noted that the staff "bureaucracies" of these organizations are established at the birth of the organization and very often remain in place for decades, outlasting the tenure of diplomats and national leadership. Therefore, there is a substantial premium affixed to being part of any international organization from the outset rather than joining later in its existence. Thus, within the executive branch, the renewed urgency to secure the advice and consent of the Senate resulted in vigorous congressional briefings by an interagency task force, chaired by the National Security Council representative.[6]

MORE REALISTIC APPRAISAL OF SEABED RESOURCES

Second, the deep seabed mining industry has undergone fundamental transformation. Previous chapters dealt with the "Agreement Relating to the Implementation of Part XI of the Convention" and the fact that this Agreement removed the objectionable deep seabed mining provisions of the original Convention. This Agreement, however, did not spring spontaneously from the pen of some statesman, but rather it was facilitated by substantially different market conditions over the course of the last one-and-a-half decades.

Deep seabed mining emerged as an issue during the late 1960s and the early 1970s, as speculation increased regarding the potential to mine mineral deposits on the deep-ocean floor. The hoped-for economic advantages of seabed mining vis-a-vis land-based mining were perceived to include low labor costs, lack of drilling or excavation expenses, and relatively low transportation costs.[7] In a 1967 address to the General Assembly, Ambassador Arvid Pardo of Malta estimated, based on what he later acknowledged were some "hasty calculations," that by 1975, a new international agency responsible for seabed mining would succeed and have at least five billion dollars available after expenses for further development purposes.[8]

In the early 1980s, many were predicting a major boom in the mining of deep seabed nodules of cobalt, manganese, nickel, copper and other minerals. Mathematical models constructed by scientists and engineers at the Massachusetts Institute of Technology, for example, predicted base case return-on-investment for deep seabed mining of 18 percent.[9] The enthusiasm for deep seabed mining was not restricted to mining companies and consortia. Two respected law-of-the-sea academics, R. R. Churchill and A. V. Lowe opined in 1983:

There are sufficient recoverable deposits on the deep seabed to offer a high level of self-sufficiency in the main minerals derived from them to States capable of exploiting them, with the consequent benefits to the balance of payments of those States, and the strategic advantage of lessening dependence upon foreign land-based deposits.[10]

Newer research indicates that these optimistic predictions were early—by at least several decades. The actual occurrence of economically feasible deep seabed mining of nodules appears increasingly remote, due primarily to the discovery of substitutes for many products and applications and the availability of ample land-based supplies.[11] Writing for the Panel on the Law of Ocean Uses in 1994, Professor Jonathan Charney of Vanderbilt University commented on recovery of deep seabed minerals:

The likelihood of early deep sea-bed mining for minerals is bleak. Recent economic conditions and the use of substitutes have depressed minerals demand, while alternative cheaper land-based sources of some nodule minerals have been identified. There is little doubt that the market will not make deep sea-bed mining economically viable before 2025 and probably much later than that.[12]

Should seabed mining of nodules ever become of genuine strategic importance to the United States, plentiful quantities are expected to be available within national 200-mile exclusive economic zones as an alternative supply when market prices improve.[13] Economical seabed mining has yet to occur. While promising sites have been identified by various companies that understandably wish to protect their investments, demand for the metals principally responsible for interest in manganese nodules, especially nickel and copper, has been depressed in recent years and may be satisfied for some time to come by sources on land. These metals can be stockpiled, and concerns have abated about the climate for remunerative investment in, and stable supply from, mines located in many countries of world.[14] Writing in the respected *American Journal of International Law*, Bernard Oxman summarized the consensus view of the Panel on the Law of Ocean Uses:

Deep seabed mining did not exist when Part XI was negotiated. Many of the objectionable provisions of Part XI were negotiated on the assumption that such mining would become a commercial reality before the end of this century. Altered market conditions, exploitation of additional land-based sources, and improved efficiency of land-based mining now indicate that deep seabed mining, in the absence of artificial government subsidies, will not be economically feasible until well into the next century, if then. New sources of seabed minerals also have been discovered, some of which are located in exclusive economic zones.[15]

Oxman's views that seabed mining is no longer a contentious issue and that the Agreement more than adequately addresses previous concerns by United States and other Western nations are echoed in a wide range of presentations at conferences and congressional testimony and appear to reflect a consensus executive branch, interagency position on this issue.

Thus, the changes in the possibilities regarding deep seabed mining did much to defuse this once-contentious issue for the United States, leaving even those skeptical that the Agreement remedied the deep seabed mining regime of the Convention with little about which to be concerned. Even though some editorial commentary has continued to argue against U.S. accession to the Convention, principally because of its seabed mining provisions,[16] that commentary seemed locked in the former paradigm of a pre-Agreement regime and old ideologies.

PROTECTION AND PRESERVATION OF THE MARINE ENVIRONMENT

Third, there was a growing desire to build global consensus on management of the environment. Part XII of the Convention deals extensively with the protection and preservation of the marine environment. Part XII covers a wide array of issues running from general principles, to global and regional cooperation, to technical assistance, to monitoring and environmental assessment, to responsibility and liability.[17] The inclusion of strong environmental-protection measures in the Convention was an early and enduring goal of the United States. The recognition of the need for cooperation in attempts to stem marine pollution was noted in a statement by President Richard Nixon at the beginning of the UNCLOS III process: "It is not possible for any nation, acting unilaterally, to ensure adequate protection of the marine environment. Unless there are firm minimum international standards, the search for relative economic advantage will preclude effective environmental protection."[18]

In the decade following the vote on the final Convention, the United States, as well as many other nations, became even more concerned about preserving the environment; environmental concerns supplanted economic considerations in many cases.[19] Given that the language of Part XII creates a diffuse but effective international mechanism for control of a significant amount of marine pollution, and that the Convention articles on marine-pollution control establish a symbiotic relationship between the Convention and other issue-specific environmental agreements, the United States found it especially advantageous to support the Convention in order to ensure the maintenance of a stable regime for environmental protection.[20]

Rear Admiral William Schachte, former Judge Advocate General of the Navy and active participant with the United States UNCLOS III delegation, has pointed out that the Convention provides a unique, outstanding framework for addressing and resolving the environmental concerns of the United States. He noted that the Convention is far superior to any of the other numerous conventions and protocols addressing marine pollution that have been attempted over the past four decades and that it strikes a delicate balance between the natural-conflicting interests of maritime States and coastal/port States on environmental issues.[21] This theme was reinforced in congressional testimony in August 1994 by Rear Admiral John Shkor, chief counsel of the U.S. Coast Guard who noted that, "The Convention is the glue that binds diverse maritime interests in the environmental field."[22]

Concern for the environment appears to be growing worldwide. Concurrently, the Convention creates environmental rights and duties, and a legal system to adjudicate them, making it even more important to use the Convention as a framework for addressing environmental challenges. This was articulated by the secretary-general of the United Nations in a 1990 report on the status of the law of the sea in which he noted the growing interest in improving the role and effectiveness of international environmental controls and in devising strategies that will take better account of both resource depletion and the benefits of conservation:

Since the Convention on the Law of the Sea provides the necessary framework of rights and obligations for all ocean uses, its importance has been stressed in all discussions regarding the future development of international law and policy....The time required to negotiate conventions and bring them into effect is of mounting concern for dealing with a number of environmental issues where rapid acceptance and implementation will be a distinct goal. Thus, there is a growing interest in such supplementary actions as provisional application of some or all treaty provisions, simultaneous adoption of recommendations that deal with selected convention subjects, and declarations of voluntary compliance.[23]

These concerns were shared by the United States, as environmental issues occupied a prominent place in the decision by the Clinton administration to accede to the Convention. In an address at the National Forum on Ocean Conservation, former United States UNCLOS III negotiator, Ambassador Elliot Richardson, noted that the United Nations Conference on Environment and Development (UNCED) in Rio de Janeiro (the 1992 Earth Summit), attended by 170 States, presented a complex agenda, with the protection of the oceanic environment as one of its principal concerns. Significantly, UNCED's "Agenda 21," a forty-chapter action plan which was signed by all the nations attending UNCED, sets forth several hundred action items for the protection of the oceans, seas, and coastal areas, as well as the protection, development, and rational use of their living resources. The introduction to Chapter 17 of UNCED's "Agenda 21" begins by stating: "International law as reflected in the Law of the Sea Convention sets forth rights and obligations of States and provides the international basis upon which to pursue the protection and sustainable development of the marine and coastal environment and its resources."[24]

Ambassador Richardson has noted further that the 1982 Law of the Sea Convention embodied basic accepted principles that would form a consensus on many environmental issues.[25] In his view and the view of others, the United

States needed to be a party to the Convention in order to retain an international leadership role in environmental concerns and deliberations.

EVOLVING GLOBAL SECURITY ENVIRONMENT

Fourth, the changing global security environment influences the U.S. position. A diminishing access to overseas bases, coupled with continuing instability in many parts of the world requiring naval presence (the Arabian Gulf, Bosnia, Zaire, and Rwanda are recent examples), when coupled with the growing naval power of many developing nations with regional ambitions (such as China and Iran), point to an ever-increasing need for naval mobility by the United States. An essential element of this requirement is the assurance that key sea and air lanes of communication will remain open as a matter of international legal right—not at the sufferance of coastal and island nations along the route and in the area of operations.[26]

The last two decades in particular have witnessed an increase in naval conflicts as well as demarcation and fishing disputes. For example, from 1974 to 1990, at least thirty-seven major demarcation disputes, fifteen major fishing disputes, and thirty-one naval conflicts occurred. A total of 83 percent of all U.S. military responses from 1946 to 1991 have involved naval forces, with about half the reactions being solely naval, and responses occurring on the average of once each month. Since the 1986 Goldwater-Nichols Act, with its emphasis on joint operations, fewer operations have been exclusively naval in character, but a far greater proportion, 95 percent, have involved naval units. Additionally, the focus of these efforts overwhelmingly has been in littoral waters, that is, near-land waters where coastal States might claim authority to exclude naval vessels. In all of the 270 instances of the use of naval forces in crisis response from 1946 to 1991, the naval forces were used not to counter other naval forces, but rather to counter land-based threats. These naval forces, therefore, had to operate in coastal waters, not the blue-water high seas, to project power from the sea onto the land.[27]

The years immediately preceding the entry into force of the Convention saw an increase in these disputes, with controversies ranging from the conflict among Southeast Asian nations over the Spratley and Paracell Islands, to Canadian and European disputes over fishing rights off the Grand Banks, to disputes between Japan and South Korea over uninhabited islands in the Sea of Japan, to conflict between Greece and Turkey over disputed islands in the Aegean. These trends helped the United States to revalidate the need for a firmly stated and fully accepted compact that ensured maritime and naval mobility.[28]

The United States recognized that its ability to achieve maximum flexibility and mobility within this changing global security environment would be greatly enhanced by accession to the 1982 Convention and the concomitant stabilizing of the world's oceans. Concurrently, it was thought that this move had the strong potential to minimize and control disputes that directly or indirectly prejudiced U.S. political, economic, and defense interests.[29] As the world's remaining global maritime power, the United States placed a uniquely high premium on the ability to move by sea anywhere on the globe.[30]

Achieving a stable and predictable regime for the world's oceans, with each nation respecting universally agreed-to rules and procedures, was recognized as being vital for the continued effective use of naval and air forces as instruments of national policy. Without international respect for the freedom of navigation and overflight set forth in the Convention, exercise of our forces' mobility rights could be jeopardized.[31] For example, disputes with littoral States could delay action and be resolved only by protracted political discussions, and the response time for U.S. and allied or coalition forces at a distance from potential areas of conflict could lengthen. Deterrence could be weakened—particularly when our allies do not have sufficient power projection capacity to resist illegal claims. Forces may arrive on the scene too late to make a difference, affecting our ability to influence the course of events consistent with our interests and treaty obligations. For example, if prevented from transiting through the Indonesian Archipelago and the Malaccan Straits, a naval carrier task group transiting from Yokosuka, Japan to Bahrain would have to reroute around Australia. Assuming a steady fifteen-knot pace, a six ship, conventionally powered task group would require an additional fifteen days and over 94,000 gallons of fuel to transit the additional 5,800 nautical miles. The additional fuel cost alone would amount to over three million dollars.[32]

A SMALLER U.S. NAVY

Fifth, the dramatic decrease in the size of the U.S. Navy provided impetus to come on board with the Convention. As challenges to unhampered use of the oceans continue, the Navy would shoulder the lion's share of the responsibility to demonstrate U.S. resolve and maintain U.S. interests. The four pillars of both the National Security Strategy and the National Military Strategy—Strategic Deterrence, Forward Presence, Crisis Response, and Force Reconstitution—require active engagement by the U.S. Navy. In discussing these four pillars of our national security and national military posture respectively, both former President George Bush and then-chairman of the Joint Chiefs of Staff, Colin Powell, placed a strong premium on the use of the United States Navy to support all pillars of the strategy along the full spectrum from peace to war. These themes were reinforced by President Clinton and by chairman of the Joint Chiefs of Staff, General John Shalikashvili, in their respective updated strategies in 1994 and 1995.[33]

Concurrently, challenges to U.S. naval mobility seem most likely to arise from archipelagic States, straits States, or from other maritime-oriented coastal States.[34] Indeed, some analysts have predicted that the defining purpose of "small navies" will develop over the next several decades as forces designed specifically to safeguard the rights conveyed by the Law of the Sea Convention.[35]

Others have noted the increase in sovereignty by coastal States over significant ocean areas has led to dramatic growth in the number, size, and capabilities of navies. Writing in *Ocean Yearbook*, retired Navy Captain Joseph Morgan noted:

[C]urrently accepted international law of the sea results in increased sovereignty by coastal States over ocean areas. Territorial seas have increased in width from 3 to 12 nautical miles, and a new political region in the oceans, the exclusive economic zone (EEZ), gives the coastal states sovereignty over resources out to 200 nautical miles from coastal baselines. In confined waters such as semi-enclosed seas, there are overlaps in EEZ claims and in some cases territorial seas. While most of these jurisdictional disputes are solved peacefully or simply left unresolved, virtually all nations with coastlines believe they need navies to influence negotiations or if necessary use force to solidify their claims. Customary international law permits expanded maritime zones to be drawn around small islands. As a result, claims to sovereignty over islands of minuscule size now abound, since sovereignty over marine resources of sometime great value accrues to the nation owning the island. In several cases, naval skirmishes have already taken place over the issue of ownership of an island that has virtually no terrestrial resources and is scarcely able to support even a quite small human population.[36]

Morgan proved quite prophetic. The issue of *Ocean Yearbook* carrying his commentary appeared in early 1995, at precisely the time when China and the Philippines were hotly contesting the rights to the Spratley Islands, of no significance themselves, but containing under their surrounding waters some of most promising oil deposits in Southeast Asia.

These challenges come as the United States Navy is going through one of the most dramatic downsizings in its history. Less than a decade ago, the "600-ship navy" was an organizing impulse and an achievable goal within the navy and the Department of Defense. The Bush/Cheney Defense Plan and its 25 percent draw-down envisioned a "base force" navy of about 450 ships. The U.S. Navy has been decommissioning ships at an accelerated pace and had only 351 ships by mid-1997. The Clinton administration's Defense Department Future Years Defense Plan (FYDP) projects a navy of about 300 ships at the end of the century. Some influential analysts are calling for even greater cuts in naval forces.[37] Regardless of the precise final count of these forces, the United States will have fewer naval units to address the future challenges to the use of the oceans. These challenges would very likely be reduced by a Convention-based regime of oceans order rather than the dynamics of customary international law.

PRESSURES ON THE FREEDOM OF NAVIGATION PROGRAM

Sixth, growing concern over the political and military costs of the U.S. Freedom of Navigation (FON) Program influenced the decision. This program was created during the final year of the Carter administration. The feeling at the time was that even with a widely ratified Law of the Sea Convention, it still would be necessary to exercise the rights set forth in the Convention in order not to lose them. President Carter himself made this point clear in announcing the new program: "Due to its preeminent position in world affairs, the United States feels compelled actively to protect its rights from unlawful encroachment by coastal States.[38]

The development of the FON program was motivated by two events during UNCLOS III: a 1977 National Intelligence Estimate study on expanding maritime jurisdiction, which concluded that the treaty would not be decisive in safeguarding U.S. navigational freedoms; and the renegotiation of the Informal Composite Negotiating Text (ICNT), which was developed without consulting the developed countries and placed heavier financial and economic burdens on the developed States. During his tenure as President Carter's Special Representative to the Third United Nations Conference on the Law of the Sea from 1977 to 1980, Elliot Richardson became concerned by the continuing proliferation of territorial claims by coastal nations. The ambassador believed that a unified international consensus on the law of the sea was necessary for the effective deployment of the United States Navy, but that, further, but it would not be sufficient merely to insist that freedom of navigation is essential or that the United States is prepared to assert its rights against objectionable claims. He noted further:

Our strategic objectives cannot be achieved unless the legitimacy of these principles is sufficiently accepted by the world at large so that their observance can be carried out on a routine operational basis. If deployments to distant regions of the world require the U.S. to defy the claims of States along the way, they entail a high risk of political, economic or even military conflict.[39]

The FON program continued under Presidents Reagan, Bush, and Clinton. It combines diplomatic action and operational assertion of our navigational rights by means of exercises to discourage State claims inconsistent with the 1982 Law of the Sea Convention and to demonstrate the United States' resolve to protect navigational freedoms reflected in that agreement.[40] Additionally, the FON program involves bilateral and multilateral consultations with other governments in an effort to promote maritime stability and consistency with international law. These consultations stress the need for, and obligation of, all States to adhere to the customary international law regarding navigation and overflight and practices reflected in the Law of the Sea Convention.

On the diplomatic front, the Department of State files with other governments diplomatic protests of maritime claims inconsistent with international law. Since the inception of the FON program, well over one hundred such protests have been filed by the United States.[41] Over the same time period, U.S. military ships and aircraft have exercised law of the sea rights and freedoms in all oceans against the objectionable claims of more than fifty countries at the rate of some thirty to forty per year.[42] Throughout the 1980s, with a substantial U.S. Navy involvement, the FON program worked reasonably well. By the early 1990s the environment had changed significantly. Thirty to forty FON assertions per year with reduced naval and air forces may be difficult to sustain and may threaten to limit the operational flexibility of our military forces, especially as U.S. friends and allies were reluctant to join in any multilateral FON operations.

At a time when forces available to conduct FON missions were dwindling, the United States was dealing with an increasingly diverse number of claims by coastal and island states to sovereignty and jurisdiction over the ocean areas that were inconsistent with the terms of the 1982 Law of the Sea Convention. These attempts to exercise national jurisdiction and sovereignty include, but are not limited to:

- unrecognized historic waters claims
- improperly drawn baselines for measuring claims
- territorial sea claims of greater than twelve miles
- security zones that are not provided for in the Convention
- contiguous zones at variance with the Convention provisions
- exclusive economic zones where the coastal state purports to negate or restrict navigation and overflight rights
- archipelagic claims not conforming to the rules of the Convention
- other categories of excessive claims including restrictions on territorial sea innocent passage, principally requirements for advance notice of innocent passage, and restrictions on transit passage.[43]

These excessive and illegal claims caused the United States particular concern because they covered the full spectrum of maritime possibilities and because they were made by the full spectrum of the community of nations. For example:

- Argentina, Italy, Panama and Russia have made historic bay claims that do not comply with international norms
- Albania, Canada, China, Colombia, Costa Rica, North Korea, Mexico, Portugal, Vietnam, and others made significant excessive baseline claims
- Cape Verde, Indonesia, and the Philippines have sought to impose restrictions on archipelagic sea lanes passage not permitted by the 1982 Convention
- China, Djibouti, Egypt, Indonesia, North Korea, Pakistan, and the Philippines have articulated various non-conforming restrictions on innocent passage
- Argentina, Canada, Italy, Spain and others have sought to impose improper restrictions on navigation of straits used for international navigation
- Brazil, Ecuador, and Peru have sought to impose improper restrictions on aircraft overflight in their exclusive economic zones inconsistent with the Convention
- Cape Verde, Finland, Iran, Sweden, and others have declared warships to be subject to coastal State environmental regulation.[44]

This is just a sampling of excessive maritime claims, but the diversity of claims in their character and the numbers of nations involved represented an enormous challenge for the United States' FON program. The financial and diplomatic costs, as well of the overall risks associated with the use of naval and air forces to credibly counter these claims, appeared to the United States to be substantially higher than would be the case with a specific, binding treaty.[45] Two experts on the law of the sea, J. Ashley Roach and Robert W. Smith, presented the position of the State Department in 1994:

Unilateral U.S. demonstrations of resolve—especially operational assertions—are sometimes viewed as antagonistic. They risk the possibility of military confrontation and of political costs that may be deemed unacceptable, with prejudice to other U.S. interests, including worldwide leadership in ocean affairs and support for use of cooperative, international solutions to mutual problems.[46]

The challenges to navigation and overflight are not incidental or insignificant. Over the past three decades, restrictions on navigation and overflight involving United States military or commercial ships and aircraft have included the following:[47]

- In 1967, the Soviet Union denied passage through the Northeast Passage in the Arctic to two U.S. Coast Guard icebreakers. As a result, they were unable to complete their mission. This route has been denied to U.S. surface vessels since then.
- In 1973, Libya enclosed a huge area of water in the Gulf of Sidra as a "historic bay." Although the world has largely rejected the claim, Libya's willingness to use force has deterred many from exercising their rights therein.
- In August 1979, Soviet aircraft staged mock missile attacks against the destroyers USS *Caron* and USS *Farragut* as they conducted FON operations exercising the right of innocent passage in the Black Sea.
- In August 1981, two Libyan SU-22 fighters attacked two U.S. Navy F-14s while the latter aircraft were properly conducting naval maneuvers sixty miles from the Libyan coast.
- In 1982 and again in 1987, Soviet forces interfered with the operations of U.S. naval frigates near Peter the Great Bay. The Soviets claim the bay is "historic" and the waters as internal. The United States considers these to be international waters.
- In February 1984, the destroyer USS *David R. Ray* was conducting FON operations by exercising the right of innocent passage in the Black Sea when Soviet aircraft fired cannon rounds into the ship's wake and a Soviet helicopter swooped within thirty feet of the ship's deck.
- After the August 1985 transit of the U.S. Coast Guard icebreaker *Polar Sea* through the Northwest passage, public opinion resulted in a restrictive Canadian law claiming high seas areas of EEZs as internal waters and closing international straits. To maintain our access to the Northwest Passage, the United States agreed not to transit with Coast Guard icebreakers without Canada's consent to the conduct of marine scientific research during the passage.
- In 1986, Ecuador interfered with a U.S. Air Force flight 175 miles from the Ecuadorian coast.
- In 1986, two Cuban MIG-21 fighters intercepted a U.S. Coast Guard HU-25A Falcon flying outside of Cuba's twelve-nautical-mile territorial sea, claiming it had entered Cuban Flight Information Region (FIR) without permission.
- In March 1986, during FON operations in the Gulf of Sidra, Libyan missile

installations fired on U.S. aircraft providing combat air patrol for vessels.
* In January 1988, two Soviet border guard vessels "bumped" the destroyer USS *Caron* and the cruiser USS *Yorktown* which were engaged in innocent passage in the territorial sea off the Crimean Peninsula.
* In April 1992, a Peruvian fighter aircraft intercepted and shot at a U.S. Air Force C-130 aircraft, killing one crewmember and wounding two others. Peru attempted to justify its action by asserting that the U.S. aircraft was within its 200-nautical-mile territorial sea/airspace.

Many of the nations making claims that the United States considered excessive have asserted that the Convention is a legal contract, the rights and benefits of which are not necessarily available to nonparties. The continual counterclaim by the United States that these rights and benefits are now embodied in customary international law may become increasingly difficult to sustain. In testimony before the Senate Foreign Relations Committee in the summer of 1994, the chairman of the Department of Defense Task Force on the Law of the Sea Convention, John McNeill, pointed to "increasingly egregious excessive claims" by many coastal States as a critically important reason to seek early ratification of the Convention.[48]

The danger of continuing to rely on the FON program were summed up best by Rear Admiral William Schachte: "The political costs and military risks of the Freedom of Navigation Program may well increase in the changing world order."[49] Conversely, by acceding to the Convention, the United States hopes to convince States with excessive claims to roll them back and, perhaps more importantly, to keep in check the natural desire by coastal States to extend their sovereignty over offshore areas through the type of increased regulation that would be inimical to navigation and overflight rights.[50] Roach and Smith sum up their commentary on the future of United States ocean policy by noting that U.S. accession to the Convention would have particularly beneficial effects: "While not eliminated outright, the need to assert U.S. navigation and overflight rights in the face of excessive claims should be reduced substantially, and with it, the risk and cost of unwanted turmoil and confrontation on and over the high seas."[51]

UNITED STATES LEADERSHIP IN SUPPORTING THE RULE OF LAW

Seventh, and finally, the United States desires to retain its leadership position in the community of nations in developing the international rule of law. In light of its diverse maritime uses and interests, the United States is unquestionably the world's leading oceanic State. Rear Admiral William Schachte emphasized the U.S. leadership role in international oceans policy, noting:

As the preeminent global power in the 1990s and beyond, the United States is uniquely positioned to assume a more visible leadership role in achieving a widely accepted international order to regulate and safeguard the many and diverse activities and interests regarding the world's oceans. And the LOS Convention affords us the opportunity to do it in a way that protects and promotes U.S. national security interests. To ensure a leadership role in this important arena, the United States must become a party to the Convention.[52]

Clearly, the Clinton administration has realized that U.S. failure to accede to a Convention widely regarded as one of the most important international agreements ever negotiated would raise fundamental questions regarding not only the future legal regime applicable to the world's oceans, but also the leadership of the United States with respect to the promotion of international law and order. The regime of the Law of the Sea Convention presented a superb opportunity for the United States to provide world leadership in an area of increasing importance to the community of nations.

By actively promoting "leadership for peace" in the politically and economically important area of an orderly development of oceans order, the United States hoped to be able to ensure itself a major role in shaping a global legal order in what some have called a post-hegemonic world.[53] Conversely, U.S. opposition to the Convention has been viewed by some as not only jeopardizing significant national interests in the Law of the Sea without substantial offsetting benefits, but also as constituting an implicit rejection of the promotion of world order through international law as a foreign-policy goal. Failure of the United States to fully support the Convention could encourage a belief that unilateralism, when backed by force, is a generally acceptable policy alternative.[54] On the other hand, full participation in the Law of the Sea Convention ultimately provides the United States with an excellent opportunity to continue to exercise world leadership within the context of far broader international activity and participation than was possible during the Cold War. More directly, the United States recognized that if it remained outside the Convention, it would not be in a position to influence its further development and interpretation as it goes through a period of transition and refinement.[55] Rear Admiral Schachte perhaps summarized it best:

By remaining outside the Convention, our long-standing leadership role in international ocean affairs and in forums, such as the International Maritime Organization, would be further eroded. Moreover, as an outsider looking in, we would not be in a position to influence the Convention's further development and interpretation. In effect, as mentioned earlier, by refusing to become a Party to the Convention, the only way we could seek to influence changes in the LOS regime would be through unilateral action, and that could lead to further destabilization and increased international friction.[56]

In sum, the totality of these factors persuaded United States policy makers that accession to the 1982 United Nations Convention on the Law of the Sea was in the best interests of the United States politically, economically, and strategically. The decision by the Clinton administration to submit the treaty to the Senate for its advice and consent was made only after exhaustive interagency review, chaired by the State Department and with the strong support of the

Defense and Commerce Departments, using the old UNCLOS executive review process. Unanimous support for moving ahead was obtained. A joint letter in July 1994 from Secretary of State Warren Christopher and Secretary of Defense William Perry to then-chairman of the Senate Foreign Relations Committee, Senator Claiborne Pell, strongly urged accession to the Convention and stated, in part, that, "Becoming a Party to the Law of the Sea Convention is in our national interests in all respects."[57] This statement exemplifies the position of these two key executive branch departments.

NOTES

1. See Walter Slocombe, "Toward Senate Consideration of the 1982 Law of the Sea Convention—Welcoming Remarks" (address at the Center for Oceans Law and Policy Symposium, *Toward Senate Consideration of the 1982 Law of the Sea Convention*, Washington, D.C., June 1995). Mr. Slocombe was the Under Secretary of Defense for Policy. See also George Galdorisi, "The United Nations Convention on the Law of the Sea: A National Security Perspective," *American Journal of International Law* 89 (1995): 208. This commentary built upon a July 1994, *Journal* piece by Panel on the Law of Ocean Uses members John Stevenson and Bernard Oxman, which addressed the need for the United States to review its decision regarding accession to the Convention.

2. Senate, *Treaty Document 103-39, United Nations Convention on the Law of the Sea, with Annexes, and the Agreement Relating to the Implementation of Part XI of the United Nations Convention on the Law of the Sea of 10 December 1982, with Annex*, 103d Cong., 2d sess., October 1994, III-IV (hereinafter *Treaty Document 103-39*).

3. See George Galdorisi and James Stavridis, "Time to Revisit the Law of the Sea," *Ocean Development and International Law* 24 (1993): 306.

4. See James Wang, *Handbook on Ocean Politics and Law* (New York: Greenwood Press, 1992), 29.

5. Jan Lodel, "The Law of the Sea and National Security" (address at the Georgetown University Law Center Symposium, *Implementing the United Nations Convention on the Law of the Sea: An International Symposium*, Washington, D.C., January 1995). Mr. Lodel, the senior representative from the Department of Defense at this well-attended conference, presented a particularly strong case for U.S. accession to the Convention and focused on the use of the Convention as a necessary condition for follow-on international negotiations and activities in international agencies. He concluded his remarks with the following statement:

We risk losing our ability to speak with authority in the international arena if we fail to join the Convention....The bottom line from the Department of Defense is this: The Law of the Sea Convention is a good deal. It is the result of long-standing bipartisan consensus. Now is the time for action. Let's join the Convention and move, smartly and confidently, into the future.

6.   Department of Defense, *National Security and the Convention on the Law of the Sea*, 2d ed. (Washington, D.C.: Department of Defense, 1996), 25, 26. Annex VI of the Convention contains comprehensive provisions for the composition and operation of the International Tribunal.

7.   James B. Morell, *The Law of the Sea: An Historical Analysis of the 1982 Treaty and Its Rejection by the United States* (Jefferson, North Carolina: McFarland and Company, 1992), 10. One of the earliest books presenting an optimistic appraisal of the commercial potential of deep seabed mining operations was *The Natural Resources of the Sea* written by entrepreneurial scientist John Mero in 1965. See also John Mero, "A Legal Regime for Deep Sea Mining," *San Diego Law Review* 7 (1970): 499.

8.   See generally Marne Dubs, "Minerals in the Deep Sea: Myth and Reality," in Giulio Pontecorvo, ed., *The New Order of the Oceans* (New York: Columbia University Press, 1986), 85-121.

9.   Professor J. Daniel Nyhart, interview with George Galdorisi, Sloan School of Management, Massachusetts Institute of Technology, 28 October 1994. Professor Nyhart was one of the principal designers of the MIT model, which was completed in 1978 and revised in 1983. At the time, it was *the* only public model for predicting deep seabed mining yields, and was, therefore, used extensively by both industry and government alike. Some mining concerns have their own, more limited models, but these are proprietary and have no visibility outside of the individual company. Professor Nyhart believes that many of the assumptions underlying the original 1978 model were erroneous, leading to too-high predicted yields. See also J. D. Nyhart and M. S. Traintafyllou, *A Pioneer Deep Ocean Mining Venture* (Cambridge, Massachusetts: MIT Press, 1983); Jan Markussen, "Commercial Exploitation of Polymetallic Nodules: Comments on Some Critical Issues," in *The Law of the Sea in the 1990s: A Framework for Further International Cooperation*, Tadao Kuribayashi and Edward Miles, eds. (Honolulu: Law of the Sea Institute Press, 1992), 346; William Brewer, "Deep Seabed Mining: Can an Acceptable Regime Ever be Found?" *Ocean Development and International Law* 11 (1982): 42. Brewer points out that the MIT model was an elaborate and sophisticated computer model that was designed to answer many pressing economic and business questions regarding deep seabed mining. Specifically, it allowed a number of hypotheses to be tried out to determine their impact on project yields.

10.   R. R. Churchill and A. V. Lowe, *The Law of the Sea* (Manchester, U.K.: Manchester University Press, 1983), 155.

11.   Ted McDorman, "Will Canada Ratify the Law of the Sea Convention?" *San Diego Law Review* 25 (1988): 535, 540.

12.   Jonathan Charney, "Provisional Application of the Agreement Relating to the Implementation of Part XI of the 1982 United Nations Convention on the Law of the Sea" (research paper, Panel on the Law of Ocean Uses, June 1994), 1-12.

13.   Panel on the Law of Ocean Uses, "U.S. Interests in the United Nations

Convention on the Law of the Sea," *Ocean Development and International Law* 21 (1990): 373. See also David Larson, "Deep Seabed Mining: A Definition of the Problem," *Ocean Development and International Law* 17 (1986): 278. The need for much-improved market conditions to make deep seabed mining economically viable was documented in the late 1970s. In congressional testimony in May 1977, Marne Dubs, of Kennecott Corporation and the American Mining Congress, estimated that it would require an investment of more than $2.5 billion between start-up and commercial recovery of one mine site in the Clarion-Clipperton zone between Hawaii and the West Coast. Further, James Wang pointed out that by a decade later the market price for most metals has fallen behind the estimated seabed mining production cost, citing the estimated cost of $3.50 to produce a ton of nickel whose average land-based production price was only $2.30 a ton as one example. Wang, *Ocean Politics and Law*, 200.

14.   John Stevenson and Bernard Oxman, "The Future of the United Nations Convention on the Law of the Sea," *American Journal of International Law* 88 (1994): 488. See also Milton Drucker, "Commentary" in *Law of the Seas in the 1990s*, Kuribayashi and Miles, eds., 352–353. Mr. Drucker, of the U.S. State Department, makes the point that the strategic impact of deep seabed mining has diminished dramatically due to alternate sources of strategic materials such as manganese and new technology to replace minerals such as cobalt.

15.   Bernard Oxman, "United States Interests in the Law of the Sea Convention," *American Journal of International Law* 88 (1994): 167, 173. See, for example, testimony by Karen Davidson (note 26 to chapter five); Wes Scholz, director, Office of International Commodities, Bureau of Economic Affairs, Department of State (address at the University of Virginia, Center for Law and Policy, May 1994); Wes Scholz (address at the Georgetown University Law Center International Symposium, *Implementation of the United Nations Convention on the Law of the Sea*, Washington, D.C., January 1995).

16.   See, for example, Doug Bandow, "Beware Part XI of the Sea Treaty," *San Diego Union*, 25 February 1994, p. 18, col. 3; William Safire, "LOST is Lost in a Foggy Bottom Fog," *San Diego Union*, 31 March 1994, p. 22, col. 1; Woody West, "Latest U.N. Maritime Treaty Should Remain Lost at Sea," *Insight*, 30 May 1994, p. 40, col. 1. These three editorials present decidedly one-sided arguments against the treaty. Each uses the acronym "LOST" as a pejorative to describe the treaty, even though this term is found nowhere else in the extensive law-of-the-sea academic literature. The editorials focus on the deficiencies of the Part XI deep seabed mining articles without acknowledging that this part has been substantially amended, specifically to make it more acceptable to Western nations in general and the United States in particular. See also James Malone, Letter to the Editor, *Wall Street Journal*, 11 April 1996.

17.   Churchill and Lowe, *Law of the Sea*, 13.

18.   Morell, *Law of the Sea: An Historical Analysis*, 200.

19.   Geoffrey Holland, "Commentary" in *Law of the Sea in the 1990s*,

401–406. Mr. Holland, director general, Physical and Chemical Sciences Directorate, Department of Fisheries and Oceans, Government of Canada, describes the increasing importance of the Convention as a framework for protection of the marine environment.

20.   Morell, *Law of the Sea: An Historical Analysis*, 200. See also Clifton Curtis, "Environmental Interests," (address at the Center for Oceans Law and Policy Symposium, *Toward Senate Consideration of the 1982 Law of the Sea Convention*, Washington, D.C., June 1995). Mr. Curtis spoke as the Oceans and Biodiversity political advisor, Greenpeace International.

21.   See William Schachte, Jr., "Special Report: The Value of the 1982 U.N. Convention on the Law of the Sea—Preserving Our Freedoms and Protecting the Environment" (address at the Council on Ocean Law, Washington, D.C., August 1991, photocopy), 4–8; William Schachte, Jr., "National Security Interests in the 1982 U.N. Convention on the Law of the Sea" (address at the Council on Ocean Law, the Brookings Institution, Washington, D.C. February 1993, photocopy), 10–14. See also Churchill and Lowe, *Law of the Sea*, chapt. 14, for a comprehensive listing of historical attempts to limit marine pollution.

22.   U.S. Senate Committee on Foreign Relations, *Current Status of the Convention on the Law of the Sea*, 103d Cong., 2d sess., 1994, 21. In this prepared statement, Rear Admiral Shkor was specific regarding the benefits of the environmental provisions in aiding the Coast Guard in its environmental enforcement role:

The Convention is also a far reaching environmental accord addressing vessel source pollution, ocean dumping and land-based sources of marine pollution As you know, the Coast Guard has recently embarked on a comprehensive, wide-ranging port State control program with the goal of purging our waters of substandard ships. This policy is in fact consistent with and supported by the Convention provisions that provide for port State enforcement competence. The Convention also prescribes a delicate balance between the rights of coastal States to adopt certain measures to protect the marine environment adjacent to their shores and the general right of a flag State to exercise prescriptive and enforcement jurisdiction over their vessels. It addresses State responsibility to curb all sources of marine pollution while requiring that all such regimes be consistent with navigation and other important maritime uses.

23.   United Nations, *The Law of the Sea: Annual Review of Ocean Affairs, Law and Policy, Main Documents, 1990* (New York: United Nations, 1993), 3–10. The secretary-general's statement reinforces the connection between the Convention and international concern for the environment. See also Biliana Cicin-Sain, "Reflections on UNCED: Emphasis on Oceans and Coasts" (paper presented at the 29th annual conference of the Law of the Sea Institute, *Sustainable Development and Preservation of the Oceans*, Bali, Indonesia, June 1995).

24.   Biliana Cicin-Sain and Robert Knecht, "Implications of the Earth Summit for Ocean and Coastal Governance," *Ocean Development and*

International Law 24 (1993): 323–351.

25.   Elliot Richardson, "Beyond the Law of the Sea: Prospects for a Sustainable Ocean Environment," *Oceans Policy News*, January 1993: 4. See also Cicin-Sain and Knecht, "Implications of the Earth Summit for Ocean and Coastal Governance,"323-351; Clifton Curtis, "Environmental Interests" (address at the Center for Oceans Law and Policy Symposium, *Toward Senate Consideration of the 1982 Law of the Sea Convention*, Washington, D.C., June 1995); J. A. Roach and R. W. Smith, *International Law Studies 1994 Excessive Maritime Claims*, vol. 66 (Newport, Rhode Island: Naval War College Press, 1994), 263.

26.   Senate Committee on Foreign Relations, *Current Status of the Convention on the Law of the Sea*, 79. This prepared statement from the Department of Defense Representative for Ocean Policy Affairs (DOD REPOPA) presents a comprehensive 1993 DOD Ocean Policy Review Paper, which frames the issues and emphasizes the value of the Convention in enhancing U.S. mobility and flexibility.

27.   Ken Booth, *Law, Force, and Diplomacy at Sea* (London: George Allen and Unwin, 1985), 172. See also George Galdorisi and Jim Stavridis, "Time to Revisit the Law of the Sea?" *Ocean Development and International Law* 24 (1993): 301-315; George Galdorisi, "The United Nations Convention on the Law of the Sea: A National Security Perspective," *American Journal of International Law* 89 (1995): 209; Edward Smith, "What '...From the Sea' Didn't Say," *Naval War College Review* 48 (Winter 1995).

28.   See Fred Ikle and Albert Wholstetter, *Discriminate Deterrence: Report of the Commission on Integrated Long Range Strategy* (Washington, D.C.: USGPO, 1988), 16.

29.   Panel on the Law of Ocean Uses, "U.S. Interests and the United Nations Convention on the Law of the Sea," 373.

30.   See Department of State, Bureau of Oceans and International Environmental and Scientific Affairs, *Limits in the Seas no. 112: United States Responses to Excessive Maritime Claims* (Washington, D.C.: United States Department of State, 1992), 2. See also RADM H. E. Grant, JAGC, U.S. Navy, "The Law of the Sea, Status of Forces Agreements, and the Role of the Legal Advisor" (remarks at the 10th Annual U.S. Pacific Command's Military Operations and Law Conference, Honolulu, April 1997). RADM Grant, the Judge Advocate General of the Navy remarked:

Over the past several years, the number of U.S. military personnel stationed in the Pacific rim area has diminished, as it has all over the globe. As our land-based overseas presence has diminished, the relative—and real—importance of forward-deployed, seagoing forces has increased. This presence, which serves the security interests of all of our countries, is dependent on a stable ocean regime.

31.   Department of Defense, *National Security and the Convention on the*

Law of the Sea (Washington, D.C.: Department of Defense, 1994), 10. This theme has been reinforced continuously at numerous symposia by high-ranking civilian and military DOD officials who stressed the critical importance of navigation and overflight rights, especially through strategic straits. See, for example, Rear Admiral William Center, Directorate for Strategic Plans and Polices, Joint Chiefs of Staff, "Military Mobility and the 1982 U.N. Law of the Sea Convention" (address at the Georgetown University Law Center Symposium, *Implementing the United Nations Convention on the Law of the Sea*, Washington, D.C., January 1995); the Honorable Walter B. Slocombe, Under Secretary of Defense for Policy, "Toward Senate Consideration of the 1982 Law of the Sea Convention"; and Vice Admiral J. Paul Reason, Deputy Chief of Naval Operations for Plans, Polices and Operations, "National Security Interests in the Law of the Sea," (addresses at the Center for Oceans Law and Policy Symposium, *Toward Senate Consideration of the 1982 Law of the Sea Convention*, Washington, D.C., June 1995).

32.   Department of Defense, *National Security and the Convention on the Law of the Sea*, 10.

33.   See *National Security Strategy of the United States* (Washington, D.C.: USGPO, 1992), 4-6 (updated and expanded in 1994); *National Military Strategy of the United States* (Washington, D.C., 1992), 2-8 (updated and expanded in 1995).

34.   John Meyer, "The Impact of the Exclusive Economic Zone on Naval Operations," *Naval Law Review* 40 (1992): 248.

35.   Nien-Tsu Alfred Hu and James K. Oliver, "A Framework for Small Navy Theory: The 1982 United Nation's Law of the Sea Convention," *Naval War College Review* 41 (Spring 1988): 39.

36.   Joseph Morgan, "Constabulary Navies in the Pacific and Indian Oceans" in *Ocean Yearbook 11*, Elizabeth Borgese, Norton Ginsburg, and Joseph Morgan, eds. (Chicago: University of Chicago Press, 1994), 368. Morgan, a retired U.S. Navy Captain and adjunct professor of law at the William Richardson School of Law at the University of Hawaii, provides keen insights into the reasons for the growth of many navies in the past decade.

37.   See, for example, Douglas Johnston, *NATO Realignment and the Maritime Component* (Washington, D.C.: Center for Strategic and International Studies Press, 1992), 6-12; William Kaufmann and John Steinbruner, *Decisions for Defense: Prospects for a New Order* (Washington, D.C.: Brookings Institution Press, 1991), 24-37, 142-144; Michael O'Hanlon, *The Art of War in the Age of Peace: U.S. Military Posture for the Post-Cold War World* (Westport, Connecticut: Greenwood Publishers, 1992), 18, 35 and 116. See Vice Admiral J. Paul Reason, U.S. Navy, Deputy Chief of Naval Operations for Plans, Policies and Operations, "National Security Interests in the Law of the Sea Convention" (address at the Center for Oceans Law and Policy Symposium, *Toward Senate Consideration of the 1982 Law of the Sea Convention*, Washington, D.C., June 1995) for a countervailing view on the need for a more robust navy.

38.   John Rolph, "Freedom of Navigation and the Black Sea Bumping Incident, How 'Innocent' Must Innocent Passage Be?" *Military Law Review* 135 (1992): 147.

39.   Department of State Press Release, no. 171, 2-12, (13 July 1979). See generally William Aceves, "The Freedom of Navigation Program: A Study on the Relationship Between Law and Politics," *Hastings International and Comparative Law Review* 19 (1996): 259.

40.   See Roach and Smith, *Excessive Maritime Claims*, 268. See also Rolph, "Freedom of Navigation and the Black Sea Bumping Incident," 148.

41.   Council on Ocean Law, *Oceans Policy News* (May 1992): 4.

42.   Department of State, *Limits in the Seas, no. 112, United States Responses to Excessive Maritime Claims*, 2. This publication provides a good summation of the rationale behind the FON Program, providing, in part:

Operations by U.S. naval and air forces designed to emphasize internationally recognized navigational rights and freedoms complement U.S. diplomatic efforts. These assertions of rights and freedoms tangibly exhibit U.S. determination not to acquiesce in excessive claims to maritime jurisdiction by other States. Although some operations receive public scrutiny (such as those that have occurred in the Black Sea and the Gulf of Sidra), most do not.

For further discussion of the Freedom of Navigation Program, see Rolph, "Freedom of Navigation and the Black Sea Bumping Incident"; and Yehda Blum, "The Gulf of Sidra Incident," *American Journal of International Law* 80 (1986): 668.

43.   See Department of State, *Limits in the Seas, no. 112, United States Responses to Excessive Maritime Claims*; Department of Defense, *DOD Maritime Claims Reference Manual* (Washington, D.C.: Department of Defense, Office of the Secretary of Defense for International Security Affairs, 1990 (revised ed. June 1994); Roach and Smith, *Excessive Maritime Claims*. These are three primary sources regarding excessive and illegal claims by a wide spectrum of nations; they contain a comprehensive listing of the claims that the United States considers unlawful.

44.   See Panel on the Law of Ocean Uses, "U.S. Interests and the United Nations Convention on the Law of the Sea," 374; Sam Bateman, "Build a WESTPAC Naval Alliance," *United States Naval Institute Proceedings* 119 (January 1993): 82; Roach and Smith, *Excessive Maritime Claims*, 4.

45.   Morell, *Law of the Sea: Historical Analysis*, 195. The Department of the Navy sponsors an annual, interagency Freedom of Navigation Conference with representatives from the National Security Council, Department of State, Department of Defense, all branches of the armed forces, Coast Guard, and other agencies in attendance. Spearheaded by the Navy Office of the Judge Advocate General, this conference is designed as one coordinating method for maintaining a comprehensive Freedom of Navigation Program.

46.   Roach and Smith, *Excessive Maritime Claims*, 266.

47.   Department of Defense, *National Security and the Convention on the Law of the Sea*, 10. See Senator Claiborne Pell, "United Nations Convention on Law of the Sea Will Enhance U.S. National Security" (address at the Georgetown University Law Center Symposium, *Implementing the United Nations Convention on the Law of the Sea*, Washington, D.C., January 1995); "U.S. Ships Report Mock Attack," *Los Angeles Times*, 11 August 1979, sec. A, p. 5; "High Seas Diplomacy Continuing," *Washington Post*, 27 July 1984, sec. A, p. 1; Dennis Neutze, "The Gulf of Sidra Incident: A Legal Perspective," *U.S. Naval Institute Proceedings* 108 (1982): 26-31; Robert Stumpf, "Air War with Libya," *U.S. Naval Institute Proceedings* 116 (1986): 42-48; Roger Haerr, "The Gulf of Sidra," *San Diego Law Review* 24 (1987): 751.

48.   Statement of Mr. John McNeill, Senior Deputy General Counsel and Chairman, Department of Defense Task Force on the Law of the Sea Convention, in Senate Committee on Foreign Relations, *Current Status on the Convention on the Law of the Sea*, 20.

49.   William Schachte, Jr., "National Security Interests in the 1982 U.N. Convention on the Law of the Sea," 14.

50.   Jan M. Lodel, "Law of the Sea and U.S. National Security" (address at the Georgetown University Law Center Symposium, *Implementing the United Nations Convention on the Law of the Sea*, Washington, D.C., January 1995).

51.   Roach and Smith, *Excessive Maritime Claims*, 257.

52.   William Schachte, Jr., "National Security: Customary International Law and the LOS Convention" (address at the Georgetown International Law Symposium, *Implementing the United Nations Convention on the Law of the Sea*, Washington, D.C., January 1995).

53.   Joshua Goldstein, *Long Cycles: Prosperity and War in the Modern Age* (New Haven, Connecticut: Yale University Press, 1988), 268.

54.   Morell, *Law of the Sea: Historical Analysis*, 206. Morell's book is replete with dramatic statements regarding the failure of United States to accede to the Convention. At one point he even compares the United States to the former Soviet Union: "The U.S. policy appears to be founded on the unproven and undemocratic assumption, traditionally predominant within the Soviet Union rather than the United States, that nation-states are unable to overcome self-interest through enlightened cooperation."

55.   U.S. Senate Committee on Foreign Relations, *Current Status of the Convention on the Law of the Sea*, 94 (this statement occurs in a letter to Senator Claiborne Pell, then-chairman of the Senate Foreign Relations Committee); interview of Professor Detlev Vaghts, editor of *American Journal of International Law*, by George Galdorisi, Cambridge, Massachusetts, 28 October 1995.

56.   Schachte, "National Security: Customary International Law and the LOS Convention."

57.   U.S. Senate Committee on Foreign Relations, *Current Status of the Convention on the Law of the Sea*, 94.

Chapter Seven

IMPLICATIONS OF A RATIFIED TREATY: WHERE THE UNITED STATES STANDS NOW

The international law of the sea evolved and existed for a long time without a comprehensive, formal codification. Moreover, the UNCLOS III negotiations were so lengthy and, in the end, so controversial that the implications of a functioning treaty may have been overshadowed during the pre-1982 debate and the post-1982 ratification process. Therefore, at this juncture, it is useful to examine just what the Treaty has wrought and, in effect, determine a "baseline" of the treaty to more fully understand its implications. This chapter will provide that baseline, not by conducting an article-by-article examination of the Treaty and the Agreement, but by focusing on the main issues for the international community in general and the United States in particular. A comprehensive, article-by-article examination of the Convention, which addresses all aspects of this treaty in some detail, is contained in United States Senate *Treaty Document 103-39*, published on 7 October 1994.[1] A useful summary of key features of the Convention provided by the United Nations Information Bureau is presented in Appendix 5.[2]

Operating in the environment of a fully ratified Convention on the Law of the Sea provides the international community with distinct advantages over the previous condition of depending on a combination of less comprehensive international conventions, bilateral and multilateral treaties, and customary international law. Bernard Oxman has offered this consensus view of the Panel on the Law of Ocean Uses of four principal advantages of a widely ratified Law of the Sea Convention:

TREATIES ARE PERCEIVED TO BE BINDING

Legislators, administrators, and judges are more likely to feel bound to respect treaty obligations. This would be particularly true in the case of a widely ratified treaty such as the Law of the Sea Convention which lays down the basic rights and duties of States. Even nonparties are more likely to be cautious about acting in a manner contrary to a widely ratified Convention; if they do, they are more likely to be isolated when their claims are challenged.

TREATY RULES ARE WRITTEN

Treaty rules are easier to identify and are generally more determinate than customary law rules. Even if one argues that a customary law rule is identical to a treaty rule, that argument in and of itself is elusive and hard to prove. Furthermore, without a widespread, binding treaty, inevitable violations are more easily interpreted as evidence that State practice, the ultimate source of customary law, is not necessarily rooted in the Convention. Even a layman reading the text of a binding treaty knows he or she is reading a legal rule, and can often form some appreciation of what the rule may require.

THE LOS TREATY PROVIDES FOR COMPULSORY ARBITRATION

Parties to the Law of the Sea (LOS) Convention are bound to arbitrate or adjudicate most types of unresolved disputes regarding the interpretation and application of the Convention. This can help avoid questionable claims in the first place. Perhaps more importantly, it provides an option for responding to unilateral claims, an option that may well be less costly than either acquiescence or confrontation. Because States are not bound to arbitrate or adjudicate disputes absent express agreement to do so, this benefit of the Convention cannot be achieved as a matter of customary law and is dependent upon ratification or accession.

THE LOS TREATY PROVIDES FOR LONG-TERM STABILITY

Experience in this century has shown that the rules of customary law of the sea may be undermined and changed by unilateral claims of coastal States. Treaty rules and subsequent obligations are harder to change unilaterally. At the same time, the Law of the Sea Convention establishes international mechanisms for ordered change that promote, rather than threaten, the long-term stability of the system as a whole. These include an amendment procedure, the growth and adaptation of authoritative case law from judicial interpretation of environmental and safety regulations as they come to be accepted, a mixed coastal State/international "legislative" system for establishing new specific navigational safety and pollution regulations off the coast of individual States, and a flexible system of shared responsibility for regulating navigation in particularly sensitive or dangerous coastal areas.[3]

WHAT THE LAW OF THE SEA CONVENTION PROVIDES

As the world's leading maritime State, the United States stands to gain the most from a universally accepted compact governing the 70 percent of the globe covered by the oceans. As both a maritime and a coastal State tied to the oceans and the use of the seas for political and economic purposes, the United States benefits from stability in laws governing the use of the seas, and stability over the long term is best ensured by a widely ratified Law of the Sea Convention. The Convention is not a panacea for the United States; its rules are not perfect. Widespread ratification, however, is likely to increase order and predictability, enhance adaptation to new circumstances, narrow the scope of disputes to more manageable proportions, and provide means to resolve them. The Convention provides a new regime in many areas, but four are of primary importance to the United States: security, economics, the environment, and dispute resolution.

National security interests have been a critical component of U.S. policy over the almost four decades spent in seeking a comprehensive Convention. They remained at the heart of the Clinton administration's policy of finding a satisfactory solution to the Part XI issue so that the United States could join the Convention. The national security interests in having a stable oceans regime are, if anything, even more important today than in 1982, when the world had a roughly bipolar political dimension and the United States had more abundant forces to project power wherever it was needed. The navigational rights and freedoms embodied in the Convention are essential to the daily operations of our military forces for the preservation or establishment of peace. The key boundaries and maritime regimes and core security rights assured by the Convention include the following:

The Definition of Baselines

The Convention defines the standards for establishment of baselines from which the various zones (the territorial sea, the contiguous zone, the exclusive economic zone) are measured. Experience has shown that drawing baselines has been and continues to be abused; such practices result in coastal States improperly claiming control of vast amounts of ocean space. The Convention lays down the fundamental rule that baselines are established at the low-water line along the coast, as marked on the nation's official large-scale charts. Straight baselines connecting protruding points of land and closing lines across river mouths and bays are permitted as exceptions to the rule, but only in compliance with clearly defined standards. For example, Khadafi's claim of a closing line across the Gulf of Sidra, which was proclaimed to be a "line of death," is clearly illegal under the Convention's rules.[4]

The Definition of Maritime Zones

The Convention clearly defines maritime zones, and specifies the rights and duties of coastal, flag and port States and permissible maritime activities in each. For example, a coastal State may claim a territorial sea no greater than twelve nautical miles from the baseline. A contiguous zone limited to customs, sanitation, fiscal, and immigration control can be extended out to twenty-four nautical miles, and an exclusive economic zone of 200 nautical miles may be established for resource-related development, environmental protection and other purposes.

The Right of Innocent Passage

This right of ships in foreign territorial seas to engage in the continuous and expeditious passage which is not prejudicial to the peace, good order, or security of coastal States is a fundamental right of nations reemphasized and better defined by the Convention. Naval vessels need this right to be able to conduct their passage expeditiously and effectively regardless of armament, means of propulsion, or cargo.   This provision regarding means of propulsion is particularly important to the United States because a significant percentage of the U.S. Navy's major combatants are nuclear powered.[5] No prior notification or authorization for innocent passage of any vessels is required under the Convention, even though a number of States have sought unilaterally to impose such conditions. The Convention plays a special role in codifying the customary right of innocent passage and contains an exhaustive list of the types of shipboard activities that are forbidden while a ship is engaged in innocent passage.

The Right of Transit Passage

The Convention establishes this new regime permitting free transit through and over international straits while meeting the concerns of major maritime States who could not accept the extension of territorial seas to twelve nautical miles without a corresponding guarantee of unimpeded right of transit through and over international straits. Over 135 straits, through which transit may have been significantly proscribed or restricted altogether as a result of the extension of the territorial seas to twelve nautical miles, are open to free passage under the regime of transit passage. These include the sixteen straits considered to be of the most strategic importance for commercial or military purposes. Among these are the straits of Hormuz, Dover, Bab el Mandeb, Malacca, Gibraltar, and Bonaficio, plus the strategic "shortcuts" through the Philippine and Indonesian archipelagoes. Less restrictive than innocent passage, transit passage permits ships and aircraft to pass through straits continuously and expeditiously in their *normal* mode. Accordingly, submarines may pass through straits submerged, naval task forces may conduct formation steaming, aircraft carriers may engage in fight operations, and military aircraft can transit unchallenged. All transiting ships and aircraft must proceed without delay; must refrain from the threat or the use of force against the sovereignty, territorial integrity, or political independence of nations bordering the strait; and must otherwise refrain from any activities other than those incident to their normal modes of continuous and expeditious transit. Transit passage through international straits cannot be suspended by the coastal or island nation.[6]

Archipelagic Sea Lanes Passage

The right of transit by ships and aircraft through archipelagos, such as the Philippines, the Bahamas, and Indonesia, can have a significant influence on the ability of military forces to proceed to an area of operations in a timely and secure manner. Archipelagic sea lanes passage permits transit in the normal mode between one part of the high seas or exclusive economic zone and another through the normal routes used for international navigation, whether or not designated by the archipelagic nation, or through International Maritime Organization—approved sea lanes. Like transit passage, archipelagic sea lanes passage cannot be impeded or suspended by an archipelagic State.[7]

High Seas Freedoms

The Convention makes an important contribution in expressly defining the types of activities that are permissible on and over the high seas. This is especially important to the United States because the effective operation of military ships and aircraft involves much more than transiting ocean areas. Under the principle of "due regard" for the rights of other high-seas users, U.S. forces remain free to engage in task force maneuvering, flight operations, military exercises, space activities (including the recovery of space craft and satellites from the ocean), surveillance and intelligence activities, and weapons testing. Additionally, all nations also enjoy the right to lay submarine cables and pipelines on the bed of the high seas as well as on the continental shelf beyond the territorial sea, with coastal or island nation approval for the course of pipelines on the continental shelf.[8]

Sovereign Immunity of Warships and Other Public Vessels and Aircraft

Sovereign immunity restricts authorities of States other than the State of nationality from exercising jurisdiction over warships and military aircraft. For example, police and port authorities may board a warship of another State only with permission of the commanding officer. A warship cannot be required to consent to onboard search or inspection. Furthermore, although warships may be required to comply with coastal State traffic control, sewage, health, and quarantine restrictions instituted in conformance with the 1982 Law of the Sea Convention, a failure of compliance is subject only to diplomatic complaint or to coastal nation orders to the warship to leave territorial waters immediately.

The concept of sovereign immunity of warships has come been increasingly challenged by coastal States wishing to circumscribe this historic right, based on assertions of security or pollution concerns. Article 236 of the Convention reconfirms the sovereign immunity of warships and military aircraft and also contains a vitally important codification of the customary principal that naval auxiliaries are entitled to the same immunity from enforcement as warships enjoy. For dependable military operations around the globe, there must be the assurance that military vessels can move freely, without being subject to levy or other interference by coastal States.[9]

UNITED STATES INTERESTS AS A MARITIME STATE

As the world's preeminent naval and air power, the United States depends on freedom of navigation and overflight to project military power, maintain and sustain a military presence, and take part in other lawful uses of ocean space and the air above it for military and commercial purposes. This global mobility has proven essential in protecting U.S. both interests and the shared interests of the international community. This security interest in global mobility is not an artifact of the Cold War. The potential threats to U.S. interests, including those we share with others, are now more dispersed. To promote peace and deter aggression, States face an increasing need to demonstrate the capability to respond promptly in different parts of the world, both unilaterally and pursuant to multilateral efforts. The future security role of the United States may depend in large measure on such capability. The Convention greatly enhances the ability of the United States to meet its security commitments.[10]

The national security aspects of the Law of the Sea Convention have direct bearing on the economic interests of the United States. The entire basis of our economy is critically dependent upon the security conferred by a stable oceans regime. To be secure and influential in the political arena, the United States must maintain its continued economic vitality. Approaching the end of the twentieth century, the United States finds itself more economically interdependent than ever upon access to global markets. The overwhelming amount of this global trade moves by sea. A widely adopted Law of the Sea Convention provides the predictability and stability that international shippers and insurers depend upon in establishing routes and rates for the global movement of commercial cargo. Additionally, this stability in the oceanic regime is critical to those who underwrite and support offshore exploration and drilling, fishing, and many other activities at sea.[11]

The Law of the Sea Convention reconciles the naturally conflicting economic pressures between maritime and coastal States with a complex accommodation of rights and duties. The Convention limits the breadth of the territorial sea to twelve nautical miles, guarantees transit for all ships and aircraft through straits overlapped by the territorial sea and through archipelagos, and preserves the freedoms of navigation, overflight, laying of cables and pipelines, and other related uses seaward of the territorial sea. At the same time, it gives the coastal State jurisdiction over living and nonliving resources, drilling, marine scientific research, and most installations and structures in an exclusive economic zone extending up to 200 miles from the coast and, on the seabed, beyond 200 miles to the outer edge of the continental margin. It also doubles, to twenty-four miles from the coast, the breadth of the contiguous zone in which fiscal, sanitary, customs, and immigration laws may be enforced. Finally, it establishes detailed coastal State rights and duties to adopt and enforce anti-pollution standards in these areas.

Critically important to economic viability is the fact that the Convention offers three protections from the risk that the established system of checks and balances will gradually evolve into the functional equivalent of a 200-mile territorial sea under discretionary coastal State control, effectively territorializing all of the major seas of the world. First, the rights and duties of coastal States and flag States are carefully enumerated. For example, there are requirements for prompt release on bond of foreign ships arrested for pollution or fisheries violations, and protections for their crews. Second, the regulation of navigation is closely tied to rules adopted or approved by a competent international organization, generally recognized to be the International Maritime Organization (IMO). Third, both the coastal State and the flag State are obligated to settle disputes peacefully. If a disagreement over navigation and overflight or related rights goes to adjudication, the States have several methods of resolution available.[12]

As discussed in previous provisions, the "Agreement" effected essential changes to the original seabed mining provisions of the Convention. Now, the resultant seabed mining regime in the Convention and Agreement provides U.S. companies and consortia with a predictable and stable regime for harvesting the resources of the ocean floor beyond the limits of the United States' continental shelf at whatever future time such mining might prove to be economically feasible. While deep seabed mining does not appear to be economically feasible in the next several decades, land-based supplies are finite, and mining the deep seabed at some time in the twenty-first century is a possibility.[13] The "Agreement" creates a regime where this mining can occur. The guarantees and protections afforded by this regime are superior to those offered by almost any land-based mining ventures, particularly those in a growing number of third—world countries.

There is strong interagency consensus within the executive branch, principally in the Department of State and the Department of Commerce, that the United States was well served by the compromise effected by the Agreement. Significantly, the United States is guaranteed membership on the International Seabed Authority, influence over financial decisions from the outset of the ratification process, and power over financial decisions. Membership will continue indefinitely if the United States accedes to the Convention. This provides assurance that future actions of the Authority will be consistent with the principles of efficiency and nondiscrimination, and proceed on a sound economic basis.[14]

Perhaps most importantly, the Convention and Agreement provide stability in the seabed mining regime. The multibillion dollar investment that likely will be necessary to mount commercial mining operations cannot take place without assurances of secure title to the resources. Given that these resources are outside the jurisdiction of any State, the act of a single State that seeks to grant exclusive title to a large area of the seabed may not be viewed as sufficiently secure under the regime of traditional high-seas freedoms to attract private capital on this scale. A State wishing to put public resources at risk through investment guarantees or direct investment might be able to overcome the problem, but given current trends, few, if any, would be willing to do so. If deep seabed mining is to take place on a commercial scale, it will have to be based on a legal regime that enjoys widespread support within the international community. The provisions of the Convention and the Agreement are unique in guaranteeing this support.[15]

UNITED STATES INTERESTS AS A COASTAL STATE

The management of fish stocks is becoming an increasingly important, and often controversial, issue for a growing number of States that rely upon fishing to feed their populations. Throughout the latter half of this century, in particular, the United States has played an important role in promoting workable solutions to fisheries management challenges. Prior to the ratification of the Convention, the legal framework of fisheries bilateral and multilateral agreements as well as nonbinding conventions by nongovernmental entities was extensive and fragmented.[16] Thus, the Convention offers the potential to transform this former hodgepodge of world fisheries law into a more articulate, more stable, more uniform system for managing living resources in the ocean.

Under the auspices of a widely adopted Convention, the United States is in a primary position to exercise influence to achieve amicable solutions to potentially contentious fisheries disputes. Tools to effect this include a legal regime that sanctions the actions of regional fishing organizations to deal with conservation issues. Additionally, the Convention levies important duties on coastal States to manage their fishery resources within limits of their maximum sustainable yield. For example, these principles are the legal cornerstone for the United Nations sponsored Conference on Straddling Fish Stocks and Highly Migratory Fish Stocks. Thus, the Convention's regime is fundamental to maintaining order between fishing and coastal States.[17]

Under the Law of the Sea Convention, the United States' fishing interests will be protected by an international agreement that sets down binding legal obligations for the international community. The Convention supplies a broad legal framework that facilitates consistency and balance in U.S. fisheries policy.

Specifically, the Convention enhances the United States' very important interest in exercising sovereign rights over the living resources of its exclusive economic zone (EEZ). Significantly for the U.S., which has the world's largest EEZ, the Convention's dispute resolution provisions underscore the high degree of discretion that a coastal State exercises in its EEZ by a specific exemption from binding dispute resolution procedures. These provisions give the United States considerable flexibility in defining and determining the optimum utilization of living resources in its EEZ. Wide latitude is also given for fixing the level of the allowable catch, determining harvesting capacity, and therefore concluding what, if any, fishery surplus might be available for exploitation by other States that might desire to fish in the region. The Convention also advances U.S. interests with respect to anadromous species, such as salmon, by recognizing the primary interest of the States in whose rivers those fish originate. The United States is one of the few States with remaining wild stocks of salmon. The Convention provides that originating States may ban high-seas fishing for anadromous fish and requires other States to cooperate with the State of origin to protect stocks from activities on the high seas.[18]

Often neglected in the high-profile debates regarding seabed mining and the ongoing debates regarding fishing rights are other economic uses of the sea of critical importance to the United States. Chief among these are offshore oil and gas production and the use of telecommunications cables, although some other emerging industries such as ocean thermal energy conversion and kelp harvesting promise to grow in importance in the future.

The offshore oil and gas industry is a multibillion dollar industry in which the United States is engaged globally, making the necessity of a stable ocean regime even more critical. The recovery of offshore hydrocarbons has grown from only 5 percent of worldwide production less than three decades ago to almost 33 percent of worldwide production today. Additionally, although U.S. exploration previously was almost exclusively on the United States' continental shelf, new exploration, such as that of the Deep Sea Drilling Project, has found promising sites in areas such as the Marianas Trench in the Pacific. The enormous costs involved in the recovery of oil and gas from these deep-ocean sites, when coupled with the potential financial returns, make a stable oceanic regime especially important.[19]

The telecommunications industry has an enormous stake in a stable oceans environment. The total value of existing undersea cables is measured in the billions of dollars. One new project, a single fiber-optic cable connecting the United States with Japan, is valued at 1.3 billion dollars. Billions more will be spent in the coming years by telecommunications companies to replace existing undersea cables with fiber-optic cables. In addition, major expansion of the web of undersea cables is anticipated, greatly increasing the importance of clear rules on the multiple uses of ocean space. Specifically, the Convention supplements existing agreements in this area by reinforcing the obligation of other ocean users to avoid damage to undersea cables and strengthening the principle of liability for damage to properly charted cables.[20]

UNITED STATES INTERESTS IN ENVIRONMENTAL STEWARDSHIP

Perhaps most importantly, the Law of the Sea Convention provides a critical benchmark for protecting the marine environment. The Convention establishes a delicate balance between the rights of coastal States to adopt measures necessary to protect the marine environment close to their shores, while recognizing the primary right of a flag State to exercise jurisdiction over its own vessels for incidents at sea, routine operational practices, design, and training of crewmembers. The Convention establishes a similar balance between the responsibility of States to curb all sources of marine pollution and the rights of maritime States to exercise their high-seas freedoms. Because the Convention and most States take the position that States cannot avoid their overarching responsibilities under the Convention to protect the marine environment through a claim of sovereign immunity, the United States uses the Convention to maintain a leadership position in environmental protection matters. As one example, the United States has successfully urged positions which hold flag States accountable for upholding applicable environmental protection norms.[21]

The Convention requires States to ensure that activities under their jurisdiction do not cause environmental damage to other States or result in the spread of pollution beyond their own offshore zones; to minimize to the fullest possible extent the release of harmful substances into the marine environment from land-based sources; to protect rare or fragile ecosystems; to conserve living resources; and to prevent the introduction of alien species into the marine environment where they may cause harm. It also provides for environmental impact assessments of planned activities, environmental monitoring of ongoing activities, and contingency planning for pollution emergencies. States are required to cooperate in establishing global and regional rules and standards for specific sources of pollution.

The environmental obligations placed on States relate to activities subject to their jurisdiction. Taken as a whole, the Convention clarifies not only the nature of environmental obligations of States, but also the activities and areas that are the object of these obligations. Four factors are particularly important in assessing the significance of this effort to combine the allocation of economic and other rights with the assumption of environmental duties.

First, the environmental regime is incorporated into a binding treaty. While a growing number of global and regional treaties deal with important environmental matters, none purports to impose comprehensive environmental obligations on so many activities in so many places. Other comprehensive global environmental instruments, including those adopted at Stockholm in 1972 and Rio de Janeiro in 1992, have been nonbinding declarations.[22] Although some have suggested that such instruments are declaratory of customary international law, these declarations do not necessarily represent an international commitment accepted as binding by the highest political organs of a State, especially when it comes to making the hard political choices necessary to implement environmental standards.[23]

Second, the Convention is the most widely ratified environmental treaty ever negotiated by the international community and is the strongest global environmental treaty negotiated to date. It establishes a duty to enforce detailed international regulations to protect the environment from all sources of pollution. In light of the contentiousness of the global conference on the environment (UNCED) at Rio de Janeiro, it is unlikely that a comprehensive environmental treaty stronger than the Law of the Sea Convention—particularly one dealing with the 70 percent of the planet covered by water—could emerge anytime soon. Because the Law of the Sea Convention contains many environmental provisions, and to a lesser degree because a number of developing countries are concerned about protection of the marine environment for economic reasons like tourism and fisheries, the collision between the environmental priorities and need for economic growth of developing countries that has dogged the negotiation and ratification of many other international environmental treaties did not impede this one.[24]

Third, in addition to establishing the basic environmental jurisdiction and duties of States, the Convention obliges the parties to adopt and enforce pollution control regulations with respect to particular sources of pollution, such as ships, ocean dumping, oil drilling, and offshore installations. It provides that these regulations shall at least have the same effect as, or be no less effective than, international rules and standards that emerge from the work of competent international organizations now and in the future. This duty applies to all parties to the Convention, whether or not they are otherwise bound to apply a particular standard.[25]

Finally, compliance with environmental standards under the Convention is subject to compulsory arbitration or adjudication. The coupling of compulsory arbitration and adjudication with environmental obligations is an extraordinary advance over past practice and makes the Convention an extraordinarily effective mechanism for preserving and protecting the marine environment.[26]

While the Convention is clearly "pro-environment," it seeks to guide problem solving in a way which respects sovereignty and the balance of interests of all States. One aspect of sovereignty that is particularly important is sovereign immunity of vessels and aircraft overseas. While the Convention does not allow a coastal State to use environmental regulatory procedures to limit navigational freedoms, it gives great specificity to the types of vessels that are affected. For example, in the past, some States have abused sovereign immunity to shield commercial activities and to avoid environmental stewardship. However, the Convention's sovereign immunity article seeks to prevent such abuses. For example, it denies protection to public vessels and aircraft engaged in commercial or other non-governmental service. It also specifically encourages responsibility for the environment.[27]

The net result of the complex environmental measures of the Law of the Sea Convention were well summarized by the Panel on the Law of Ocean Uses:

The Convention introduces into the law of the sea a comprehensive new code of environmental rights and duties. It provides a legal and institutional framework for concrete national and international measures to protect the marine environment from activities conducted or permitted by any government anywhere in the oceans, in a manner that balances the various interests at stake.[28]

UNITED STATES INTERESTS IN PEACEFUL DISPUTE RESOLUTION

Another major concept that the Convention introduces is that of structured dispute resolution. The arbitration and adjudication provisions of the Convention promote not only the peaceful resolution of international, political, and commercial disputes, but more broadly, the rule of law. One perceived weakness of international law is that States have been reluctant to accept the compulsory jurisdiction of courts and arbitrators. Furthermore, dispute settlement under international law can run the gamut from diplomatic intervention, to economic sanctions, to arbitration, to bringing an action before the International Court of Justice. This methodology was described by United States Law-of-the-Sea Negotiator, Rear Admiral William Schachte, as "ad hoc, at best."[29]

At least with respect to many issues of international law that arise in connection with the oceans, a widely accepted Convention on the Law of the Sea addresses this weakness of customary international law in a fundamental way. No comparable treaty with such broad mandatory compromissory clauses has ever been widely ratified. The prospective evolving written interpretations and applications of the law by authoritative tribunals established pursuant to the Convention must be considered progress beyond the traditions of self-help rooted in unilateral perceptions of law and force. The Convention does just this by promoting compliance with its provisions establishing or permitting fora for dispute resolution. To achieve consensus, however, certain especially contentious areas of vital national concern may be excluded from binding dispute settlement. Importantly for the United States, military activities are such matters excluded from the binding dispute settlement process.[30]

Moreover, the Convention reiterates the duty of States to resolve controversies peacefully. Some categories of disputes will be settled through a compulsory dispute-resolution process. Whether voluntary or compulsory, however, such a system of peaceful resolution becomes increasingly important in a world of increased tensions, such as small or regional conflicts involving border disputes, ethnic clashes, or disputes over ocean resources. Such a system will be useful to settle maritime boundaries and contentious navigational issues.

The Convention names four potential fora for compulsory, binding dispute settlement: the International Tribunal for the Law of the Sea (Annex VI); the International Court of Justice; an arbitral tribunal (Annex VII); and a special arbitral tribunal (Annex VIII) for specified categories of disputes. A State may choose, by written declaration, one or more of these means. A State may opt out of one or more of the procedures or fora with respect to three categories of disputes: maritime boundary disputes; disputes concerning military activities and certain law-enforcement activities; and disputes where the U.N. Security Council is exercising the functions assigned to it by the U.N. Charter.[31]

The salutary benefits of the Convention's dispute resolution mechanisms were summed up by U.S. Secretary of State Warren Christopher in a transmittal letter in September 1994:

The Convention establishes a dispute settlement system to promote compliance with its provisions and the peaceful settlement of disputes. These procedures are *flexible*, in providing options as to the appropriate means and fora for resolution of disputes, and *comprehensive*, in subjecting the bulk of the Convention's provisions to enforcement through binding mechanisms. The system also provides parties the means of excluding from binding dispute settlement certain sensitive political and defense matters.[32]

Thus, as the 1982 United Nations Convention of the Law of the Sea becomes a widely accepted international instrument, this comprehensive document brings with it important rights and obligations for the international community. For the United States, operating in this treaty environment represents not an end, but a beginning. It represents the beginning of a long-awaited process of improved ocean governance under the rule of law. Just as importantly for the United States, however, it represents an opportunity and an obligation to conduct a comprehensive review of our oceans policy in a number of important areas and a launching point for evolving new policy directions in these areas. These challenges will be addressed in the remaining chapters.

NOTES

1.   U. S. Senate, *Treaty Document 103-39, United Nations Convention on the Law of the Sea, with Annexes, and the Agreement Relating to the Implementation of Part XI of the United Nations Convention on the Law of the Sea, with Annex*, 103d Cong., 2d sess., 7 October 1994 (hereinafter *Treaty Document 103-39*). This excellent reference resource not only lists the entire Convention and Agreement, but also provides a discussion of them by subject area, including such major provisions as navigation and overflight, marine environment, living marine resources, continental shelf, deep seabed mining, marine scientific research, dispute settlement, and other matters.

2.   This summary is derived from United Nations, Office of Ocean Affairs and Law of the Sea, "Background Information on the United Nations Convention on the Law of the Sea," reprinted in Biliana Cicin-Sain and Katherine Leccese, eds., *Implications of Entry into Force of the Law of the Sea Convention for U.S. Ocean Governance*, (Honolulu: Ocean Governance Study Group, 1995), 4-5.

3.   Bernard Oxman, "United States Interests in the Law of the Sea Convention," *American Journal of International Law*, 88 (1994): 172. See also

John Stevenson and Bernard Oxman, "The Future of the United Nations Convention on the Law of the Sea," *American Journal of International Law* 88 (1994): 492.

4.   See Department of Defense, *National Security and the Convention on the Law of the Sea*, 2d ed. (Washington, D.C.: Department of Defense, 1996), Tab A; J. Ashley Roach and Robert Smith, *International Law Studies 1994: Excessive Maritime Claims*, vol. 66 (Newport, Rhode Island: Naval War College, 1994), 27-31.

5.   Les Aspin, *Annual Report to the President and the Congress, 1994* (Washington, D.C.: USGPO, 1994), 169.

6.   See Department of Defense, *National Security and the Law of the Sea Convention*, 2d ed., 5; Senate, *Treaty Document 103-39*, 18-19.

7.   Senate, *Treaty Document 103-39*, 22-23; Department of Defense, *National Security and the Law of the Sea Convention*, 2d ed., 5, 8.

8.   See Department of Defense, *National Security and the Law of the Sea*, 8.

9.   See Senate, *Treaty Document 103-39*, 27-28.

10.   See, for example, Department of Defense, *National Security and the Convention on the Law of the Sea* (Washington, D.C.: Department of Defense, 1994), 1-21;   United States Senate Committee on Foreign Relations, *Current Status of the Convention on the Law of the Sea*, 103d Cong., 2d sess., 11 August 1994   (Statement of John McNeill, senior deputy counsel and chairman, Department of Defense Task Force on the Law of the Sea Convention and Statement of Rear Admiral William Center, USN, deputy director, International Negotiations, J-5 Directorate, Joint Staff); Standing Committee on Law and National Security, *American Bar Association National Security Law Report*, December 1994, 1-3.

11.   The economic importance of seaborne commerce to the United States is often viewed as a "self-evident truth" not receiving extensive treatment in the considerable law-of-the-sea literature. Data supporting the amount of seaborne commerce are addressed in the following: Institute for National Strategic Studies, *Strategic Assessment 1995: U.S. Security Challenges in Transition* (Washington, D.C.: National Defense University Press, 1995), 107-114; Duncan Hammer, "Transportation and Communications Interests" (address at the Center for Oceans Law and Policy Symposium, *Toward Senate Consideration of the 1982 Law of the Sea Convention*, Washington, D.C., June 1995); Scott Allen, "Mare Liberum," *U.S. Naval Institute Proceedings* 109 (July 1983): 46.

12.   John Stevenson and Bernard Oxman, "The Future of the United Nations Convention on the Law of the Sea," 493.

13.   James Wang, *Handbook on Ocean Politics and Law* (New York: Greenwood Press, 1992), 182. Wang presents a detailed analysis of the seabed mining potential for various minerals, comparing not only the gross potential yield of various minerals, but also the potential seabed yield as a percentage of worldwide supply and the projected percentages in the year 2030.

14.   See Senate, *Treaty Document 103-39*, 59-68. See Karen Davidson, "Law of the Sea and Deep Seabed Mining: The Agreement Modifying Part XI of the U.N. Law of the Sea Convention" (address at the Center for Oceans Law and Policy Symposium, *Toward Senate Consideration of the 1982 Law of the Sea Convention*, Washington, D.C., June 1995).

15.   See, for example, Terry Garcia, "U.S. Accession to the Law of the Sea Convention: NOAA's Perspective" (address at the Georgetown University Law Center Symposium, *Implementing the United Nations Convention on the Law of the Sea*, Washington, D.C., January 1995); Wesley Scholz, "Law of the Sea Convention and the Business Community: The Seabed Mining Regime and Beyond" (address at the Georgetown University Law Center Symposium, *Implementing the United Nations Convention on the Law of the Sea*, Washington, D.C., January 1995) Terry Garcia is General Counsel for NOAA, and Wesley Scholz is Director of International Commodities, Bureau of Economic and Business Affairs at the Department of State.

16.   See Wang, *Ocean Politics and Law*, 483-545.

17.   See, for example, W. T. Burke, "Implications of Ratification on U.S. Fisheries Management," R. P. Barston, "United Nations Conference on Straddling and Highly Migratory Fish Stocks," and Lisa Speer, "Improving International Management of Straddling and High Migratory Fish," in Cicin-Sain and Leccese, eds., *Implications of Entry into Force of the Law of the Sea Convention for U.S. Ocean Governance*; Will Martin, "Fisheries Conservation and Management of Straddling Stocks and Highly Migratory Stocks Under the United Nations Convention on the Law of the Sea" (address at the Georgetown University Law Center Symposium, *Implementing the United Nations Convention on the Law of the Sea*, Washington, D.C., January 1995). Mr. Martin was Deputy Assistant Secretary of Commerce for International Affairs, NOAA.

18.   Christopher Joyner, "Ocean Fisheries, United States' Interests and the 1982 Law of the Sea Convention" (address at the Georgetown University Law Center Symposium *Implementing the United Nations Convention on the Law of the Sea*, Washington, D.C., January 1995).   See also William Burke, "Implications of Ratification on U.S. Fisheries Management," in Cicin-Sain and Leccese, *Implications of Entry into Force of the Law of the Sea Convention for U.S. Ocean Governance*, 38-40.

19.   Wang, *Ocean Politics and Law*, 175-179. The author predicts that by the early twenty-first century, offshore oil and gas production may account for half of world supply. He also points out that even as early as the mid-1970s, the annual value of offshore oil production was already four times as much as the total annual value of the living resources claimed from the sea.

20.   Terry Garcia, "U.S. Accession to the Law of the Sea Convention"; Wesley Scholz, "The Law of the Sea Convention and the Business Community"; Senator Claiborne Pell, "United Nations Convention on the Law of the Sea Will Enhance U.S. National Security" (addresses at the Georgetown University Law Center Symposium, *Implementing the United Nations Convention on the Law of*

the Sea, Washington, D.C., January 1995). See also Eric Wagner, "Submarine Cables and Protections Provided by the Law of the Sea," *Marine Policy* 19 (1995): 127-136.

21.   Bernard Oxman, "United States Interests in the Law of the Sea Convention," 169.

22.   John Stevenson and Bernard Oxman, "The Future of the United Nations Convention on the Law of the Sea," 494.

23.   Panel on the Law of Ocean Uses, "U.S. Interests and the United Nations Convention on the Law of the Sea," *Ocean Development and International Law* 21 (1990): 402.

24.   Oxman, "United States Interests in the Law of the Sea Convention," 170.

25.   Stevenson and Oxman, "The Future of the United Nations Convention on the Law of the Sea," 495.

26.   Ibid.

27.   William Schachte, Jr., "National Security Interests in the 1982 United Nations Convention on the Law of the Sea" (address at the Council on Ocean Law symposium, Washington, D.C., 1993).

28.   Panel on the Law of Ocean Uses, *United States Interests in the Law of the Sea Convention* (Washington, D.C.: Council on Ocean Law, 1992).

29.   William Schachte, Jr., "National Security: Customary International Law and the LOS Convention" (address at the Georgetown University Law Center Symposium, *Implementing the United Nations Convention on the Law of the Sea*, Washington, D.C., January 1995).

30.   John McNeill, "Dispute Settlement Mechanisms of the Law of the Sea Convention and U.S. Interests" (address at the University of Virginia Center for Ocean Law and Policy and U.S. Naval War College Conference, *Implementing the 1982 Law of the Sea Convention*, Annapolis, Maryland, March, 1996), 10.

31.   Marjorie Ann Browne, *CRS Issue Brief: The Law of the Sea Convention and U.S. Policy* (Washington, D.C.: Congressional Research Service, Library of Congress, 1995), 4. See also Lee Kimball, *The Law of the Sea: Priorities and Responsibilities in Implementing the Convention* (Gland, Switzerland: International Union for Conservation of Nature and Natural Resources Press, 1995).

32.   Senate, *Treaty Document 103-39*, ix. See also J. Ashley Roach, "Dispute Settlement in Specific Situations" (address at the Georgetown University Law Center Symposium, *Implementing the United Nations Convention on the Law of the Sea*, Washington, D.C., January 1995); Burdick Brittin *International Law for Seagoing Officers*, 5th ed. (Annapolis, Maryland: Naval Institute Press, 1986), 309. Brittin quotes Louis Sohn, who served as the U.S. negotiator on the dispute-settlement provisions of the Convention, to emphasize the importance of these provisions to the United States:

Of course, while most substantive provisions of the Convention might become customary international law which non-parties to the Convention might be able to invoke, the dispute settlement provisions are available only to parties to the Convention. Should a dispute arise between a State party to the Convention and a State which is not a party thereto, such a dispute would have to be solved in accordance with procedures available to the parties to the dispute outside the Convention. At present, such procedures are seldom available. As the United States has found out in its disputes with Canada and Latin American States in the last decades, without a satisfactory dispute settlement system even a powerful nation cannot adequately protect its citizens and ships against acts of foreign governments when those governments are not willing to submit their acts to an impartial adjudication. On the other hand, in cases between parties to the Convention the system of dispute settlement provided by the Convention, through it is extremely flexible and provides several options, can lead in 90 percent of the cases to a binding decision, which is likely to be accepted and complied with by the parties to the dispute. This is the way to the rule of law and to ensuring that the peace of the world is not jeopardized by a dangerous escalation of law of the sea controversies.

Chapter Eight

POLICY DIRECTIONS FOR THE UNITED STATES IN THE LAW OF THE SEA

As international treaties such as the 1982 United Nations Convention on the Law of the Sea (UNCLOS) compete for a place in the national agenda, it is important to determine where an oceans policy in general, and the Convention in particular, fit into the fabric of the national political, economic, and security tapestry. Is the Law of the Sea Convention just "one more treaty" or is it, and the United States oceans policy that it undergirds, a linchpin for our new national security paradigm?

STRATEGIC SETTING

In submitting the 1982 United Nations Convention on the Law of the Sea and the companion Agreement to the United States Senate for its advice and consent in October 1994, President Clinton noted: "Since the 1960s, the basic U.S. strategy has been to conclude a comprehensive treaty on the law of the sea which will be respected by all countries."[1]

The Convention and the Agreement were submitted to the Congress with little fanfare, but with a firm commitment by the administration to continue to make this treaty the cornerstone of United States oceans policy. Several months after the president's submission, in an address at the Georgetown University Law School Symposium on *Implementing the United Nations Convention on the Law of the Sea*, United States UNCLOS III negotiator, Rear Admiral William Schachte, framed the president's submission with even a tighter focus:

The president has forwarded the Law of the Sea Convention to the Senate for its advice and consent. If given, it will enable the fulfillment of a long-standing commitment shared with previous Republican and Democratic Administrations to participate in a stable, widely-accepted and comprehensive legal regime for the world's oceans.[2]

The United States' strategic landscape for the 1990s and beyond looks vastly different than it has looked in our collective experience in the almost five decades following the end of World War II. The U.S. oceans policy must adapt to this new strategic landscape if it is to support our articulated national goals. The strategic imperatives of the United States' new National Security Strategy must be reflected in our oceans policy if it is to effectively support this strategy. United States accession to the 1982 United Nations Convention on the Law of the Sea should enhance this mutual integration.

The first clear articulation of the United States post-Cold War security paradigm was made by President George Bush at the Aspen Institute Symposium on 2 August 1990—the same day that Saddam Hussein's forces invaded Kuwait. The president laid out a new security vision:

In an era when threats may emerge with little or no warning, our ability to defend our interests will depend on our speed and our agility. And we will need forces that give us global reach. No amount of political change will alter the geographic fact that we are separated from many of our most important allies and interests by thousands of miles of water....We have to have air and sealift capabilities to get our forces where they are needed when they are needed. A new emphasis on flexibility and versatility must guide our efforts.[3]

President Bush later formalized these concepts in the *National Security Strategy of the United States*. The president tied together the political, economic, and defense pillars of our national security interests and objectives by emphasizing a strategy of engagement and leadership that focused on, in particular, the need for global and regional stability as well as an open international trading and economic system. In discussing the opportunities offered by the new post-Cold War security paradigm, the president offered a security vision clearly dependent on the worldwide presence that a dynamic oceans policy under the Law of the Sea Convention could facilitate:

For the first time in more than forty years, we are no longer faced with the constant threat of World War III. Democracy has been embraced by a majority of countries around the world and our former adversaries are now our partners. We face a future enjoying not only great credibility in the eyes of the world, but also with more, and in many cases stronger, friends and allies than ever before to help shoulder the responsibilities and burdens. Multilateral institutions such as the United Nations, the Conference on Security and Cooperation in Europe, NATO, the Organization of American States, the Asia-Pacific Economic Cooperation Forum and others are energized and ready to confront new challenges. In combat and humanitarian operations, we have proven our ability to build coalitions to achieve common objectives. Our economic future lies more than ever in the global marketplace, our economic well-being guaranteed by expanded trade through such historic initiatives as the North American Free Trade Agreement and the Uruguay Round of multilateral trade talks.[4]

As a companion document to the president's *National Security Strategy of the United States*, the Chairman of the Joint Chiefs of Staff, General Colin Powell, published *The National Military Strategy of the United States*. General Powell built upon the president's arguments for a viable oceans policy:

Though geography provides the United States a defensive shield not shared by many other nations, our national security is critically linked to events and access overseas. The United States must maintain the strength necessary to influence world events, deter would-be aggressors, guarantee free access to global markets, and encourage continued democratic and economic progress in an atmosphere of enhanced stability.[5]

Both President Bush and General Powell devised the same four pillars of their respective strategies: strategic deterrence, forward presence, crisis response, and reconstitution. Built into these pillars is the assumption that United States naval and air forces can deploy throughout the world and have the flexibility and mobility to move rapidly across all of the world's oceans to respond where and when they are needed.

A mid-1994 Department of Defense white paper, *National Security and the Convention on the Law of the Sea*, highlighted the importance of a widely accepted Law of the Sea Convention to our comprehensive oceans policy and our national security posture:

Without international respect for the freedoms of navigation and overflight set forth in the Convention, exercise of our forces' mobility rights could be jeopardized. Disputes with littoral States could delay action and be resolved only by protracted political discussions. The response time for U.S. and allied or coalition forces based away from potential areas of conflict could lengthen. Deterrence could be weakened—particularly when our coalition allies do not have sufficient power projection capacity to resist illegal claims. Forces may arrive on scene too late to make a difference, affecting our ability to influence the course of events consistent with our interests and treaty obligations.[6]

As the United States moves through the mid-1990s, the imperatives that drove the initial Bush and Powell strategies have intensified. President Clinton and Chairman of the Joint Chiefs of Staff, General John Shalikashvili, published in 1995 strategies that placed an even stronger premium on the comprehensive package of rights and duties articulated in the Law of the Sea Convention than their predecessors.

In his first articulated security strategy, *A National Security Strategy of Engagement and Enlargement*, published in February 1995, President Clinton made a further break with those Cold War security paradigms that had put a premium on a force structure and a strategy designed, in many respects, to fight World War III should it ever occur. Such a force structure and strategy were not as dependent on worldwide mobility and flexibility on a daily basis. Significantly, in the introduction to this brief strategy—and prior to any discussions about specific strategies—the president acknowledged the vital role of the United Nations Convention on the Law of the Sea, noting that,

[The Convention] was the culmination of years of negotiations to ensure an equitable balance between the rights of coastal states to control activities in adjacent offshore areas to protect their economic security and environmental interests, and the rights of maritime states to free and unimpeded navigation and overflight in the oceans of the world.[7]

To an even greater degree than his predecessor, President Clinton emphasized the need to deter and defeat aggression in major regional conflicts, provide credible overseas presence, contribute to multilateral peace operations, and support counterterrorism efforts and other similar actions such as noncombatant evacuation and counternarcotics operations. Clearly, these activities are critically dependent on free and unhampered use of the oceans, particularly for navigation and overflight, as a matter of internationally recognized right—not at the sufferance of coastal or island States.

In the same month as the president's strategy, Chairman of the Joint Chiefs of Staff, General Shalikashvili, in *National Military Strategy of the United States of America: A Strategy of Flexible and Selective Engagement*, developed the themes advanced by President Clinton. Its major themes of promoting stability and thwarting aggression through peacetime engagement and conflict prevention are facilitated by the two complementary strategic concepts of overseas presence and power projection.[8] The chairman goes further to emphasize the need to promote cooperative security measures, work to open foreign markets, spur global economic growth and promote democracy abroad—all goals that presuppose the ability to operate U.S. naval and air forces on, over, and under the world's oceans in accordance with the provisions of the 1982 United Nations Convention on the Law of the Sea.

The importance of the Law of the Sea Convention to national security was illustrated in the summer of 1994 when the Department of Defense established a Law of the Sea Task Force to carry out the department's responsibilities in connection with further consideration of the Convention by the administration and during the Senate's advice-and-consent process. The Task Force was established under the joint guidance of Walt Slocombe, Under Secretary of Defense for Policy, and Admiral William Owens, Vice Chairman of the Joint Chiefs of Staff. The task force leader, the late John McNeill, Senior Deputy Counsel for the Department of Defense, was able to bring together a great deal of talent from the various defense agencies and military services, and his task force became one of the most visible and vocal proponents of the 1982 U.N. Convention. Throughout the mid-1990s the Task Force delivered numerous briefings to key senators, congressmen, and staffers, emphasizing the critical role of the Law of the Sea Convention in national security.

The articulated security strategies of the president and the Joint Staff, as well as the efforts of the Department of Defense Task Force, were framed in the context of the actual use of U.S. military forces in the mid-1990s. The end of the Cold War brought more of a new world disorder than a new world order; it reemphasized the fact that the majority of the United States' political, economic, and military interests are located across the oceans, far way from the shores of America. Events in Haiti, the Persian Gulf, Somalia, the former Yugoslavia, Rwanda, and other flash points served as important reminders of the need for strategic mobility based upon an assurance that our forces could surge to anywhere in the world, unencumbered by political considerations of negotiating navigation or overflight rights.

The value of strategic flexibility and mobility is recognized outside of military and government circles. Several academics long familiar with the law of the sea have written forcefully on the need for the United States to preserve its strategic mobility within the context of the Law of the Sea Convention. Typical is the view of charter Panel on the Law of Ocean Uses member, Professor Clingan's:

One thing is fairly certain....The United States Navy will be much "leaner and meaner" with substantial emphasis on speed and mobility. With superpower confrontation, at least for the present, no longer a major threat, the emphasis will be placed upon the capacity to move ships, supplies and troops rapidly to the scene of a regional conflict, if need be.[9]

Beyond the strategic implications of periodic U.S. response to worldwide flash points is the continuing requirement for stability in the oceans to support the economic vitality of the industrialized nations in general and the United States in particular. While the economic needs of nations vary, whether for raw material, energy, high technology, machine tools, food, or other resources, most nations are today critically dependent upon international trade for their economic survival. In a general sense, the most developed nations feel this dependency most acutely.

A complex network of sea lanes, which stretch through every ocean, are the acknowledged lifelines of all industrialized nations. Their daily welfare is contingent upon their ability to communicate by sea. For the United States, in particular, this trade represents the lifeblood of our economy. The overwhelming majority of this international trade moves by sea because the economic benefits of sea transport remain superior to every other form of travel. The cost of movement by sea is about 500 British Thermal Units per ton/mile; by rail, about 700; by truck, about 5,000; and by aircraft, about 15,000.[10] Additionally, the very existence of other modes of transport, for example, transport by air, is critically dependent on seaborne trade, for the complex international air traffic network is dependent on fuel prepositioned by ships, and is completely vulnerable to the loss of that fuel.

Clearly, the strategic and economic imperatives of the United States throughout the 1990s and beyond are inextricably linked to an oceans policy that guarantees the rights and obligations conferred by the 1982 United Nations Convention on the Law of the Sea. The entire strategic and economic equation, from military force structure, to alliance partnerships, to contingency war plans, to theater deployment plans, to bilateral and multilateral operations, assumes that the balance of rights and duties conferred by the Convention to preserve navigational freedoms will be universally recognized. With the Convention in place, it is hoped order and predictability will be the norm in the operations of all nations on, under, and over the oceans.

But, at this juncture it is too early to make this assumption. The history of international relations dating back over two millennia suggests that ocean issues have been especially contentious. Within the United States over the past five decades, the mechanisms for formulating and implementing oceans policy have not always been well defined, clearly articulated and thoroughly exercised. The natural tension between coastal and maritime States has not been erased completely by the Convention. Issues, many of which are vital political, economic, or security concerns for the United States, remain to be dealt with as the world community begins to adapt to the Convention. For these reasons, it is critically important that the United States continue the evolution of an effective oceans policy.

OCEANS POLICY

Oceans Policy Requirements

One way to approach the question whether an oceans policy is necessary is to reframe the question and ask whether it is acceptable to have the political, economic, and security imperatives connected with our use of the oceans depend on a positive confluence of factors coalescing, coincidentally, in the right fashion and at the right time. Clearly, this is not acceptable and may be dangerous. Certainly, it is prudent and may be necessary to provide positive direction to the way in which we view the use of the oceans and to the way we regulate those uses both within the United States, and, perhaps more importantly, in the international milieu.

The realities of the United States' position in the mid-1990s suggest a need for more positive direction in oceans policy. The present and future ocean activities and interests of the United States require no less. Much has been said in previous sections and chapters regarding the need for a coherent oceans policy that guides our international efforts in the area of ocean governance. Our international efforts must also be coordinated with oftentimes competing national interests, authority, and responsibility.

As a nation, we must increasingly confront issues requiring the setting of priorities among competing uses and of balancing the distribution of ocean benefits between current and future generations. An equitable balance must be struck, too, between impacts on local interests and the benefits to the nation as a whole. Throughout the second half of the twentieth century the United States has not had a single, integrated oceans policy per se, but rather has had a series of basically independent subpolicies, such as an offshore oil policy, a marine mammals policy, an ocean dumping policy and many others. A compelling need exists for an overarching policy that pertains to the entire assembly of ocean uses and resources and the long term public interest in the ocean as a whole. A need exists for policies that are based on equity and stewardship of the public trust; policies that take into account the functioning of the ocean and its various subsystems; and policies that achieve balances and set priorities that ultimately will determine the success or failure of any ocean management programs.[11]

Clearly, national policy formulation and decision making in ocean development and management raise complex issues, cover a variety of rights and concomitant duties, span a range of governmental and international activity, involve several sectors of activity, and encompass many diverse disciplines. Given these implications, the development of ocean resources calls for a coordinated oceans policy at the national level that treats the 1982 United Nations Convention on the Law of the Sea as a beginning, not an end.

Historical Perspective

Returning to the international scene, another way to view the importance of oceans policy is to briefly review the historical affect of oceans policy on the relations of nations. These historical antecedents go back over two millennia, as was seen in Chapter 2 in reviewing the development of the international *law* of the sea, but they become increasingly important approaching the present in consideration of their affect on the *policy* of States. Collectively, they convey a sense that the policies of nations with respect to their use of the oceans have far reaching and longlasting effects on their national security and on the international environment.

The Greek city states had adopted a policy of seeking naval preeminence in the eastern Mediterranean Sea as a matter of national survival. Using sea power as a basis, Alexander the Great dominated much of the ancient world in the fourth century B.C. Several decades later, Rhodes articulated its ocean policy in the Rhodian Sea Law, the first internationally recognized code of maritime conduct. Later, in the second century A.D., in a watershed policy statement, Rome identified the seas of the Empire as *res communis* under the law of nature, a classification maintained in subsequent codification of Roman law, which preserved the freedom of the sea in an era when marine resources were rarely depleted by use.[12]

Competing national policies of several Mediterranean civilizations led to clashes over control of the sea as successive claimants were challenged militarily by neighboring nations. Carthage's exclusive claim to portions of the Mediterranean Sea, by which, for example, Romans were not permitted even to wash their hands in the Sicilian Sea, is widely recognized as one cause of the Punic Wars.[13]

With the expansion of maritime commerce, freedom of navigation was initially exercised throughout medieval Europe, but the growth of fish consumption and the evolution of feudal doctrine soon gave rise to restrictions on freedom of fishing as exclusive rights were claimed to offshore fisheries. In the late Middle Ages, Danish and Norwegian claims led to armed conflict with other Baltic States, as well as with Holland and England.[14]

The Treaty of Tordesillas of 1494, which essentially divided the world's oceans between Spain and Portugal, was discussed in Chapter 2. The need for the treaty was precipitated by Spain's support of Columbus's voyage, which violated exclusive maritime rights claimed by Portugal. Consequently, the rulers of both nations believed that dividing the world's oceans between the nations was the only way to avert war between these two Catholic States.[15] This treaty was the strongest and most comprehensive assault on the *res communis* regime and represented a major policy decision by Spain, Portugal, and the Pope. The vigorous attempts to impose this regime on other States was an enormous undertaking by Spain and Portugal, and one that was certain to evoke a strong reaction by other maritime-oriented States.

Less than a year after Pope Alexander VI proclaimed the Treaty of Tordesillas, in a strong protest to this policy, France invaded Italy, marching through Rome and threatening Spanish interests in Naples. England did not have the military resources available to France at the time, and, therefore, avoided open involvement in the war. However, in what one might view as a precursor to the United States Freedom of Navigation Program a half-millennia later, Henry VII commissioned several expeditions to sail through northern Atlantic waters claimed by Spain and rewarded mariners who made new discoveries for England. Although these voyages were not successful commercially, Henry VIII continued this policy of challenging the closed seas regime and undertook a major expansion and modernization of England's Navy.[16]

France maintained a more active challenge to Spanish control of the Western hemisphere by sending Giovanni da Verrazano and Jacques Cartier across the Atlantic and asserting through diplomatic channels that the seas were open to free use by all and that policies put forth in papal bulls could have no binding effect. French policy gave license to their corsairs to attack Spanish and Portuguese shipping throughout the Atlantic; this ultimately led to the Treaty of Cateau-Cambresis of 1559 in which it was agreed that a peace treaty would be in effect "east of the Azores and north of the Tropic of Cancer," successfully sidestepping the issue of access to the new world.[17]

The policy decision on the part of the British in reaction to Spain's exclusive claims created the concept of marque and reprisal and the institution of privateering. During the second half of the sixteenth century, western voyages by English merchants and privateers—including those of John Hawkins and Sir Francis Drake—were backed financially and politically by Queen Elizabeth I, whose unwavering support for the principle of the freedom of the seas was one of the primary causes of the breakdown of the Anglo-Spanish alliance and of the war that ensued between these two States during the last fifteen years of her reign.[18]

Although England was the most visible proponent of freedom of the seas, both in her articulated policies and in her actions, the publication of *Mare Liberum* by Hugo Grotius in 1608 was seen there as a threat to England's claims to control of the seas around Great Britain. After John Selden published *Mare Clausum* in 1635 as a counterargument to Grotius, Queen Elizabeth I and King James made policy decisions to support the arguments of *Mare Clausum*. This launched more than two centuries of conflict on the high seas where, as a matter of policy, England attempted to exercise exclusive use of the world's oceans. England's seventeenth century claims to exclusive fishing rights and maritime sovereignty provoked several wars with the Dutch and ongoing conflict with the French.[19]

Following independence, the United States went to war with the Tripolitan States to uphold the principle of freedom of the seas rather than acquiesce to their demands for tribute. Earlier, England's interference with high-seas navigation eventually caused France and Spain to enter the American War of Independence on the side of the United States. Similar issues subsequently precipitated the War of 1812.[20] At that time, America did not seek or want another war with England, but fought to assure the sovereignty of American vessels on the high seas, and, more importantly, to assert the right of the United States to trade freely with Europe. Talleyrand articulated French policy and declared his nation's intention to "fight on the sea, not for herself alone, but to liberate the ocean and to emancipate all peoples who are victims of England's cupidity."[21] These clashes of oceans policies among the world's major powers continued essentially unabated until the Declaration of Paris in 1856 aligned international policy and law with the realities of contemporary use of the sea.[22]

By the latter half of the nineteenth century, the United States was becoming a significant player in the international community, principally on the strength of its navy and its adherence to the precepts of Captain Alfred Thayer Mahan.[23] The United States fashioned a policy of expanding its influence, principally across the Pacific, but also in other areas, such as the Caribbean, by supporting a growing merchant fleet and building a navy to rival the established naval powers of the day. This policy of supporting national growth and expansion through a powerful Navy continued into the twentieth century. In response to Germany's policy of unrestricted submarine warfare in the Atlantic Ocean during World War I, the United States emerged from its isolation and entered the European conflict. Following the war, President Wilson stated in his Fourteen Points that there must be "[a]bsolute freedom of navigation upon the seas outside territorial waters, alike in peace and war, except as may be closed in whole or in part by international action for the enforcement of international covenants."[24]

Similarly, U.S. concern regarding freedom of the seas played an important role in the deteriorating relations between the United States and Germany prior to World War II. Thus, two World Wars in the first half of this century provided the fuel for further naval expansions and left the United States, at midcentury, as undisputed mistress of the seas and in position to craft a viable oceans policy.[25]

The past several administrations, both Democratic and Republican, have emphasized that a comprehensive international treaty governing the use of the world's oceans was a major foreign policy goal for the United States. Implicit in these pronouncements, however, is the reality that, though the 1982 United Nations Convention on the Law of the Sea is the most comprehensive international treaty ever negotiated, it provides, at best, a *basic* framework for the activities of States with respect to the oceans. Much is left unstipulated and much needs still to be decided, first at a national, and then at an international, level. In many ways the Convention provides more of a beginning than an ending.

For the United States, the spectrum of issues to consider in the oceans policy arena is broad indeed. They range from what agency or agencies of the federal government will make and enforce oceans policy, to how consensus on oceans policy will be achieved, to defining the differing roles of the federal, state, and local governments in oceans policy formulation and implementation, to the crafting of international agreements to supplement and complement the 1982 United Nations Convention, to a host of others. Each issue is individually important, and grappling with the full spectrum of issues defies simple solutions.

United States Oceans Policy through the Mid-1990s

One starting point for understanding the complexities of oceans policy development is to review the formulation and implementation of oceans policy within the United States in the half century preceding the submission of the 1982 United Nations Convention on the Law of the Sea, and the companion Agreement, to the Senate by President Clinton. This review can begin the process of understanding the opportunities and challenges involved with formulating U.S. oceans policy as we move into the twenty-first century.

United States oceans policy received increasing attention during the second half of the twentieth century. In 1945, at the conclusion of World War II, United States oceans policy consisted of the sum and substance of the war at sea. In support of the war effort, ocean science, and many non-ocean sciences, were under the direction of the Office of Naval Research. University research in these areas was dominated by the Office of Scientific Research and Development. University laboratories were established as dedicated or rededicated to a particular phase of military technology. Closely identified with the oceanic effort were the Underwater Acoustics Laboratory of Harvard University, the Applied Physics Laboratory of the University of Washington, the Naval Ordnance Test Facility associated with the California Institute of Technology, and the Applied Physics Laboratory of Johns Hopkins University. The National Academy of Sciences had established the National Research Council and under it the National Research Defense Committee to focus scientific expertise on national security. It was within the framework of these institutions that the first postwar United States oceans policy decisions were made. Most notable of these were the decisions to initiate nuclear submarine development, which would once again revolutionize naval warfare, and to develop the satellite as precursor to the ballistic missile and an instrument for global observation, navigation, and communication.[26]

National desires to turn "swords into plowshares" followed closely upon the end of the war. The technology involved in building and maintaining offshore radar picket platforms was readily adapted to the development of increasingly ambitious and complex offshore oil and gas platforms. The Department of the Interior thus became involved in oceanic policy decisions and was a significant actor in the production of the first postwar oceans policy pronouncement in the Truman Proclamation, a watershed policy departure made despite the objections of the State Department.[27] This action initiated the continuing division of responsibility between the Coast Guard and the Army's Corps of Engineers for regulation of the offshore oil industry. The principal issue that had reached the national agenda was the question of ownership of offshore oil and gas resources. This issue dominated the national ocean agenda between 1947, when the Supreme Court handed down its decision in *U.S. v. California*, and 1953, when Congress enacted the Submerged Lands Act and the Outer Continental Shelf Lands Act. Of lesser national concern was the small and disorganized fishing community.[28]

The unanticipated reaction to the Truman Proclamation's Declaration on the Continental Shelf were claims, such as Ecuador's and Peru's, extending territorial seas to 200 miles for the purpose of extending jurisdiction over fisheries, including tuna. This was of as much concern to the Defense Department as it was to tuna fishermen who later received some protection from the Fisherman's Protective Act. As a result, a de facto oceans policy was coordinated between the Departments of Defense, Interior, and Commerce in support of the State Department efforts to participate in the First United Nations Conference on the Law of the Sea in 1958. The United States' policy was to secure the continental shelf to its outer limit for the extraction of oil, but to limit jurisdiction over the water column to a three mile territorial sea that would satisfy Defense Department concerns over freedom of navigation and fisherman's concerns over the harvest on the high seas.[29]

United States negotiators at the United Nations Conference in 1958 focused attention on the need to more effectively formulate oceans policy. In the aftermath of the Korean War, and reflecting public sympathy to continue to "beat swords into plowshares," public pressure was forcing the Department of Defense to divorce its activities from those having commercial value. The establishment of the National Science Foundation in 1963 and the passage of the Mansfield Amendment to the Defense Appropriations Act divorced military and nonmilitary science and development. As one example, the Navy's Deep Submergence program ceased attempting to develop military hardware to meet commercial requirements. Concurrently, a national consensus developed that the Federal government ought to do more to capitalize on the great benefits that the oceans were seen to hold. Toward that end, the Sea Grant College program was enacted into legislation in 1966,[30] and as late as 1968 the major support for the oceanic effort of the University of Rhode Island, the Woods Hole Oceanographic Institution, the Lamont Geophysical Laboratory of Columbia University, the University of Miami, Texas A&M, Scripps Institution of Oceanography, Oregon State University, and the University of Washington was derived from the Office of Naval Research.[31]

At the seat of government, it was the United States Congress that took the major ocean policy initiative that was to bring the United States to its zenith of coherence and organization with respect to the nation and the sea. The Marine Resources and Development Act of 1966 established the Stratton Commission whose task was to establish an organizational framework and program by which the United States might most effectively utilize the sea. The commission's report, "Our Nation and the Sea," was to become the most important document in U.S. oceans policy since the Truman Proclamation.[32] The commission reported to a cabinet-level council, chaired by the vice president, which included the Secretaries of State, Navy, Interior, Commerce, Health, Education and Welfare, and Treasury, as well as the director of the National Science Foundation. The Stratton Commission's report, issued in 1969, was a complete program based on a nationally coordinated oceans policy. The report addressed all aspects of a comprehensive oceans policy with the exception of maritime commerce.[33]

At this juncture, elements of a national oceans policy began to emerge. The consensus strengthened during this period that the federal government should be more active in directing a national oceans policy. Congress members and staff in both houses were excited by these prospects. The second half of the 1960s probably represented the peak of high-level executive branch attention to national oceans policy. In a major policy speech delivered at the commissioning of the oceanographic research ship *Oceanographer*, President Johnson forcefully articulated the importance of the oceans.[34] And, in his 1968 State of the Union address, the president discussed the importance of the oceans in further detail.[35]

By decade's end, momentous changes were occurring in oceans policy development on the international and national scene. The Pardo Resolution[36] had set in motion the machinery for the Third United Nations Conference on the Law of the Sea. It was also the impetus for the establishment by the United States of the International Decade of Ocean Exploration. The publication in 1962 of Rachel Carson's book *Silent Spring* and environmental disasters such as two major oil spills, the Torrey Canyon off the shores of Scotland in 1968, and the Santa Barbara oil blowout in 1969, focused world attention on the ocean environment.[37]

The executive branch and the Congress implemented the Stratton Commission report by establishing a National Advisory Commission on the

Oceans and Atmosphere (NACOA) and a National Oceanic and Atmospheric Administration (NOAA) in the Department of Commerce. The Congress also established a formal State Department Advisory Group to provide advice to the American delegation to UNCLOS III across the spectrum of public oceanic interests. In turn, the executive branch established an interagency advisory group to advise the State Department. The National Academy of Science and the newly formed National Academy of Engineering were similarly reorganized to support the new hierarchical structure. The National Academy of Science organized a Freedom of Ocean Science Task Group, whose members became the science cadre of the State Department Law of the Sea Advisory Group. This group was to be the core of the Ocean Policy Committee of the National Academy of Sciences. This committee, in turn, formed a bridge between the Academy of Sciences Ocean Board, the Academy of Engineering's Marine Board, and the Interagency Advisory Group.[38]

Thus, as the United States entered the 1970s, and as the international community prepared for the convening of UNCLOS III, the United States had a well-defined hierarchy for determining and establishing a national and international oceans policy.[39]   There were, however, a few structural weaknesses. Surprisingly, the Congress did not reorganize itself to provide a coherent legislative face with respect to the oceans. In addition, by deciding to place NOAA within the Department of Commerce, the executive branch effectively divided the domestic responsibility for ocean resources among five agencies: Commerce had responsibility for developing fisheries; Interior had responsibility for seabed resources; the Coast Guard had regulatory responsibility for marine safety of offshore installations; the Corps of Engineers of the Department of the Army had responsibility for fixed installations on the seabed; and the Environmental Protection Agency had responsibility for protection of the marine environment with respect to pollution associated with the development and transport of marine resources.[40]

The net result of these developments was that, within the executive branch, the nation was well organized for its oceanic future. These committees and organizations were characterized by interlocking directorates, with some ocean experts serving simultaneously on several task groups, academies and boards. The Congress, however, did not achieve this level of organization.[41]   For example, no single committee in the United States Senate had exclusive responsibility for oceans policy matters. In the House of Representatives, the Merchant Marine and Fisheries Committee represented one such structure, but overseeing the U.S. Merchant Marine was not a focal point of integrated U.S. oceans policy.[42]

In the wake of the 1968 presidential election, the responsibility for implementing the recommendations of the Stratton Commission's report, "Our Nation and the Sea," passed to the Nixon administration. Early in 1969 the administration established a commission to review the Stratton Commission Report. During the course of this review, the White House demonstrated that although science and defense were important issues, the ocean and ocean resources were not viewed as major economic interests of the United States. To some it seemed that the structure of national oceans policy was being dismantled even as it was being put in place. Even so, NOAA continued to flourish within the Department of Commerce, and the Coast Guard was relocated in the Department of Transportation. Additionally, of particular importance to the long-term generation of national oceans policy was the establishment of the National Sea Grant Program in the nation's colleges and universities.[43]

This was the national oceans policy formulation structure that existed in the United States at the beginning of UNCLOS III. Although the president and the Executive Office of the White House did not appear to have a compelling desire to closely direct United States oceans policy, this role was quickly assumed by the secretary of state, who made a number of significant declarations of United States' policy with respect to the law of the sea. Recommendations for U.S. policy grew out of formal meetings and preparatory studies on the part of the Interagency Task Force and the Public Advisory Committee to the State Department. Ambassador Stevenson, along with the secretary of state, used these recommendations to formulate policy goals for the United States delegation to UNCLOS III. These goals consisted of the following:

- Develop the concept of "straits passage" and preserve freedom of navigation, particularly freedom of navigation for naval ships, submarines, and aircraft, despite the trend to increase the breadth of territorial seas.
- Maximize the preservation of high-seas freedoms and minimize the sovereign rights of coastal states in the exclusive economic zone.
- Re-establish freedom of scientific research outside the territorial sea, without a requirement for consent on the part of the coastal State.
- Establish a flag State, port State, and coastal State regime for the protection of the ocean environment which would guarantee standards not less than those adopted by the United States and at the same time prevent the establishment of special regimes that would inhibit freedom of navigation.
- Prevent the establishment of a common heritage regime that would inhibit United States enterprise in exploitation of the resources of the seabed beyond national jurisdiction and prevent the mandatory transfer of technology on other than commercial terms.
- Negotiate a comprehensive treaty which the Congress of the United States would be willing to ratify.[44]

Previous chapters have examined the United States' participation in the UNCLOS III process in detail, emphasizing the ultimate, unsatisfactory outcome of the decade-plus of negotiations from the perspective of the United States. Oceans policy formulation did not stop while these protracted negotiations were underway. Impatient over the progress of the UNCLOS III negotiations, the U.S. Congress unilaterally intervened by passing the Magnuson Act, which established a 200-mile Fisheries Conservation Zone and which was crafted to reflect what the United States hoped would result from the UNCLOS III negotiations, and the Deep Seabed Hard Minerals Resource Act, which sought to establish an independent, reciprocal-States regime for the deep seabed. There was, however, very little coordination between the Congress and the executive branch for the conduct of negotiations with respect to the Magnuson legislation. With respect to the Deep Seabed Hard Minerals Resource Act, the United States was perceived by some to be hostile to the common heritage regime and to the Treaty itself.[45]

The United States' attitude towards the common heritage regime must be examined in more detail in the context of the day. The Arab oil embargoes, which occurred during the protracted UNCLOS III negotiations, gave United States hard mineral mining interests an opportunity to focus attention on a new problem. Because of its lack of domestic sources, the United States, they argued, faced a potentially serious shortage of strategic minerals such as cobalt, nickel, and manganese. According to this argument, a hard minerals cartel along the lines of OPEC could place the U.S. in a vulnerable position. Although not widely supported, this "problem," when coupled with the growing impatience with UNCLOS III, was sufficiently compelling to push a domestic seabed mining bill through Congress and into law by 1980.

The major role in communicating between the executive and the Congress was carried out by the National Advisory Committee on the Oceans and Atmosphere. This body was statutorily required to report to both the executive and the Congress. Members of this body served for staggered terms of three years each. Such appointments were made in an attempt to depoliticize the membership. Unfortunately, the Ford, Carter, and Reagan administrations each made appointments perceived as politically partisan, and, to no one's surprise, this now-politicized body ceased to be an effective entity and was finally dissolved by the Reagan administration.[46]

Although good intentions in oceans policy abounded in the decades of the 1960s and 1970s, and although some notable strides were made, United States oceans policy during this twenty-year period was never as well organized as it might have been. Responding to the promise of great benefits to come from the development of ocean resources, the Stratton Commission had developed a blueprint for a substantially expanded and better coordinated national ocean effort. Unquestionably, important ocean legislation was enacted in the 1970s. Much of it, however, was enacted in response to perceived environmental problems, rather than to the overarching recommendations of the Stratton Commission. However, just as these ocean-protection programs were coming on line, the energy crisis developed and, in response, legislative actions were taken to address it. As a consequence, what started out as a comprehensive ocean program aimed at increasing the benefits of ocean use was first torqued toward the narrower goal of protection and conservation and then toward the specific objective of energy independence.[47]

The ushering in of the Reagan administration represented a watershed in the formulation of United States oceans policy. The Reagan administration favored deregulation by the federal government and reduced much of the advisory and policy-making machinery of government. The new administration believed that "free-market" forces would allocate the nation's resources, including ocean and coastal resources, more efficiently than government regulation and that industry should be freed from the vast array of governmental regulation in order to allow markets to operate most efficiently to generate national wealth. Administration support for the National Academy of Science Ocean Policy Committee was greatly curtailed. Partly as a result of this curtailment, and partly as a result of a policy decision by the Academy of Science's Board, its role was shortly thereafter relegated to a subcommittee which largely ceased to function. The focus of the Marine Board of the academy was similarly modified to take emphasis away from engineering technologies of significance to national commerce and trade and to concentrate on engineering as it applied to ocean science.[48]

As the Reagan administration continued its reorganization of the executive branch structure, policy analysis and policy decision were concentrated in the National Security Council as part of the Executive Office of the White House. The earlier policy determination by the Nixon administration that government efforts on the oceans would be focused on science and defense was reinforced to a high degree. The Reagan administration believed that resource development and commerce and trade could best thrive in an atmosphere of limited government interaction. The primary oceanic priority in the National Security Council was the preservation of the "oil pipeline" from the oil producing Gulf States to the Western industrialized nations. This contributed to a significant buildup of the U.S. Navy throughout the 1980s.[49] A primary role of this Navy was to assure passage of oil through the Strait of Hormuz, across the Indian Ocean, through the Strait of Malacca, past the Philippines, and across the Pacific. This policy supported the securing of rights for bases in the Philippines and in Diego Garcia, military aid to Kuwait and Saudi Arabia, and the nullification of any potential threats to this pipeline. It also reinvigorated the policy of securing the right of innocent passage by warships through territorial seas.[50] This absolute need for guaranteed naval mobility was recognized outside the executive branch, as well. Within the prestigious "naval review" issue of the U.S. Naval Institute's *Proceedings*, Thomas Clingan commented extensively on the importance of naval mobility to the United States.[51]

With respect to the law of the sea (LOS), in March 1981, the Reagan administration quickly requested the U.N. to place a hold on further LOS negotiations until a comprehensive review of United States' policy on the law of the sea could be made. This review was carried out diligently by an interagency committee but was truncated without effective resolution.[52] Large portions of the treaty were not only acceptable, but highly desirable, from the standpoint of United States oceans policy. Nevertheless, despite attempts at modification to address U.S. objections, and even though the principal negotiator for the United States for this portion of the treaty, Leigh Ratiner, recommended that the United States become a signatory to the Treaty, it was not acceptable to the White House. The key reason for the U.S. rejection of the Convention was based on the Reagan administration's objections to Part XI of the treaty, in large part because of its belief that commercial enterprise should not be conducted by governmental entities.[53]

The Reagan administration recognized that its vote against the Treaty, and its subsequent refusal to sign the Convention, could leave a vacuum with respect to oceans policy formulation and articulation by the administration. Therefore, the White House moved quickly, and on 10 March 1983, the president articulated a Presidential Ocean Policy Statement as well as Proclamation 5030, establishing a 200-nautical mile exclusive economic zone for the United States. Previous chapters have dealt with the content and the timing of these actions and the efforts to influence the final treaty makeup and vote. While these efforts did not completely achieve the desired effect, the residual result was that these two statements formed the core of the administration's, and in the absence of strong congressional action, the United States' oceans policy throughout the 1980s and into the 1990s. The Presidential Ocean Policy Statement and Proclamation 5030 are presented in their entirety in Appendices 1 and 2, respectively.[54]

At the level of the cabinet departments of the Executive Branch, the articulated policy of the Department of State and the Department of Defense was the pursuit of United States oceans policy on three tiers: (1) a vigorous freedom of navigation (FON) program, (2) promulgation of guidance to military forces, and (3) active development and support of conventional international law addressing ocean issues.

The articulated purpose of the FON program is to preserve and protect the global mobility of U.S. forces, and the navigation and overflight rights of all ocean uses. The program is designed to be peaceful rather than provocative and to impartially reject excessive maritime claims of allied, friendly, neutral, and unfriendly States alike. The effectiveness of the FON Program as a "lever" to gain full coastal State compliance with the navigation and overflight provisions of the Convention has been positive for the most part, although the value of asserting these rights has begun to be weighed against the negative effects of a policy built around continual protest and assertion.

In addition to the FON program, the United States provided extensive, specific guidance to its naval forces which embodied the navigation and overflight provisions of the Convention. These comprehensive rules are embodied in U.S. Naval Warfare Publication (NWP-9)/Fleet Marine Force Manual (FMFM) 1-10, entitled *The Commander's Handbook on the Law of Naval Operations*. This publication not only provides definitive and binding guidance to the operating forces of the United States, but has also served as a model for, and has been widely cited and emulated by, other maritime nations in the preparation of their own military guidance.[55]

The Commander's Handbook on the Law of Naval Operations does far more than ensure compliance by U.S. military forces with U.S. oceans policy and the navigational articles of the 1982 Convention. It also provides other nations an illustration of authoritative interpretation by the United States in applying those rules in its daily maritime activity worldwide. In this way, the United States has taken the lead in breathing real life into the navigational articles of the Convention. *The Commander's Handbook on the Law of Naval Operations* has been widely distributed, informally, to other nations with maritime interests. It has been discussed at international conferences and symposia. This publication's success is reflected in its being widely cited and emulated by other maritime nations in the preparations of their policy guidance. Thus, *The Commander's Handbook on the Law of Naval Operations* has emerged as a key reference on contemporary ocean law.[56]

Finally, a third tier of the United States oceans policy revolved around the active development and support of conventional international law addressing ocean issues. Beyond the 1982 United Nations Law of the Sea Convention, the United States was instrumental in a significant number of multilateral efforts at international codification in a number of important areas, as well as bilateral agreements embracing virtually every aspect of ocean use. Whether through negotiation of multilateral conventions or less comprehensive bilateral agreements, U.S. involvement in the shaping of conventional international law has played an important role in the implementation of United States oceans policy.[57]

As the Reagan administration transitioned to the Bush administration, the organizational structure for the generation of oceans policy had been essentially dismantled in favor of *laissez faire* resource exploitation. The national security apparatus that had dominated ocean policy in the 1980s was also changing dramatically with the end of the Cold War. The relatively static bipolar confrontation with the Soviet Union, which might have, in some ways, supported something of a de facto, omnibus United States oceans policy had been replaced by a "new world disorder" of essentially unrelated international confrontations, a condition which demanded immediate attention of policy makers. Thus, as the United States entered the 1990s, the collective post World War II experience of formulating oceans policy within the larger context of national security priorities had largely disappeared.

What emerged in the first half of the 1990s was a domination of United States oceans policy by the Department of State and the Department of Defense and a concerted effort by these two departments to gain administration backing for a properly modified 1982 U.N. Convention on the Law of the Sea. The Defense Department, and particularly the Department of the Navy, long recognized the benefits of the treaty in enabling it to carry out its national defense imperatives. During this time, the Defense Department conducted a number of studies and analyses touting the benefits of the treaty and worked with the State Department to back the treaty as the central instrument of U.S. oceans policy. These efforts culminated in 1994 in the issuing of a joint letter from the secretaries of state and defense to Senator Claiborne Pell, then-chairman of the Senate Foreign Relations Committee, strongly urging that the Law of the Sea Convention and the companion Agreement be adopted by the United States. Appendix 3 contains the text of this letter.[58] Seventy-one days later, President Clinton submitted the Convention and the Agreement to the United States Senate for its advice and consent. Appendix 4 contains the text of the president's transmittal letter. The president noted, in part, that "[s]ince the late 1960s, the basic U.S. strategy has been to conclude a comprehensive treaty on the law of the sea which will be respected by all countries. Each succeeding administration has recognized this as the cornerstone of United States oceans policy."[59]

This is where the United States stood as we entered the last half of the decade. The president had articulated a position that the 1982 Law of the Sea Convention represents the cornerstone of United States oceans policy at a time when no clear apparatus for formulating, implementing, and directing the domestic aspects of this nation's oceans policy has been firmly established. Some portions of a once-cohesive apparatus, however, still exist: the national security structures still involved in oceans policy, legislative and administrative organizations designed to respond to special interests, and a growing consensus on protection and preservation of the marine environment. How the United States rebuilds this apparatus and infrastructure will depend in large part on the way in which the issues relating to its oceans policy are framed.

United States Oceans Policy Challenges

As the United States continues to use the 1982 United Nations Convention on the Law of the Sea as the foundation for its oceans policy, the Convention will serve as a prism that will disperse this nation's oceans policies into various levels of action and into various functional and zonal issue areas. A brief review of these policy-making levels and issue areas can capture some of the essence of the challenges that will face United States' policy makers throughout the 1990s and into the next century.

Operating within the context of the Convention, the United States will be required to matrix its policy implementation across three levels: (1) our interactions with other nations, both at a bilateral and multilateral level; (2) our polices at a national level, particularly with respect to implementing legislation, where needed; and (3) our internal policies, particularly with respect to the interaction of the federal government with state and local governments. Coordination will be required between and among these three levels.

At the international level, the Convention provides a framework for further international negotiation and accommodation. This is not just an implicit understanding, but an explicit requirement that is repeated many times in the Convention's 320 Articles and nine Annexes. The language in Article 59, for example, dealing with the resolution of conflicts regarding rights and jurisdiction in the exclusive economic zone, is illustrative: "conflict should be resolved on the basis of equity and in the light of all the relevant circumstances, taking into account the respective importance of the interests involved to the parties as well as to the international community as a whole."

Within the United Nations forum, several entities have been established that facilitate this ongoing development of the law of the sea: the United Nations General Assembly, the International Maritime Organization, the U.N. Food and Agriculture Organization, the International Oceanic Commission, the International Tribunal for the Law of the Sea, the Commission on the Limits of the Continental Shelf, and The International Seabed Authority.[60] United States participation in these institutions will be vital to insuring that we retain a voice in international oceans policy formulation. Additionally, there are numerous bilateral and multilateral international treaties, conventions, and protocols impacting on the uses of the oceans to which the United States is party that must be reviewed for applicability and relevancy in a post-Convention environment.

At the national level, the relationship between the various parts of the Convention and the body of current U.S. law must be examined. For example, two pieces of legislation—the Fishery Conservation and Management Act and the Deep Seabed Hard Mineral Resources Act—were enacted in 1977 and 1982 as interim measures prior to entry into force of the Law of the Sea Convention; the detailed provisions of the Convention in those areas had not completed Conference negotiation at the time of enactment. In his 23 September 1994 letter to the president, Secretary of State Warren Christopher highlighted the need for review, noting: "The [State] Department, along with other concerned agencies, stands ready to work with Congress toward enactment of legislation necessary to carry out the obligations assumed under the Convention and Agreement and to permit the United States to exercise rights granted by the Convention."[61]

Clearly, there is more national legislation that is affected by, and connected to, the Law of the Sea Convention. While this legislation will not be treated in detail here, it is important to note that at the time each piece of legislation was passed, the United States was not a party to the Convention and the Agreement and, therefore, at a minimum, each piece of legislation should be reviewed for its consistency with the Convention and its utility and applicability in a post-Convention environment.

At the level of the interaction of federal, state, and local policies, a post-Convention environment will require a comprehensive review of enabling legislation as interpreted in judicial decisions dating back over a century and a half. Disputes as to the division of offshore jurisdiction between the federal and state governments have historically arisen mostly in the context of title to offshore submerged lands. In the pre-Convention environment, the States have had jurisdiction over continental shelf resources to the limits of their Submerged Lands Act grant, which has been, generally, three miles.[62]

In a post-Convention environment, disputes between federal and state entities could pose much contentiousness. Prior to 27 December 1988, when President

Reagan's Proclamation 5928 extended the American Territorial Sea from three to twelve miles, and prior to the 16 November 1994 entry into force of the 1982 United Nations Convention on the Law of the Sea, individual states of the United States were generally satisfied with a jurisdictional limit of three miles. Now, with twelve miles as the international norm, and with the establishment of an exclusive economic zone out to 200 nautical miles, it is unlikely that states will be satisfied if the federal government does not share some of its jurisdictional authority over these enlarged oceanic areas.

The aforementioned policy-making levels will be important vehicles for dealing effectively with what promise to be significant political, economic, and security issues in oceans policy formulation as the United States and the world community approach the twenty-first century. Major oceans policy issues that must be coordinated include navigation and overflight, protection, and preservation of the marine environment, oceans resource acquisition and conservation, marine scientific research, counter drug operations, prevention of piracy, immigration monitoring and control, naval arms control, and sovereign immunity of warships and other nationally flagged vessels. Of significance, many of these issues have often-powerful constituencies at the international, national, and local levels, making the crafting of a balanced and effective oceans policy a special challenge.

UNITED STATES POLICY IMPERATIVES

In view of the complexities presented above, it might be natural to attempt to underplay the importance of these issues and operate under the assumption that the Convention alone is sufficient to guide United States oceans policy throughout the 1990s and into the next century. Unfortunately, our collective experience suggests otherwise and strongly supports the need to craft a comprehensive, viable United States oceans policy. The imperatives facing the United States in oceans policy are many and varied, but the current state of United States oceans policy formulation may not be optimum to meet U.S. policy imperatives. In the words of law-of-the-sea expert, Professor Thomas Clingan, "there is almost literally no policy and no effective mechanism for its development within the U.S. government."[63]

The end of the Cold War apparently has resolved the U.S.-Soviet standoff and the constant threat of nuclear Armageddon, but the "new world order" has been anything but ordered. Regional strife and crises requiring the surge of U.S. forces to the four corners of the world have increased the need for the employment of United States Army, Air Force, Navy, and Marine Corps units worldwide—and oftentimes with virtually no warning. Worldwide mobility and flexibility is totally contingent on the free use of the oceans and the airspace above by both the United States and our allies.

The global trading network that is the lifeblood of the economies of all developed nations is increasing both in scope and importance. For the United

States, in particular, an increasing portion of our total gross national product is generated through foreign trade. By the mid-1990s, over 20 percent of U.S. gross domestic product was traded overseas. Pacts such as the International Trade Organization (ITO) and the North American Free Trade Association (NAFTA) promise to accelerate this dependence on global trade and travel. The potential for serious disruption in the economies of the United States, some of our key allies, and other Western nations, is more imminent than at any time in our history, due to the volume of the trade involved, the time-sensitive nature of the movement of both raw materials and finished goods, and the interlocking network of worldwide suppliers and distributors. This network is now so vital that not only the disruption, but merely the fear of disruption, would pose an unacceptable economic catastrophe.[64]

The stresses induced by population growth—and in the case of many newly independent nations—exploding population growth, when coupled with the significant movement of most populations towards coastal areas—have made exploitation of oceanic resources and preservation of the marine environment an increasing priority for the nations of the world. Concurrent with this increased need for ocean-resource exploitation, the comprehensive oceans regime created by the 1982 United Nations Convention on the Law of the Sea has provided coastal nations with control over vast new ocean areas from which to extract resources and build national wealth. Increasing percentages of worldwide energy needs are being met with hydrocarbons extracted from under the sea, and the trend towards exploiting these resources further and further from coastlines is increasing. Technology has provided States with the ability to fish at great distances from their home waters—whether on the high seas or in the exclusive economic zones of other States. Other ocean uses, from deep seabed mining, to the laying and maintaining of communications cables, to ocean thermal energy conversion, and others, are causing most States to look increasingly towards the oceans as an important source of national wealth.

Recognizing the need to protect their access to their ocean resources, more and more coastal States have acquired naval and air forces capable of enforcing their primary right of resource extraction, and many have shown increasing aggressiveness in using these units against their neighbors with conflicting claims. This, in turn, has engendered a degree of uncertainty among other nations and may be the precursor of a new naval arms race—not the first world arms race of capital fleets that defined naval arms races of our collective memory, but the acquisition of smaller platforms specifically designed to enforce the use of the oceans within each nation's area of interest.[65]

The complexities engendered by accelerating world change, when coupled with the complexities of the new order of the oceans wrought by the Convention, make it imperative that the United States be equipped to resolve the issues of the use of the oceans that will increasingly arise throughout the 1990s and into the next century. To prepare to do this, the United States policy implementors must first have an understanding of the magnitude of these oceans issues, and then must ensure the existence of the policy-making apparatus to deal effectively with these important areas of oceans policy.

NOTES

1.   U.S. Senate, *Treaty Document 103-39, United Nations Convention on the Law of the Sea, with Annexes, and the Agreement Relating to the Implementation of Part XI of the United Nations Convention on the Law of the Sea, with Annex*, 103d Cong., 2d sess., 7 October 1994, iii (hereinafter *Treaty Document 103-39*).

2.   William Schachte, Jr., "National Security: Customary International Law and the LOS Convention" (address at the Georgetown University Law Center Symposium, *Implementing the United Nations Convention on the Law of the Sea*, Washington, D.C., January 1995), 2.

3.   This quotation appears in Jack Grunawalt, "The 1982 United Nations Convention on the Law of the Sea: An Operational Lawyers Perspective" (address at the Center for Oceans Law and Policy Symposium, *Toward Senate Consideration of the 1982 Law of the Sea Convention*, Washington, D.C., June 1995).

4.   President George Bush, *The National Security Strategy of the United States* (Washington, D.C.: USGPO, 1993), 3.

5.   General Colin Powell, *The National Military Strategy of the United States* (Washington, D.C.: USGPO, 1992), 2.

6.   Department of Defense, *National Security and the Convention on the Law of the Sea* (Washington, D.C.: Department of Defense, 1994), 9. Department of Defense, *National Security and the Convention on the Law of the Sea* (Washington, D.C.: Department of Defense, 1996). See also Rear Admiral Walter Doran, "An Operational Commander's Perspective on the 1982 LOS Convention," *The International Journal of Marine and Coastal Law*, 10 (1995): 335. In the same month that the DOD white paper was released, Secretary Perry forwarded a letter to the chairman of the Senate Foreign Relations Committee, stating that both he and General Shalikashvili urged the early advice and consent of the Senate in order to send a strong signal that the United States is committed to an ocean regulatory regime that is guided by the rule of law. In a press statement on the same day, the Secretary of Defense noted, in part:

The Nation's security has depended upon our ability to conduct military operations over, under, and on the oceans. We support the Convention because it confirms traditional high seas freedoms of navigation and overflight; it details passage rights through international straits; and it reduces prospects for disagreements with coastal nations during operations.

7.   President William Clinton, *A National Security Strategy of Engagement and Enlargement* (Washington, D.C., USGPO, 1995), 4.

8.   General John Shalikashvili, *National Military Strategy of the United*

States of America: A Strategy of Flexible and Selective Engagement (Washington, D.C.: USGPO, 1995).

9.   Thomas Clingan, *The Law of the Sea: Ocean Law and Policy* (San Francisco: Austin and Winfield, 1994), 560-561. See also John Stevenson and Bernard Oxman, "The Future of the United Nations Convention on the Law of the Sea," *American Journal of International Law* 88 (1994): 488; Bernard Oxman, "United States Interests in the Law of the Sea Convention," *American Journal of International Law* 88 (1994): 168-169.

10.   Scott Allen, "Mare Liberum," *United States Naval Institute Proceedings* 109 (July 1983): 46. See also Scott Allen, "The Elements of Seapower: Mahan Revisited," in *Ocean Yearbook 7*, Elizabeth Borgese and Norton Ginsburg, eds. (Chicago: University of Chicago Press, 1988), 330-334, for a more comprehensive treatment of the costs of various modes of worldwide transportation.

11.   Robert Knecht, Biliana Cicin-Sain, and John Archer, "National Ocean Policy, A Window of Opportunity," *Ocean Development and International Law* 19 (1988): 113. Professors Knecht and Cicin-Sain, then with the University of California and now with the University of Delaware, and Professor Jack Archer, then with the Woods Hole Oceanographic Institution, and now with the University of Massachusetts at Boston, are three of the founding members and are on the steering committee of the Ocean Governance Study Group. This group has studied the evolution of United States oceans policy in great detail and is one of the leading organizations attempting to devise plans for ocean governance in the United States in the future.

12.   James B. Morell, *The Law of the Sea: An Historical Analysis of the 1982 Treaty and Its Rejection by the United States* (Jefferson, North Carolina: McFarland and Company, 1992), 179. The *res communis* regime was a significant policy pronouncement, stating that the sea is common to all, both as to ownership and to use, and is not susceptible to national appropriation.

13.   Ibid., 186.

14.   Ibid.

15.   See, for example, John Craven, "The Evolution of Ocean Policy," in *The Law of the Sea in the 1990s: A Framework for Further International Cooperation*, Tadao Kuribayashi and Edward Miles, eds. (Honolulu: Law of the Sea Institute Press, 1992), 379-380.

16.   E. B. Potter, and C. W. Nimitz, *Seapower, A Naval History* (Englewood Cliffs, New Jersey: Prentice-Hall, 1960), 183. See also Robert Friedheim, *Negotiating the New Ocean Regime* (Columbia, South Carolina: University of South Carolina Press, 1993), 13-14. Friedheim notes that Spain and Portugal ruined their economies trying to exclude all other users from the vast areas of the oceans that they claimed. Friedheim's position parallels that of Paul Kennedy, author of the best-selling *The Rise and Fall of the Great Powers* (New York: Random House, 1987) who has noted: "try as they might, Spain and Portugal simply could not keep their papally assigned monopoly of the

outside world to themselves."

17.   Morell, *Law of the Sea: Historical Analysis*, 187.

18.   Ibid., 187. Morell disputes the attempts by England to disclaim any national-level direction for this privateering, noting that: "Drake did this, Hawkins that, Frobisher the other, with consequences which, somewhat astonishingly, added up to the foundation of the British Empire, accounted for as an unintended by-product of contempt for Spain and hatred of the Pope."

19.   Potter and Nimitz, *Seapower*, 81.

20.   Ibid., 132.

21.   Morell, *Law of the Sea: Historical Analysis*, 186.

22.   Craven, "The Evolution of Ocean Policy," 380.

23.   Allen, "The Elements of Seapower," 318.

24.   Woodrow Wilson, "The Fourteen Points," reprinted in Thomas Patterson, ed., *Major Problems in American Foreign Policy* (Lexington, Massachusetts: Heath, 1978).

25.   See generally Potter and Nimitz, *Seapower*; Scott Allen, "The Elements of Seapower" in *Ocean Yearbook 7*, 317-339; William Aceves, "The Freedom of Navigation Program: A Study on the Relationship Between Law and Politics," *Hastings International and Comparative Law Review* 19 (1996): 259.

26.   Craven, "The Evolution of Ocean Policy," 381.

27.   Robert Friedheim, *Negotiating the New Ocean Regime*, 20.

28.   Craven, "The Evolution of Ocean Policy," 382.

29.   Ibid., 381-382.

30.   Knecht, Cicin-Sain, and Archer, "National Ocean Policy: A Window of Opportunity," 116.

31.   Craven, "The Evolution of Ocean Policy," 382.

32.   R. B. Abel, "The History of United States Ocean Policy" in *Making Ocean Policy*, F. Hoole, R. Friedheim, T. Hennessey, eds. (Boulder, Colorado: Westview Press, 1981), 5.

33.   Craven, "The Evolution of Ocean Policy," 382.

34.   Clingan, *Ocean Law and Policy*, 586.

35.   Knecht, Cicin-Sain, and Archer, "A Window of Opportunity," 117.

36.   See Chapter 3, notes 18-22, and accompanying text.

37.   Knecht, Cicin-Sain, and Archer, "A Window of Opportunity," 117.

38.   Craven, "The Evolution of Ocean Policy," 383.

39.   Morell, *Law of the Sea: Historical Analysis*, 44.

40.   Craven, "The Evolution of Ocean Policy," 384.

41.   Morell, *Law of the Sea: Historical Analysis*, 37, 45, 56-57.

42.   Craven, "The Evolution of Ocean Policy," 384.

43.   Ann Hollick, "United States Oceans Politics," *San Diego Law Review* 10 (1973): 471. Professor Hollick provides a comprehensive review of the making of U.S. oceans policy from the mid-1960s up to the beginning of the UNCLOS III deliberations.

44.   Craven, "The Evolution of Ocean Policy," 386.

45.   Morell, *Law of the Sea: Historical Analysis*, 171.

46.   Craven, "The Evolution of Ocean Policy," 391.

47.   Knecht, Cicin-Sain, and Archer, "A Window of Opportunity," 121.

48.   Craven, "The Evolution of Ocean Policy," 391.

49.   See, for example, U.S. Naval Institute, *The Maritime Strategy* (Annapolis, Maryland: Naval Institute Press, 1986).

50.   Craven, "The Evolution of Ocean Policy," 391.

51.   Clingan, *Ocean Law and Policy*, 568-576.   This statement is a republication of Thomas Clingan, "The Next Twenty Years of Naval Mobility," *Naval Institute Proceedings* 106 (May 1980): 82.

52.   Craven, "The Evolution of Ocean Policy," 392.

53.   Morell, *Law of the Sea: Historical Analysis*, 205.

54.   Reproduced in J. Ashley Roach and Robert W. Smith, *International Law Studies 1994: Excessive Maritime Claims* vol. 66 (Newport, Rhode Island: Naval War College Press, 1994), 275-278.

55.   Department of the Navy, *The Commander's Handbook on the Law of Naval Operations*, NWP-9A/FMFM 1-10, (Washington, D.C.: Naval Warfare Publications Library, 1989). The "annotated supplement" to this comprehensive document contains extensive footnotes and is intended to be used by naval staff legal advisors.   This manual has been updated and reissued as NWP 1-14M/MCWP 5-2.1 (Washington, D.C.: Naval Warfare Publication Library, 1995). See also Professor Jack Grunawalt, "1982 United Nation's Convention on the Law of the Sea: An Operational Lawyer's Perspective" (address at the Center for Oceans Law and Policy Symposium, *Towards Senate Consideration of the 1982 Law of the Sea Convention*, Washington, D.C., June 1995). Professor Grunawalt points out that NWP-9A/FMFM 1-10 is the basic reference on board all Navy and Coast Guard ships, and in all Navy and Marine Corps aviation squadrons.   Additionally, he notes that this document has been translated into several languages and is used extensively in foreign war colleges and by foreign operating forces.

56.   Roach and Smith, *Excessive Maritime Claims*, 257-258.

57.   Ibid., 258-259.

58.   U.S. Senate Committee on Foreign Relations, *Current Status of the Convention on the Law of the Sea*, 103d Cong., 2d sess., 11 August 1994, 94.

59.   Senate, *Treaty Document 103-39*, iii.

60.   Biliana Cicin-Sain and Katherine Leccese, eds., *Implications of Entry into Force of the Law of the Sea Convention for U.S. Ocean Governance* (Honolulu: Ocean Governance Study Group, 1995), 5-6.

61.   Marjorie Ann Browne, *CRS Issue Brief: The Law of the Sea Convention and U.S. Policy* (Washington, D.C.: Congressional Research Service, Library of Congress, 1995), 11.

62.   See, for example, John Briscoe, "The Division of America's Offshore Zones as Between Nation and State," and Joseph Morgan, "U.S. Claims to Maritime Jurisdictions: Too Much or Not Enough," in *Implications of Entry into*

Force of the Law of the Sea Convention for U.S. Ocean Governance, Cicin-Sain and Leccese, eds., 53-68.

63.   Thomas Clingan, *Ocean Law and Policy*, 586. Professor Clingan, a charter member of the Panel on the Law of Ocean Uses and a frequent contributor to law of the sea journals, wrote forcefully regarding the need for U.S. oceans policy in his 1994 book:

At the time of this present writing, it could be said that there is almost literally no policy and no effective mechanism for its development within the U.S. government. Such policy as exists is reflected in national legislation, such as the Fishery Conservation and Management Act, previously considered, or the Hard Minerals Act. But policy does not depend upon past acts. Policy development for the future is essential, and that development seems to be completely lacking. The Department of State, the lead agency during the years of the Law of the Sea Conference, has fallen into lethargy on the subject, and no single agency has stepped in to fill the void. U.S. oceans policy lacks the impetus given to it by the report on the Stratton Commission, Our Nation and the Sea, in 1969.

64.   Maureen O'C. Walker, "Entry Into Force of the 1982 United Nations Convention on the Law of the Sea," (paper presented at the MTS/IEEE Symposium, San Diego, California, October 1995). Ms. Walker is chief of the Division of Marine Law and Policy of the U.S. Department of State and is one of the State Department's principal spokespersons regarding the law of the sea.

65.   See, for example, Joseph Morgan, "Constabulary Navies in the Pacific and Indian Oceans," in *Ocean Yearbook 11*, Elizabeth Borgese, Norton Ginsburg, and Joseph Morgan, eds. (Chicago: University of Chicago Press, 1994), 368-383; Nien-Tsu Alfred Hu and James K. Oliver, "A Framework for Small Navy Theory: The 1982 United Nation's Law of the Sea Convention," *Naval War College Review* 41 (Spring 1988): 39.

Chapter Nine

OCEANS POLICY ISSUES: WHAT THE UNITED STATES MUST FOCUS ON

FRAMING THE ISSUES

As the United States navigates the second half of the 1990s and moves into the twenty-first century, there are significant functional and zonal oceans policy issues that this nation must address as we use the oceans to support our political, economic, and security interests. Many of these issues are interrelated and, therefore, crafting an omnibus oceans policy that effectively deals with each of these issues in a coordinated fashion is a significant policy challenge.

The 1982 United Nations Convention on the Law of the Sea formally entered into force for many nations on 16 November 1994 and much of its contents forms the basis of United States oceans policy. While the Convention is comprehensive in scope, it is neither exhaustive nor static; it was not intended to be the last or only word on the orderly use of the oceans shared by the community of nations. The Convention is replete with references to nations working out details at the bilateral and multilateral level.[1] Much "fleshing out" of the Convention's provisions has already transpired, but much more needs to be done. While many areas have already lent themselves to amicable solutions and agreements, other areas, many of which are by their nature more controversial, still need to be worked out. As the world's major State, the United States has vital interests in all of these areas. The United States is and will continue to be at or near the center of virtually all oceans policy issues.

Despite entry into force for many nations of the 1982 United Nations Convention on the Law of the Sea, increasing contentiousness exists in some oceans policy issues. This situation brings with it the concomitant imperative for the United States to exercise leadership in working with both maritime and coastal States to resolve these issues. None of these issues shows immediate signs of resolving without proactive participation by the United States.

For example, immediately after the Convention came into force, several straits and archipelagic States, such as Malaysia and the Philippines, reiterated the position that the Convention was a package deal and that non-parties would not be entitled to transit passage rights, or that conditions, such as prior notification, would be required of certain types of vessels seeking to pass through these international straits. Archipelagic States, such as the Philippines, sought to restrict the number of sea lanes through their archipelagoes to a number thought to be unreasonably low by most maritime States. Other States, under the rubric of environmental protection, sought to impose restrictions on transit of ships or aircraft through their exclusive economic zones. The fatal attack on a United States Air Force cargo aircraft by a Peruvian fighter in 1992, which Peru weakly justified as defense of its "territorial sea," is a vivid reminder of the catastrophic consequences of unresolved controversies.[2]

International controversies went beyond navigation and overflight concerns. At a 1997 law-of-the-sea symposium, current and former department of state geographers detailed the extensive nature of worldwide island sovereignty and delimitation disputes that have the potential to become security flashpoints.[3] One of the most prominent current disputes involves the oil and gas resource-driven claims, counterclaims, and conflicts over the Spratley Islands, portions of which are currently occupied or claimed by Vietnam, the Philippines, China, Malaysia, Brunei, and Taiwan. These claims presented compelling evidence of the need to continue to conduct bilateral and multilateral negotiations to resolve oceans issues.[4] In like manner, fishing disputes, such as the 1995 disputes between Canada and Spain over fishing in high-seas areas off the Grand Banks, as well as other serious, but less well-publicized, fishing rights disputes between Norway and Iceland, France and Spain, Japan and Russia, and even between the United States and Canada and Mexico, indicate that this is another area of contention that must be the subject of continued negotiation and policy formulation.[5] Other critical issues, such as piracy, drug smuggling, and illegal immigration, all of which occur on the seas and which have yet to see a great degree of cooperation among maritime, coastal, and flag States, need to be resolved by the international community within the context of the Convention.

OCEANS POLICY ISSUES FOR THE UNITED STATES

Navigation and Overflight

Preservation of the rights of navigation and overflight for U.S. military ships and aircraft, other U.S. flagged craft, and other U.S. owned ships and aircraft has always been a top priority—if not *the* top priority—of United States oceans policy. This was the primary reason why the United States participated in the UNCLOS I and UNCLOS II negotiations, and why we pushed so hard to begin UNCLOS III. This was the paramount articulated concern throughout UNCLOS III. Preserving and protecting the rights of our naval and merchant vessels and aircraft to operate on, over, and under the seas continues to be the foundation that undergirds our political, economic, and security paradigm.

Challenges to this freedom of navigation and overflight have remained significant. Chapter 6 detailed the nature and extent of challenges to the freedoms of the ocean uses conferred by the Convention, and the ways in which the United States works to discourage or, where necessary, roll back illegal claims inconsistent with the Convention. Nonconforming claims have been made, and continue to be made, by a large number of nations; therefore, resolving these claims continues to be a high priority for the international community and a key oceans policy issue for the United States. These claims exist in virtually all recognized zonal areas: the territorial sea, the contiguous zone, international straits, archipelagic waters, the exclusive economic zone, the high seas, and a few other, specific, areas, as illustrated below. Significantly, many of these nonconforming claims occur in areas where United States forward deployed military forces routinely operate, such as in the Arabian Gulf. Legislation, such as the Iranian Marine Areas Act of 1993, which, among its other provisions, seeks to claim significant portions of the Arabian Gulf as internal Iranian waters, seeks to claim still more area as territorial seas, purports to require warships to obtain prior approval to engage in innocent passage, and prohibits military activities within the exclusive economic zone, are illustrative of some of the more egregious claims the United States must confront.[6]

Territorial Sea

Article 3 of the 1982 United Nations Law of the Sea Convention provides every State with the right to establish the breadth of its territorial sea up to a limit not exceeding twelve nautical miles, measured from baselines determined in accordance with the Convention. State practice in asserting territorial sea claims has become, in large measure, relatively stable; many excessive claims have been rolled back, due, largely, to the efforts of the United States. Acceptance of the Convention's territorial sea limits, however, is not universal. Seventeen States still claimed territorial seas of over twelve miles at the time the Convention came into force in November 1994.[7] Among the more egregious of these claims are those of Ecuador and Peru to a 200-mile territorial sea. The United States has either issued diplomatic protest or asserted its navigation rights against all of these excessive territorial sea claims, and some claims have been protested more than once.

Issues regarding the right of innocent passage through the territorial sea go beyond those associated with the width of this maritime zone. They involve, primarily, over-zealous interpretations of Article 21 of the Convention, which empowers a coastal State to adopt, with due publicity, laws and regulations relating to innocent passage through the territorial sea. Some examples of these attempted restrictions provide an indication of the ongoing controversy. In 1981 Finland purported to prohibit innocent passage through certain areas of its territorial sea, limited vessels to designated sea lanes in the territorial sea, and required compulsory pilotage service for all vessels, including sovereign immune vessels. In 1985, Italy announced similar compulsory pilotage requirements for large ships carrying oil and other pollutants while transiting the Strait of Messina. In 1985, Libya announced regulations which, in part, purported to restrict the right of innocent passage of commercial vessels in the Libyan territorial sea to daylight hours only, with prior notification required. In 1986, Sri Lanka issued a Notice to Mariners which purported to require all vessels to obtain permission before entering its territorial sea. The former Soviet Union stipulated special rules for warship navigation in its territorial sea, restricting warships to specifically prescribed areas. These Soviet restrictions met with vigorous U.S. protests and led, ultimately, to the February 1988 bumping incident in the Black Sea.[8]

Perhaps the most objectionable restrictions on innocent passage through the territorial sea for the United States are demands for prior notification or prior permission for passage of warships, limitations on the number of warships permitted to pass, and limitations on, or prohibitions against, passage by nuclear-powered warships. The United States has vigorously protested these restrictions over the past three decades. *International Law Studies 1994: Excessive Maritime Claims* lists a total of forty States asserting either prior notification or prior permission restrictions.[9] From a national security perspective, these attempts to limit the passage of warships are most onerous. The unsatisfactory nature of a prior notification regime was highlighted at a June 1995 Center for Ocean Law and Policy Symposium in the remarks by Professor Jack Grunawalt, director of the Oceans Law and Policy Department, Center for Naval Warfare Studies, U.S. Naval War College:

A notification requirement for ship transit of the territorial sea is, for all practical purposes, a requirement for authorization. To illustrate, the naval commander would ask: How far in advance must I notify the coastal State? To whom is notification to be provided and in what language? How is it to be provided? In writing? By radio? By flag hoist? Will someone be available 24 hours a day to receive my notice? Must I await acknowledgment? Am I required to provide a track, speed of advance and anticipated departure time and place? Am I allowed to deviate? Must I provide information pertaining to my mission? To my weapons? To my means of propulsion?[10]

These are by no means the only areas of contention regarding the territorial sea. As the United States continues to refine its oceans policy, the territorial sea will remain an important area of emphasis and attention, with the United States focusing on the tenets of Article 19 of the Convention. Importantly, that article provides that passage is deemed innocent unless it violates the exclusive list of activities considered to be prejudicial to the peace, good order, and security of the coastal State, set forth in Article 19. Moreover, any coastal State determination that passage by any transiting ship must be made solely on the basis of acts of the transiting vessel while in the territorial sea. Therefore, such considerations as characterization of the vessel, types of cargo, means of propulsion, flag, origin, destination, or purpose of the voyage—criteria that are not found in Article 19's exclusive list—cannot be used in determining that the passage is not innocent.[11]

Contiguous Zone

Article 33 of the Convention provides for a contiguous zone, that is, a zone contiguous to the territorial sea, where the coastal State may exercise the control necessary to prevent and punish infringement of its customs, fiscal, immigration, or sanitary law. This zone may not extend beyond twenty-four nautical miles from established baselines from which the territorial sea is measured. This apparently straightforward definition would not seem to indicate that the contiguous zone would be a contentious area.

The contiguous zone is comprised of waters in and over which the ships and aircraft of all nations enjoy traditional high-seas freedoms of navigation and overflight. At the time that the Convention entered into force, however, some sixteen countries claimed the right to expand the competence of the contiguous zone to include protection of national security interests, and thus restrict or exclude warships and military aircraft. These claimants included Bangladesh, Burma, Haiti, Iran, Sri Lanka, Sudan, Syria, Venezuela, Vietnam, and Yemen. Syria claims a six-mile contiguous zone, next to its thirty-five-mile territorial sea, and Namibia has claimed a contiguous zone coextensive with its 200-mile exclusive economic zone (EEZ). North Korea has claimed a fifty-mile military boundary since 1977.[12]

Excessive claims in the contiguous zone, especially those attempting to regulate military activities, are particularly bothersome to the United States, because, given the strictures regarding innocent passage in the territorial sea, the contiguous zone is the natural place to move, marshall, exercise, and organize naval forces in the many venues that we use such forces, ranging along the spectrum from peacetime presence, to show of force, to humanitarian operations, to noncombatant evacuation operations, to actual conflict.

International Straits

In negotiating the 1982 Convention, the maritime powers accepted a maximum twelve-mile territorial sea conditioned on the stipulation that straits used for international navigation be subject to a transit passage regime with liberal rights of passage for vessels and aircraft. These rights of transit passage provide a guaranteed and unsuspendable legal right for ships and aircraft to transit international straits without coastal State interference. Thus far, the transit passage regime has not been accepted universally; some States have sought to impose restrictions on the use of these straits inconsistent with the terms of the Convention. The United States has issued diplomatic protests against virtually all of the excessive claims, and it has conducted operational assertions, under the auspices of the Freedom of Navigation program, in the case of some of the more egregious claims, such as those by Iran, Oman, Spain, Yemen, and the former

Soviet Union.[13]

A factor contributing to the potential ambiguity regarding the regime for passage through international straits is that the Convention addresses five different kinds of straits used for international navigation, each one with a distinct legal regime. Those straits connecting one part of the high seas or EEZ with another part of the high seas or EEZ are governed by Article 37 regarding transit passage. Those straits connecting part of the high seas or EEZ and the territorial sea of a foreign nation are governed by Article 45(1)(b), regulating nonsuspendable innocent passage. Straits connecting one part of the high seas or EEZ with another part of the high seas or EEZ where the strait is formed by an island of a State bordering the strait and its mainland, if there exists seaward of the island a route through the high seas or EEZ of similar convenience with regard to navigation and hydrographic characteristics, are governed by Article 38(1) regulating another regime of nonsuspendable innocent passage. Straits regulated in whole or in part by pre-existing international conventions, such as the Turkish straits, are governed by Article 35(c) preserving rights and duties existing under those international agreements.   Finally, straits through archipelagic waters are governed by archipelagic sea lanes passage in accordance with Article 54.[14]

The complexity of these differing transit regimes has contributed to contentiousness of the issue. In addition, coastal States recognize the critical importance of these straits to the major maritime powers. As a result, the coastal States seek to capitalize on this importance and extract various concessions as a condition for use of straits. International straits represent one area where, in many cases, maritime nations have virtually no other option should the coastal State restrict passage.

Examples of attempts to restrict passage through international straits indicate the level of contentiousness of this issue and underscore the need for further development of the law. In 1982, Yemen declared that warships and warplanes must obtain prior permission before passing thorough the strait of Bab el Mandeb. Spain has made several claims of coastal State authority over aircraft exercising the right of transit passage, and of pollution control authority over ships transiting the Strait of Gibraltar. Malaysia, Indonesia, and Singapore have asserted various requirements governing transit through the Strait of Malacca, such as a minimum under-keel clearances for vessels. In 1988, Indonesia attempted to close the Sunda and Lombok Straits to all traffic for a period of time. Italy attempted to close the Strait of Messina to vessels over 10,000 tons carrying oil or other pollutants. Long-standing and ongoing efforts by the former Soviet Union and Canada seek to impose additional restrictions, such as characterizing the straits as "historic waters" or requiring prior approval for passage, for the straits in the Northeast and Northwest Passage, respectively.[15]

In addition to dealing individually with these types of excessive claims, the construction of the Convention necessitates continuing negotiation, via the appropriate international agencies, regarding other rights and duties in these straits. Article 41 of the Convention allows states bordering straits to designate sea lanes and prescribe traffic-separation schemes to promote navigational safety, so long as these are in conformity with the regime of transit passage. These sea lanes and traffic separation schemes must conform to generally accepted international standards; negotiations within the International Maritime Organization (IMO) are generally recognized as the proper forum for review of proposed schemes and resolution of disputes. Article 42 authorizes States bordering straits to adopt nondiscriminatory laws and regulations to control pollution and the discharge of oil, oily wastes, and other noxious substances in these straits, and to prohibit fishing and loading or unloading of any commodity, currency, or person in contravention of the coastal State's customs, fiscal, immigration, or sanitary laws and regulations. Article 43 provides further for the maintenance by straits States of navigational or safety aids and other improvements to aid in the prevention, reduction, and control of pollution from ships. International negotiation and compromise in the area of international straits is a compelling and continuing international oceans issue.

Archipelagic Waters

A new regime created by Part IV of the 1982 United Nations Convention on the Law of the Sea is that of archipelagic waters. Article 46 of the Convention defines an archipelagic State as a State constituted wholly by one or more archipelagos, that is, "a group of islands, including parts of islands, inter-connecting waters and other natural features which are so closely interrelated that such islands, waters and other natural features form an intrinsic geographical, economic and political entity." In Article 43, the Convention allows a State claiming archipelagic status to draw straight archipelagic baselines around the outermost islands of the archipelago. The archipelagic State's sovereignty then extends, pursuant to Article 49, to the waters thereby enclosed by those baselines, with important limitations.

A regime of archipelagic sea lanes passage applies within archipelagoes; it parallels most of the important elements of the transit passage regime applying to international straits and is similarly not suspendable. All ships and aircraft, including warships and military aircraft, possess the right of archipelagic sea lanes passage while transiting through, under, or over the waters of archipelagos and adjacent territorial seas by way of archipelagic sea lanes. Those sea lanes include all of those routes normally used for international navigation and overflight, whether or not designated by the archipelagic State.

This new regime's adoption was accompanied by concerns regarding the enclosure of millions of square miles that were formerly high seas. Depending on the exact way in which archipelagic baselines are ultimately defined and applied, a total of twenty States could legitimately claim archipelagic waters. However, some States, which are not themselves archipelagoes, but which have coastal islands that have the attributes of archipelagoes, have sought to enclose those islands and claim archipelagic status for them. Even within the United

States, some commentators have suggested that the Hawaiian Islands have a strong historical claim to archipelagic status.[16] Many of these nonconforming claims have been dealt with successfully by maritime nations. The most common type of claims that promise to remain contentious, however, are the attempts to improperly limit the number of archipelagic sea lanes or to prescribe inappropriate archipelagic baselines.

Indonesia was the first State to suggest that it might seek to exercise its right to designate sea lanes suitable for the continuous and expeditious passage of foreign ships through its archipelagic waters. Although proper sea lanes are required to include all normal passage routes and all normal navigational channels, the Indonesian Navy has sought to limit them to a mere three sea routes, all north-to-south. Similarly, the Philippines refused to recognize the Convention's archipelagic regime notwithstanding its ratification of the Convention. Specifically, it maintains the position that the Philippine archipelagic waters are essentially internal waters through which, absent Philippine permission, foreign navigation and overflight may be prohibited.[17]

The entire regime of archipelagic sea lanes passage is one that will require significant international negotiation. At the time of the entry into force of the Convention, not every State entitled to claim archipelagic status had yet done so, and, of those States claiming archipelagic status, less than half had enacted national legislation applying this status. Additionally, no archipelagic State had submitted a proposal to the IMO as the "competent international organization" to approve State designation of archipelagic sea lanes through its waters. Because those enclosed archipelagic waters not included in sea lanes are to be considered territorial waters where the rules of innocent passage apply, there is a general feeling among maritime nations that archipelagic States are dragging their feet in an effort to provide archipelagic sea lanes transit rights in as little of their waters as possible. For the United States, continuing and full participation in the IMO is one key to ensuring a regime that protects U.S. vital interests.

Exclusive Economic Zone

The 200-mile exclusive economic zone (EEZ) grants coastal States increased control over the resources off their coasts, while curtailing the trend of national claims to broader territorial seas and preserving within the EEZ as many high-seas freedoms as possible. Within the EEZ, the coastal State may explore, exploit, conserve, and manage resources out to 200 miles from coastal baselines; other States retain the rights to navigate, overfly, and conduct related activities. Over eighty-five states have claimed an EEZ. With its numerous islands, territories and possessions, and long coastlines, the United States' EEZ claim is the largest, totaling almost 3.4 million square miles.[18]

The enormous ocean areas now encompassed by EEZs—between 30 and 34 percent of all ocean areas, depending on how baselines are measured—and the jurisdictional complexity of the EEZ, make them an area of natural contention and one that requires ongoing accommodation of conflicting claims. Pursuant to Article 58, in the EEZ, "all States enjoy the high-seas freedoms of navigation and overflight, laying of submarine cables and pipelines, and other internationally lawful uses of the seas related to those freedoms, such as those associated with the operation of ships, aircraft, and submarines," so long as those uses are compatible with other provisions of the Convention. Articles 88 to 155, which, apart from the fuller enumeration of freedoms in Article 87, set forth the entire regime of the high seas on matters other than fisheries, apply to the EEZ in so far as they are not incompatible the EEZ provisions. These rights are the same as the rights recognized in international law for all States on the high seas.

Military activities, such as anchoring, launching and landing of aircraft, operating military devices, intelligence collection exercises, ship and aircraft operations, and conducting surveys, are recognized high seas uses that are preserved by Article 58. Under that article, all States have the right to conduct military activities within the EEZ, but must do so consistently with the obligation of due regard for coastal State's resource and other rights, as well as the rights of other. It is the duty of the flag State alone, however, not the right of the coastal State, to enforce this "due regard" obligation.[19]

The concept of "due regard" in the Convention balances the obligations within the EEZ of both coastal and maritime States. Article 56 provides that coastal States "shall have due regard to the rights and duties of other States" in the EEZ. Article 58 places similar requirements on other States to have "due regard to the rights and duties of the coastal state" and to comply with regulations established pursuant to the Convention. Although it is not specific, Article 59 provides a basis for resolving disputes over rights and duties not allocated by Articles 56 and 58 and other provisions of the Convention. It stipulates that the conflict "should be resolved on the basis of equity and in the light of all relevant circumstances, taking into account the respective importance of all the interests involved to the parties as well as to the international community as a whole."

Article 60 permits the coastal State to authorize and regulate the construction, operation, and use of artificial islands, installations, and structures for economic purposes, and other installations and structures that could interfere with the exercise of the coastal State's rights in its EEZ. This provision does not preclude, however, the deployment of listening or other, similar security-related devices by other States. Article 60 requires the coastal State to give "due notice" of artificial islands, installations, and structures and to remove those no longer in use in accordance with generally accepted international standards established by the IMO. Article 60 also permits the coastal State to establish and give notice of reasonable safety zones around such structures, which zones are not to exceed 500 meters in breadth except in accordance with generally accepted international standards or as recommended by the IMO, and requires ships to respect the zones and generally accepted international navigation standards. Finally, Article 60 provides that even approved artificial islands, installations, and structures, and the safety zones around them, may not be located where they may cause interference with the use of recognized sea lanes essential to international navigation.

Of the remaining articles in the Convention on the EEZ, thirteen specifically relate to living resources jurisdiction in the zone. For example, consistent with Article 73, the coastal State may, in the exercise of its sovereign rights over living resources in the EEZ, take such measures, including boarding, inspection, arrest, and judicial proceedings against vessels not protected by sovereign immunity, as are necessary to ensure compliance with rules and regulations adopted in conformity with the Convention. To ensure against abuse, arrested vessels and their crews must be promptly released upon the posting of reasonable bond or other security. In cases of arrest or detention of foreign vessels, the coastal State must notify the flag State promptly, through appropriate channels, of the actions taken and of any penalties imposed.[20]

While no State has claimed an EEZ extending beyond 200 miles from coastal baselines, several States that have declared EEZs seek to regulate activities within the EEZ in ways not permitted by the Convention. For example, Iran claims the right to prohibit all foreign military activities within its EEZ, while Brazil and Uruguay do not permit foreign military exercises in their EEZs. Chile, in its "presential sea" concept, permits foreign naval operations in its EEZ only when Chile is included. Colombia has claimed that foreign States do not have the right to conduct maritime counter-narcotics law enforcement operations in its EEZ. Trinidad and Tobago required written permission to establish or use any artificial island, installation, or structure in its EEZ. Costa Rica requires that fishing vessels wishing to transit its EEZ, but not intending to fish, notify Costa Rican authorities upon entering and leaving those waters. India, Pakistan, Mauritius, Seychelles, and Guyana all have domestic legislation under which designated zones may be established in the EEZ, and entry into them regulated by the coastal State. Additionally, a total of twenty States permit imprisonment of fisheries violators, contrary to the express provision of the Convention.[21]

While these claims are among the most conspicuous examples of coastal State attempts improperly to proscribe activities in their EEZs, they are illustrative of a general and increasingly prevalent tendency among some coastal States to presume that they have the *absolute right* to exploit ever-dwindling living resources from the EEZ. To some extent, this attitude is supported by the language of article 59 in the Convention which grants each coastal State "sovereign rights" over exploring, exploiting, conserving, and managing the natural resources—whether living or non-living—of the waters superjacent to the seabed and its subsoil.[22] These coastal States must then view any activities of maritime States as potentially prejudicial to their attempts to sustain living-resource exploitation. Consequently, it is unlikely that coastal States will unilaterally reverse current attempts to maximize their jurisdiction in their EEZs.

The United States has not fully accepted the legitimacy of this trend in international interpretation of the rights and responsibilities within the EEZ. From a naval mobility standpoint, the United States has presumed the EEZ to have essentially high seas freedoms. The navy's strategic document, *Forward...From the Sea*, notes that "the naval service, operating from sea bases in international waters, can influence events ashore in support of our interests."[23] This is further addressed at the operational level in the U.S. Navy's *Commander's Handbook on the Law of Naval Operations*, which provides guidance to naval commanders by stating that, "the existence of an exclusive economic zone in an area of naval operations need not, of itself, be of concern to the naval commander."[24]

The concerns of many coastal States seem to focus on naval activities as threatening to interfere with or harm their interests. A frequently cited example is that of weapons exercises, test, or placement that harm a natural resource. Controversy likewise surrounds the issue of emplacement of military devices, such as detection devices, in the EEZ. Moreover, it is difficult to conclusively determine just what the Convention means with respect to naval activities in the EEZ—it is vague and ambiguous. Indeed, according to one commentator, "Uncertainty in the Convention is nowhere so striking as in the area of military uses of the EEZ."[25] Thus, naval operations in foreign EEZs are by no means free of political or diplomatic controversy, as seems presumed by the articulated U.S. strategy.

High Seas

Initially, the high seas would not appear to be an area of contention. The high seas "belong" to all nations; there should be no trouble with excessive claims of any kind, because States cannot "claim" international waters. However, because of the vast expanses of ocean space that are covered by the high seas and the wide range of activities conducted on the high seas, the United States has a large stake in closely following the issue of use of the high seas.

Pursuant to Article 87, all ships and aircraft, including warships and military aircraft, possess freedom of movement and operation on, under, and over the high seas. For warships and military aircraft, this includes maneuvering of task forces, flight operations, military exercises, surveillance, intelligence gathering, and munitions testing. All of these activities, of course, must be conducted with "due regard" for the interests of other States considering the circumstances. Thus, a State must be cognizant of the interests of others in using a high-seas area, and balance those interests with its own, and also must refrain from activities that unreasonably interfere with the exercise of other States' high-seas freedoms in light of that balance of interests.[26]

As another example of the evolution of the concept of high seas under the Convention, a traditional, primary use of the high seas is that of fishing. Now, however, States are bound by the duty to conserve living resources of the high seas and to cooperate with other governments toward that end. In the words of one commentator: "Freedom to fish on the high seas is no longer an unfettered economic right. It has been made subject to several conditions, including the fundamental obligation for governments to cooperate in the conservation and management of high seas living resources."[27]

Protection and Preservation of the Marine Environment

Protection and preservation of the marine environment has become an area of increasing concern for the United States and an issue that almost certainly will demand increased attention as the United States formulates and refines its oceans policy. An early and enduring goal of the United States throughout the UNCLOS III process was to have the Convention contain strong environmental-protection measures. These ocean-related environmental concerns have increased over the last decade and were highlighted at the 1992 United Nations Conference on Environment and Development (UNCED) in Rio de Janeiro (the 1992 "Earth Summit"). The United States National Report, submitted at the commencement of UNCED, listed various environmental problems and proposed ways to deal with these problems. Significantly, the United States pushed for action to deal with land-based sources of marine pollution and the conservation of marine species, including elimination of destructive and wasteful fisheries practices, as well as protection of ecosystems and critical areas to preserve marine biodiversity.[28]

UNCED provided additional political impetus to the Convention by recognizing the thorough and carefully balanced legal framework established by the Convention and upon which UNCED builds.[29] The United States Department of State has added that "the Law of the Sea Convention is the strongest comprehensive environmental treaty now in existence or likely to emerge for quite some time."[30] The very strength of these environmental provisions of Part XII of the Convention all but guarantees that this area demands focused United States' attention as it will have mutually competing concerns as both a maritime State and as a coastal State.

Under the Convention, States are to take measures to deal with *all* sources of pollution of the marine environment, including land-based sources, the atmosphere, dumping, vessels, and installations and devices, Article 194. For land-based sources, the Convention requires States to adopt laws to prevent, reduce, and control such pollution, Article 207. Additionally, rather than relying solely on flag States for the enforcement of vessel-source pollution rules, the Convention charges coastal States and port States, as well as flag States, to act against vessels within territorial or EEZ waters suspected of violation of antipollution regulations, Article 211. Coastal State regulations, especially within the EEZ, must be in accordance with generally accepted international standards, specifically under the IMO. Compliance with environmental standards under the Convention is subject to compulsory arbitration or adjudication.[31]

Few expect that the implementation of the environmental provisions of the Convention will be a smooth or simple matter. Among the more noteworthy difficulties to be expected is an intensified resistance to economically costly proposals for environmental initiatives from those having to bear the primary financial costs of such environmental protection. Moreover, a generic inability to ascertain exactly the source of pollution that crosses national boundaries will complicate pollution source reduction. In any event, some will connect the credibility of the United States as a world leader with the vigor with which it works to protect and preserve the marine environment.[32]

Crafting an effective, comprehensive policy to deal with the issue of protection and preservation of the marine environment is complicated by the extensive existing national legislation dealing with marine pollution, by international treaties dealing with marine environmental protection to which the United States is already party, by "soft law," and by emerging legislation dealing with environmental protection.

At the national level, the United States has enacted a number of statutes dealing with marine pollution control. Appendix 6 contains a selective listing of some of the important elements of this national legislation.[33] Additionally, the United States is a party to many international agreements and protocols designed to protect and preserve the environment. A listing of some of the more important of these treaties is contained in Appendix 7.[34] Arguably the three most important current global treaties in this area are:

- The Protocol of 1978 relating to the International Convention for the Prevention of Pollution from Ships (MARPOL 73/78), which regulates discharges from the normal operations of ships. Sources include bilge water, oily or hazardous wastes, sewage, and garbage, including plastics.
- The Convention on the Prevention of Marine Pollution by Dumping of Wastes and Other Matter (the London Dumping Convention), which regulates the disposal of wastes in the ocean from all ship-involved activities except normal ship operations.
- The Convention on Oil Pollution Preparedness, Response and Cooperation, which regulates international response to oil spills.[35]

"Soft law" is an increasingly important consideration in crafting effective national policies regarding protection and preservation of the marine environment. This "law" comes primarily in the form of international codes and guidelines from organizations—primarily under United Nations auspices—which attempt to deal with various aspects of the environment. These organizations range from the World Health Organization (WHO), to the Food and Agriculture Organization (FAO), to the United Nations Educational, Scientific, and Cultural Organization (UNESCO), to the International Atomic Energy Agency (IAEA) and others.[36] Examples of "soft law" range from UNEP guidelines and principles regarding the harmonious utilization of natural resources shared by two or more States, to IAEA codes regarding transboundary movement of radioactive waste, to FAO standards for the marking and identification of fishing vessels. As a leading world power, committed to the rule of law, the United States is obliged, at least, to consider this "soft law" when crafting its own policies.

Finally, increasing, worldwide emphasis on protecting and preserving the marine environment has resulted in several regional and international agreements addressing specific aspects of this problem. The sheer number of these agreements requires constant vigilance on the part of the United States to ensure that well-intentioned efforts to protect and preserve the maritime environment do not adversely affect important rights vital to the United States such as navigational freedoms. Several examples of accords designed to protect and preserve the marine environment serve to illustrate the extent of this potential area of contention, as discussed below.

The draft of the 1983 Convention for the Protection and Development of the Marine Environment of the Wider Caribbean Region (commonly called the Cartagena Convention) included a protocol (the Protocol Concerning Specially Protected Areas and Wildlife of the Wider Caribbean Region, or SPAW) which would have significantly restricted navigation through certain treaty areas or prohibited it altogether. Intensive negotiations were required on the part of the United States to eliminate those unacceptable, restrictive measures.[37]

Throughout the negotiations leading to the conclusion of the 1986 Convention for the Protection of the Natural Resources and Environment of the South Pacific Region (SPREP), and the Protocol for the Prevention of Pollution of the South Pacific Region by Dumping, special vigilance was necessary to ensure that traditional navigation rights were not impaired. For example, while the Parties agreed to establish "specially protected" areas, the Convention specifically provided that "the establishment of such areas shall not affect the rights of other Parties or third States under international law."[38]

The 1992 United Nations Conference on Environment and Development focused attention on the global importance of environmental protection. Accordingly, today's international efforts to preserve and protect the maritime environment and the large number of diverse stakeholders in these efforts—regional organizations, national governments, non-governmental organizations, and others—make the formulation of effective United States oceans policy in this vital area particularly challenging.

Acquisition and Conservation of Marine Resources

The oceans continue to provide a wealth of resources and have the potential to meet growing demands of a burgeoning worldwide population. But in much the same way as protection and preservation of the marine environment, the acquisition and conservation of marine resources promise to pose daunting policy challenges for the United States. As illustrations, this section will focus on four primary categories of resources: fish and marine mammals, living bottom dwelling species, oil and natural gas, and deep seabed minerals.

Initially, it might seem counterintuitive to categorize the acquisition and conservation of marine resources as a daunting policy challenge for the United States. After all, approximately 90 percent of living marine resources are harvested within 200 miles of the coast—that is, within coastal State EEZs, where jurisdiction under the Convention is quite well defined.[39] The majority of oil and gas exploration and exploitation occurs well within national EEZs or continental shelves, and, the deep seabed mining regime is exhaustively covered by the Convention and the Agreement, with clear lines of responsibility and authority.

The realities of resource exploitation, however, defy any simple logic. Traditional perceptions of the inexhaustibility of marine resources and of the capacity of the oceans to neutralize wastes have changed as marine species have been progressively depleted and their habitats damaged or threatened by pollution and a variety of other human activities. Maintaining the health and productive capacity of the oceans while seeking to meet the economic aspirations of growing populations worldwide will require difficult choices.

Fisheries

Fisheries issues have the potential to be as complex as any maritime matters. Complicating this equation is the nonstatic nature of the oceans; living marine resources migrate. While the Convention gives the coastal State near-exclusive rights to exploit fish in its EEZ, fish do not respect political boundaries. Many species of particular importance to the United States are found in or migrate over vast areas of the oceans, often crossing the EEZs of several nations as well as the high seas. Likewise, marine ecosystems and ocean currents, which transport pollutants and otherwise affect economic and environmental interests, extend across maritime boundaries and jurisdictional limits. Not surprisingly, in view of these factors, since the Convention was opened for signature in 1982, many new problems have emerged in relation to the conservation and utilization of living resources on the high seas.[40]

For the United States, the sustainability of fisheries is under extreme stress. The pressure on ocean fisheries begins at the shoreline. More than half of the American population lives within fifty miles of the coastline. Coastal development is booming and remains difficult to contain and to control. As a result, massive changes are occurring in coastal ecology that are destroying or damaging habitats for finfish and shellfish alike.[41]

Nearly one-half of the coastal finfish stocks within the United States' jurisdiction are now overexploited, that is, more are being caught than are being replenished by natural means. Included in these stocks are fourteen of the most valuable ground species. In addition, thirty-six others are fully exploited. The majority of overexploited stocks would require from five to twenty years to recover fully, even if fishing stopped altogether.[42] Several species, among them the New England ground fish, red snapper, swordfish, striped bass, and Atlantic bluefin tuna, are threatened with commercial extinction, with too few fish remaining to justify the cost of catching them.[43]

Further from the coastline, the stress on ocean resources is also substantial. Straddling stocks and highly migratory species are of great significance. Straddling stocks are those stocks of associated species that occur both within the EEZ and in areas adjacent to and beyond that zone. Typically, these stocks occur in the EEZs of only a few States. Highly migratory species (HMS), on the other hand, are those species which migrate through thousands of miles of open ocean. They are fished in the EEZs of many coastal states and in the open oceans.[44]

This is an area of great significance. For example, tunas make up more than one-quarter of the total volume of edible fish imported into this country each year.[45] U.S. fishermen catch hundreds of millions of dollars worth of tuna annually, most of it outside of U.S. waters. The quintessential distant-water fishing dilemma was, and remains, the struggle between the United States and its Latin American neighbors over the tuna catch off their coasts. Other straddling and highly migratory species of great significance to U.S. fishermen include swordfish, pollock in the Bering Sea, as well as marlins, sailfish, and other billfish important to recreational fishermen.[46]

These important fisheries are under increasing stress. Tuna and other highly migratory species in the Atlantic have been depleted significantly, and the harvest of bluefin tuna in the western Atlantic has seen particularly severe catch reductions. Similarly, North Atlantic swordfish stocks have deteriorated substantially, leading to the virtual elimination of the U.S. recreational swordfish fishery.[47] Catches of pollock in the high-seas "Donut Hole" area of the Bering Sea between the United States and Russia,[48] a high-seas area surrounded by the EEZs of the two States, soared to nearly 1.5 million metric tons in 1989 and then crashed to less than 11,000 tons in 1992.[49]

The combination of the importance of fisheries to the United States, the diminishing returns of fisheries, and the complex nature of fisheries conservation has led to extensive efforts on the part of the United States and the world community to take action regarding this important world resource. The complexity of this multi-faceted effort accentuates the need for a coordinated United States oceans policy.

At the national level, the United States has enacted extensive legislation relating to fisheries. Much of this legislation predated the 1982 United Nations Convention on the Law of the Sea. One of the most important pieces of legislation, the Fishery Conservation and Management Act of 1976 (now popularly known as the Magnuson Fishery Conservation and Management Act [MFCMA] for the late Senator Warren Magnuson) ushered in a new era of marine fisheries management for the United States. This Act placed fisheries resources beyond existing State jurisdiction and within 200 miles of all U.S. coasts under federal jurisdiction; an entirely new regional management system began allocating harvestable quotas. The MFCMA is continuously under review by the U.S. Congress.[50] Beyond the MFCMA, other comprehensive national legislation, most of it pre-Convention, governs various, specific aspects of fisheries management. A listing of some of the more important United States fisheries legislation is provided in Appendix 8.[51]

The United States is a party to a plethora of bilateral and multilateral international fisheries agreements, most of which were negotiated prior to the

Convention. These agreements cover an extraordinarily wide range of fisheries issues in great detail. For example, agreements addressing the exploitation and conservation of tuna go back to 1949.[52] These have a substantial impact on the extent to which the United States can exploit living marine resources. A listing of selected international agreements is provided in Appendix 9.[53]

As the United States continues to develop its oceans policy, it will undoubtedly find it necessary to focus on areas of fisheries conservation and management that have proven to be particularly resistant to effective international management. These areas include transboundary and straddling stocks, highly migratory species, anadromous species, catadromous species, and marine mammals. Constant attention to each of these areas will be necessary.

Coastal stocks migrate between different States' EEZs landward of 200 miles, and this fact was well recognized during the UNCLOS III negotiations. It was also recognized that the EEZ boundary would not in all cases reflect the migrations of coastal stocks beyond 200 miles. In the first transboundary straddling stock situation, the States concerned are to seek to agree on measures necessary to coordinate and ensure the conservation of resources. In the second straddling stock situation, the Law of the Sea Convention requires that a coastal State and those States fishing the stocks in the adjacent high seas seek agreement on measures necessary to conserve the stocks in adjacent areas, either directly or through appropriate subregional or regional organizations.[54] To be effective, the measures adopted for the adjacent high seas would have to be compatible with those applied to the same stock within the EEZ. Nonetheless, there is systemic pressure to extend national jurisdiction out ever farther in order to protect straddling stocks from distant-water fishing nations.[55] The respective rights of coastal States and States fishing straddling stocks beyond the EEZ are being discussed under the auspices of the United Nations Conference on Fisheries. A cogent U.S. policy is needed to properly address this nation's interests in this critical resource area.

Highly migratory species bring their own sets of considerations to fisheries management, addressed in Article 64. Coastal States, through whose EEZs these species migrate, and other States fishing the species are bound to cooperate to ensure conservation and optimum utilization, both within and beyond the EEZ—throughout the range of the species. Under the Law of the Sea Convention, international organizations are to be established for the purpose of conserving these species. The United States initially objected to the view of most coastal States that highly migratory species within the EEZ were subject to national jurisdiction. The U.S. view was that any State should be able to fish for these species in other nations' EEZs, subject only to applicable international agreements. In 1990, the United States reversed this position, claiming jurisdiction over tuna in the U.S. EEZ, effective January 1992. The respective rights and obligations of coastal and distant-water fishing States in relation to highly migratory species are also under ongoing discussion under the auspices of the United Nations Conference on Fisheries[56] and similarly require active U.S.

input based on a thoroughly considered U.S. policy position.

The high value of the United States' salmon industry[57] makes the management of anadromous species, those species whose stock spawn in rivers, of critical importance to the United States. For these species, the Convention grants the State within whose rivers the stocks spawn primary interest in, and responsibility for, conservation and management. Harvesting of the stocks is permitted only within EEZs and may not take place on the high seas, Article 66. Nevertheless, in situations where economic dislocation of another State's fishing interests would result, efforts are to be made to agree on terms and conditions for fishing beyond the EEZ. In practice, high-seas fisheries for anadromous stocks are no longer recognized as legitimate. Furthermore, when stocks migrate to within the EEZ of a State other than the State of origin, that State must cooperate with the State of origin in management and conservation.[58]

Closely related to the management of anadromous species is the conservation of catadromous species, those fish that migrate from fresh water to spawn in salt water, such as shrimp and eels. For these species, under article 67, the coastal State in whose waters these species spend the greater part of their life cycle is responsible for them. Harvesting of these species may occur only in the EEZ and is subject to other Convention provisions for EEZ living resources. Where species migrate through the EEZ of more than one State, they are to be managed pursuant to an agreement between the States concerned, recognizing the special responsibility of the host State to maintain the species.[59] Currently, the United States manages these species under the provisions of the Magnuson Fishery Conservation and Management Act (MFCMA).[60]

Marine Mammals

Marine mammals also are the subject of intense interest. Under Article 65 of the Convention, States are to cooperate in conserving marine mammals within EEZs and on the high seas.[61] Individually or through a competent international organization, they may grant marine mammals greater protection than the standard applicable to other marine living resources. For other species, the "qualified maximum sustainable yield" standard represents a minimum standard, but marine mammals are not subject to "optimum utilization" requirements. For cetaceans such as whales, the particular role of appropriate international organizations, such as the International Whaling Commission, is recognized as the means to promote their conservation, management, and study.[62]

The complex nature of the harvesting of fish and marine mammals for human consumption makes this an oceans policy issue that will remain particularly challenging. It is unlikely that United States' interests in this important area will diminish, and, therefore, it is expected that this area will require increased cooperation on the part of all involved U.S. agencies, with enhanced coordination at the executive level in order to fashion a policy that advances United States' interests.

Sedentary Species

Sometimes lost in the high-profiled discussions about various types of finfish is the economic value of sedentary species of the continental shelf, that is, those species such as crab, coral, mollusks, and sponges. In Articles 68 and 77, the Convention grants exclusive jurisdiction over these resources to the coastal State.[63] Although typically confined to the continental shelf, the coastal State's exclusive right over these species may extend beyond 200 miles if the coastal State can claim a continental shelf beyond 200 miles.[64]

This is an area of increasing controversy, primarily because of the large economic returns on these species. For example, disagreements arose over whether certain species of scallop on the Canadian continental shelf beyond 200 miles meet the definition of sedentary species. Initially, the United States rejected Canadian claims that these scallops are sedentary species and, therefore, subject to exclusive Canadian authority and control.[65] Although this matter has been substantially resolved, continued refinement of U.S. oceans policy will be necessary to resolve effectively this and similar issues.

Oil and Gas

The exploration for, and exploitation of, offshore oil and gas resources is also an oceans policy issue of increasing importance to the United States. Previous chapters have dealt with the magnitude of offshore hydrocarbon deposits, but not with issues regarding their economic use, and, particularly not with issues stemming from the affect such exploration and exploitation has on other resource and nonresource related uses of the oceans.

The area of potential exploration for offshore hydrocarbon deposits is extensive. The U.S. Federal Outer Continental Shelf (OCS) encompasses approximately 560 million hectares. Of this total, 13.2 million hectares were under lease to oil and gas exploration, development, and production companies during 1989. In 1989, the OCS oil and gas program generated more than 2.9 billion dollars in production royalties and lease-related revenues for the federal government. Approximately 1.35 billion cubic meters of oil and 2.46 billion cubic meters of natural gas have been produced from the OCS between 1954 and 1989. An additional 651.8 million cubic meters were produced from State waters during this period for a United States EEZ total of about two billion cubic meters. Between 1971 and 1988, oil production from OCS wells averaged almost one million barrels per day. In 1972, the OCS supplied almost 14 percent of the United States' production of natural gas and 12 percent of the oil produced. By 1989, the OCS supplied almost 24 percent of all natural gas produced in the U.S. and more than 16 percent of the nation's oil production.[66]

Balancing the development of oil and gas resources on the outer continental shelf with protecting the coastal and marine environments and their living resources has been controversial. In June 1990, in response to public concern over the adverse environmental effects of OCS oil and gas activities, and in light of some uncertainties in the scientific analysis of potential ecological and social impacts of offshore development, President George Bush announced a delay on OCS leasing until after the year 2000 in many areas off California, Florida, the Pacific Northwest, and the North Atlantic. The Oil Pollution Act of 1990[67] initiated a comprehensive federal oil spill prevention, response, liability, and compensation program. This act established a one billion dollar trust fund to improve prevention and cleanup of oil spills, and includes monies for cleanup activities, improving the safety of marine transportation of oil, and research. It also imposed a moratorium on oil and gas leasing off the North Carolina coast.[68]

This type of legislation may foreshadow an increasing tendency to seek legislative relief for known and potential environmental hazards associated with oil and gas exploration and exploitation. Through the mid-1990s, with energy prices relatively stable, the natural tension between oil and gas interests and environmentalists was manageable. Should a new wave of "energy shocks," such as those of the 1970s, occur, this now-delicate balance may be thrown off by the real or perceived need to accelerate offshore hydrocarbon exploration.

Adding to the complexity of this issue is the potential for oil and gas exploitation beyond the limits of uncontested national jurisdiction. Promising discoveries have been made in areas of the high seas, and although exploitation of these reserves will prove technologically challenging, the potential for international tension over rights is high. In fact tension has already manifested itself in multination disputes over the Spratley Islands—of no particular importance themselves—save the fact that they sit astride potentially enormous hydrocarbon reserves. These factors make it even more imperative that the United States develop an effective policy position regarding this important area.

Deep Seabed Mining

The final area of resource exploitation to be examined is deep seabed mining. Now that the Convention and the Agreement are becoming part of international law, the United States will need to carefully accommodate its oceans policy with respect to deep seabed mining. Specifically, the exploration licenses issued to several seabed mining consortia by the National Oceanic and Atmospheric Administration (NOAA) under the authority of the Deep Seabed Hard Mineral Resources Act of 1980 will need to be reviewed to ensure consistency with the Convention and the Agreement.[69]

As the world's largest economy, with the world's largest EEZ, and with unquestioned worldwide maritime interests, the United States has, arguably, the largest stake in the ordered acquisition and conservation of marine resources. While the Convention and the Agreement provide an excellent, omnibus starting point for fashioning international agreements in this important area, the United States must nevertheless develop a comprehensive national oceans policy that protects both our current and future interests.

Marine Scientific Research

Marine scientific research is governed by several articles in the Convention, including Articles 40, 87, 143, and 147. The Convention recognizes the essential role of marine scientific research in understanding oceanic and related atmospheric processes and in informed decisionmaking about ocean uses and coastal waters. Part XIII of the Convention affirms the right of all States to conduct marine scientific research and sets forth obligations to promote and cooperate in such research. The Convention encourages publication or dissemination of the results of marine scientific research activities, a position consistent with the general U.S. policy of advocating the wide sharing of the results of scientific research.[70]

Part XIII, in Articles 238 to 263, confirms the rights of coastal States to require consent for marine scientific research undertaken in marine areas under their jurisdiction. These rights are balanced to ensure that the consent authority is exercised in a predictable and reasonable fashion so as to promote maximum access to research activities.[71]

The Convention grants the coastal State jurisdiction over marine scientific research conducted within its EEZ and on its continental shelf and requires that the coastal State reasonably consent to such research being conducted. For the United States, which seeks access to other nations' offshore areas as the location for most useful and promising marine scientific research, this provision could initially seem to be too restrictive. However, the Convention includes certain obligations on the coastal State that, under normal circumstances, will grant consent for research by other States or competent international organizations. Such consent may not be delayed or unreasonably denied. The Convention includes an "implied consent" rule to promote prompt coastal State responses to requests for consent. Under this rule, work on a marine scientific research project may proceed six months after detailed information on the project has been provided by the foreign State or international organization unless, within four months of receipt of the information, the coastal State has informed the research project that (1) it has withheld consent, (2) the information provided does not conform with the facts, (3) additional information is required, or (4) outstanding obligations exist from previous research projects.[72]

This is an area that troubled the United States during the UNCLOS III negotiations and is one that still needs to be handled with finesse by U.S. policy makers. Many developing States view ocean science with suspicion, especially if that science is likely to enhance the political or economic power of others. Those governments fear that "researchers" are often looking for knowledge about resources that could be passed on to intelligence agencies or multilateral corporations, information that, if widely shared, would give developed State agencies and corporations an advantage in any negotiation or interaction with the developing State. These States may look at knowledge as something to be controlled, not shared.[73]

The wording of these provisions in the Convention is somewhat ambiguous, leading potentially to natural areas of contention. Also adding to differences of opinion and interpretations is the fact that, although there are numerous references to "marine scientific research" and "scientific research," nowhere in the Convention are either one of these terms defined. The "generally accepted definition" is that "marine scientific research" usually refers to those activities undertaken in the ocean and coastal waters to expand knowledge of the marine environment and its processes. It is distinguished from hydrographic surveys, from military activities, including military surveys, and from prospecting and exploration, which activities are, thus, excluded from the Conventions provisions on marine scientific research.[74]

Not surprisingly, these factors have led to uneven interpretation of the Convention's marine scientific research provisions by the world community. Some examples of restrictions placed on marine scientific research include:

- Delaying responses to requests for ship clearances;
- Denying at the last minute permission to conduct the research;
- Requiring that all data, regardless of format, be provided immediately prior to departure from the last port of call;
- Requiring the data to be provided within a fixed time after leaving the coastal State's waters, rather than after completion of the cruise;
- Requiring copies of data collected in international waters, or in waters under another country's jurisdiction;
- Requiring data to be held in confidence and not placed into the public domain;
- Requiring the cruise reports to be submitted in languages other than English;
- Requiring more than one observer to be on board;
- Requiring the observer to be on board during nonresearch legs of a voyage;
- Requiring research and port call requests to be submitted other than through the Foreign Ministry; and
- Failing of Foreign Ministry to forward cruise reports to the cognizant responsible organization.[75]

The importance of marine scientific research to the United States, when coupled with the complex regime governing this issue and the ambiguity regarding the nature of this research, make it imperative that the U.S. factor this important aspect of the use of the oceans into its overall oceans policy.

SUMMARY

Navigation and overflight, protection and preservation of the marine environment, acquisition and conservation of marine resources, and marine scientific research are oceans policy areas that have to compete—and will continue to compete—for the attention of U.S. policy makers and will develop their own constituencies that will vigorously pursue single-issue policies. The imperative to fashion an omnibus, comprehensive United States oceans policy to deal effectively with these diverse and potentially conflicting issue areas is more of an imperative now, in a post-Convention environment, than it ever has been.

NOTES

1.   United Nations Convention on the Law of the Sea, done at Montego Bay on 10 December 1982, entered into force 16 November 1994, U.N. Doc. A/CONF.62/122, reprinted in United Nations, *The Law of the Sea: Official Text of the Convention on the Law of the Sea with Annexes and Index* (New York: United Nations, 1983) (hereinafter *1982 LOS Convention*).

2.   Department of Defense, *National Security and the Convention on the Law of the Sea* (Washington, D.C.: Department of Defense, 1994), 20.

3.   Robert Smith and Bradford Thomas, "Island Disputes and the Law of the Sea: An Examination of Sovereignty and Delimitation Disputes" (address at Center for Oceans Law & Policy, Center for National Security Law, and Council of Foreign Relations Seminar, *Security Flashpoints: Oil, Islands, Sea Access and Military Confrontation*, New York, February 1997).

4.   See, for example, Keith Eirinberg, "U.N. Maritime Pact Could Produce South China Sea Solution," *Washington Times*, 26 June 1995; Lloyd Vasey, "Collision in the China Sea—World Oil and Shipping Lanes at Stake in Multination Dispute," *The Christian Science Monitor*, 22 June 1995; "Chinese, Filipino Ships Face Off in Spratleys," *New York Times*, 16 May 1995, p. 14; "U.S. Warns Claimants in South China Sea," *Defense News*, 15 May 1995, p. 8. Detailed examinations of the controversies involved in South China Sea island disputes were a key component of the Twenty-first Annual Seminar of the Center for Ocean Policy, *Security Flashpoints: Oil, Islands, Sea Access, and Military Confrontation*, held in conjunction with the Council on Foreign Relations in New York in February 1997. An omnibus presentation was made at the conference by Ambassador Hasjim Djalal of Indonesia, who currently serves as president of the International Seabed Authority. On the same program, also making presentations pressing their national claims, were representatives of Malaysia, the Philippines, and China. One particularly noteworthy paper catalogued the Chinese historic claim to the Spratleys:

The islands in the South China Sea...have historically been China's territory. The Chinese people sailed to and discovered the South China Sea islands as early as more than two thousand years ago. The Chinese dynasties started exercising jurisdiction latest in the Song era (60-1127 A.D.). China was the first to discover these islands, the first to name them, the first to engage in fishing and other production activities there, and the first to exhibit control and authority over the area. Given the lack of inhabitability in most parts of the South China Sea islands, permanent settlements by the Chinese people and administrative and/or military presence by the Chinese government were and remain unnecessary for the purpose of maintaining China's sovereignty....China's inchoate title upon discovery, coupled with its well-recorded exploitation and exercise of jurisdiction afterwards, undoubtedly entitles China to claim sovereign rights. The French and Japanese invasions and occupations in the 1930s were invalid and did not establish their title because the South China Seas islands were no longer *res nullius* or *terra nullius* absent China's abandonment of sovereignty, which the Chinese government never did and will never do. The same is true with respect to the current claims and occupations by Vietnam, the Philippines, Malaysia, and Brunei.

Jianming Shen, "International Law Rules and Historical Evidences Supporting China's Title to the South China Sea Islands" (address at the Center for Oceans Law and Policy, Center for National Security Law, and Council of Foreign Relations Seminar *Security Flashpoints: Oil, Islands, Sea Access, and Military Confrontation*, New York, February 1997). See also Hasjim Djalal, "Conflict Resolution in the Spratley Islands" (paper presented at *Tenth Annual U.S. Pacific Command International Military Operations and Law Conference*, Honolulu, April 1997). Professor Djalal speaks authoritatively, serving as Indonesian Ambassador-at-large for the Law of the Sea and Maritime Affairs and the first president of the International Seabed Authority.

     5.   Walter Doran, "An Operational Commander's Perspective on the 1982 LOS Convention," *The International Journal of Marine and Coastal Law* 10 (1995): 335. See also "If World War III Comes, Blame Fish," *U.S. News & World Report* 21 October 1996, p. 59. This article identifies 9 principal areas of conflict: the Gulf of Thailand, off Portugal, the Sea of Okhotsk, the Philippines, off Ireland, the Northeast Atlantic, between Australia and Indonesia, the Malaysian coast, and the Grand Banks. In March 1995, Canadian forces chased down and seized a Spanish trawler, in an illustrative incident.

     6.   Hugh Lynch, "Freedom of Navigation in the Persian Gulf and the Strait of Hormuz" (address at the Center for Oceans Law and Policy, Center for National Security Law, and Council of Foreign Relations Seminar *Security Flashpoints: Oil, Islands, Sea Access, and Military Confrontation*, New York, February 1997). Subsequently, Captain Charles Allen, JAGC, U.S. Navy, Deputy Department of Defense Representative for Ocean Policy Affairs, highlighted the strong potential for future conflict:

Many of the provisions of the Marine Areas Act are clearly inconsistent with international law and, therefore, as a matter of law need not be observed. Given the long standing tensions and conflicts in the region, however, the possibility exists that Iran may attempt to enforce the provisions of the Marine Areas Act, particularly in the Strait of Hormuz and its western approaches.

Charles Allen, "Persian Gulf Disputes" (address at the Center for Oceans Law and Policy, Center for National Security Law, and Council of Foreign Relations Seminar *Security Flashpoints: Oil, Islands, Sea Access, and Military Confrontation*, New York, February 1997).

     7.   J. Ashley Roach and Robert W. Smith, *International Law Studies 1994: Excessive Maritime Claims* vol. 66 (Newport, Rhode Island: Naval War College Press, 1994). The authors are well-recognized experts on the law of the sea and produced this volume in cooperation with the Department of State. This

publication is one of three United States principal sources documenting excessive maritime claims.   The others are *Maritime Claims Reference Manual* (Department of Defense, Office of the Secretary of Defense for International Security Affairs, 1990, revised ed., 1994) and Department of State, *Limits in the Seas No. 112: United States Responses to Excessive Maritime Claims* (Washington, D.C., United States Department of State, Bureau of Oceans and International Environmental and Scientific Affairs, 1992).   *International Law Studies 1994: Excessive Maritime Claims* is the most recent publication of the three and is used as a principal resource throughout this chapter.

8.   Department of Defense, *National Security and the Convention on the Law of the Sea*, 20. See also John Rolph, "Freedom of Navigation and the Black Sea Bumping Incident, How 'Innocent' Must Innocent Passage Be?" *Military Law Review* 135 (1992): 147.

9.   Roach and Smith, *Excessive Maritime Claims*, 158-159.

10.   Professor Jack Grunawalt, "The 1982 United Nations Convention on the Law of the Sea: An Operational Lawyer's Perspective" (address at the Center for Oceans Law and Policy Symposium, *Towards Senate Consideration of the 1982 Law of the Sea Convention*, Washington, D.C., June 1995). Professor Grunawalt was an active participant in shaping policy for the United States Law of the Sea delegation, particularly during his service as a Navy Captain in the Judge Advocate General's Corps as special counsel to the Chief of Naval Operations. In his address he presented a compelling briefing describing the negotiations during the Ninth UNCLOS III session in 1980 where a group of seven States unsuccessfully attempted to insert language in the Convention requiring prior permission or notification for the passage of warships through the territorial sea; he noted further that recent initiatives by some coastal States have followed this same pattern.

11.   U.S. Senate, *Treaty Document 103-39, United Nations Convention on the Law of the Sea, with Annexes, and the Agreement Relating to the Implementation of Part XI of the United Nations Convention on the Law of the Sea, with Annex*, 103d Cong., 2d sess., 7 October 1994, 14-17 (hereinafter *Treaty Document 103-39*).

12.   Roach and Smith, *Excessive Maritime Claims*, 103-108.

13.   See generally Roach and Smith, *Excessive Maritime Claims*, 177-229.

14.   Senate, *Treaty Document 103-39*, 16-18.

15.   See Roach and Smith, *Excessive Maritime Claims*, 33-34, 180-222.

16.   John Van Dyke, "Hawaii's Claim to Archipelagic Waters," in *Implications of Entry into Force of the Law of the Sea Convention for U.S. Ocean Governance*, Biliana Cicin-Sain and Katherine Leccese, eds. (Honolulu: Ocean Governance Study Group, 1995), 78-80. Professor Van Dyke, of the William S. Richardson School of Law at the University of Hawaii, is a charter member of the Ocean Governance Study Group Steering Committee. He points out that while the claim of archipelagic status for the Hawaiian Island Chain would not appreciably benefit the *federal* government, the *State of Hawaii* could

assert sovereign control over these enclosed waters. He cites significant historical precedent for a claim of archipelagic status and historical waters status for the Hawaiian Islands.

17.   See Roach and Smith, *Excessive Maritime Claims*, 134-138.

18.   Alfred Greenwood, et al., *CRS Report to the Congress: Oceans and Coastal Resources: A Briefing Book* (Washington, D.C.: Congressional Research Service, Library of Congress, 1995), CRS-7.

19.   See *Treaty Document 103-39*, 2-20.

20.   Ibid., 25.

21.   Roach and Smith, *Excessive Maritime Claims*, 117, 241-49. See also J. Ashley Roach, "Dispute Settlement in Specific Situations" (remarks at the Georgetown University Law Center Symposium, *Implementing the United Nations Convention on the Law of the Sea*, Washington, D.C., January 1995).

22.   See Marjorie Ann Browne, *CRS Issue Brief: The Law of the Sea Convention and U.S. Policy* (Washington, D.C.: Congressional Research Service, Library of Congress, 1995), CRS-3.

23.   John H. Dalton; Admiral Jeremy M. Boorda, USN; General Carl E. Mundy, USMC; *Forward...From the Sea* (Washington, D.C., USGPO, 1995), 1-10.

24.   Department of the Navy, *The Commander's Handbook on the Law of Naval Operations*, U.S. Naval Warfare Publication (NWP)9A/Fleet Marine Force Manual (FMFM) 1-10, (Washington, D.C.: Naval Warfare Publications Library, 1989), 1-AS11-6-2. This source has been recently revised as Department of the Navy, *Naval Warfare Publication 1-14M/MCWP 5-2.1, The Commander's Handbook on the Law of Naval Operations* (Washington, D.C: Naval Warfare Publications Library, 1995).

25.   See John C. Meyer, "The Impact of the Exclusive Economic Zone on Naval Operations," *Naval Law Review* 40 (1992): 241; Steven Rose, "Naval Activity in the EEZ—Troubled Waters Ahead?" *Naval Law Review* 39 (1990): 67; Boleslaw Adam Boczek, "Peacetime Military Activities in the Exclusive Economic Zone of Third Countries," *Ocean Development and International Law* 19 (1988): 451; Michelle Wallace, "The Right of Warships to Operate in the Exclusive Economic Zone as Perceived by Delegates to the Third United Nations Law of the Sea Convention," in *International Navigation, Rocks and Shoals Ahead?*, John Van Dyke, Lewis Alexander, and James Myer, eds. (Honolulu: Law of the Sea Institute Press, 1988), 345.

26.   *Treaty Document 103-39*, 26.

27.   Christopher Joyner, "Ocean Fisheries, United States' Interests and the 1982 Law of the Sea Convention" (address at the Georgetown University Law Center Symposium, *Implementing the United Nations Convention on the Law of the Sea*, Washington, D.C., January 1995), 3.

28.   Greenwood, et al., *CRS Report to the Congress: Oceans and Coastal Resources: A Briefing Book*, CRS 135-161. At the conclusion of the UNCED on 14 June 1992, the Plenary session adopted Agenda 21, Chapter 17. Chapter

17 includes the protection of the oceans, all kinds of seas (including coastal and semienclosed seas), and coastal areas and includes the protection, rational use, and development of their living resources. The session concluded that new approaches to marine and coastal areas management at the national, subregional, regional, and global levels would be necessary over the next decade. Seven program areas were identified for international protection and sustainable development:

- integrated management and sustainable development of coastal areas, including exclusive economic zones
- marine environmental protection
- sustainable use and conservation of marine living resources on the high seas
- sustainable use and conservation of marine living resources under national jurisdiction
- critical uncertainties for the management of the marine environment and climate change
- international and regional cooperation and coordination
- sustainable development of small islands

The comprehensive nature of these program areas gives some indication of the potential areas of contention in oceans policy formulation. See also Biliana Cicin-Sain, "Reflections on UNCED Implementation: Emphasis on Oceans and Coasts" (paper presented at the 29th annual conference of the Law of the Sea Institute, *Sustainable Development and Preservation of the Oceans*, Bali, Indonesia, June 1995).

29.   John R. Stevenson and Bernard H. Oxman, "The Future of the United Nations Convention on the Law of the Sea," *American Journal of International Law* 88 (1994): 491-492. See also Robert Knecht and Biliana Cicin-Sain, "Implications of the Earth Summit for Ocean and Coastal Governance," *Ocean Development and International Law* 24 (1993): 350.

30.   Senate, *Treaty Document 103-39*, 31; Department of State, *Dispatch Supplement: Law of the Sea Convention: Letters of Transmittal and Submittal and Commentary*, (Washington, D.C., U.S. Department of State, Bureau of Public Affairs, February, 1995), 19-24. This State Department publication provides extensive treatment of the issue of protection and preservation of the marine environment and highlights the fact that need for further negotiation and accommodation on this issue, noting, in part, for example: "International rules and national legislation relating to pollution from deep sea-bed mining have yet to be developed."

31.   Marjorie Ann Browne, *CRS Issue Brief: The Law of the Sea Convention and U.S. Policy*, CRS 3-4.

32.   See, for example, Douglas Johnston, "Protection of the Ocean Environment: Competing Views of the Implementation Process," in *Implications of Entry into Force of the Law of the Sea Convention for U.S. Ocean Governance*, Biliana Cicin-Sain and Katherine Leccese, eds., 34-37; Robert

Krueger and Stefan Risenfeld, eds., *The Developing Order of the Oceans, Proceedings of the Eighteenth Annual Conference of the Law of the Sea Institute* (Honolulu: Law of the Sea Institute, 1985), 133-179; Lee Kimball, *The Law of the Sea: Priorities and Responsibilities in Implementing the Convention* (Gland, Switzerland: International Union for Conversation of Nature and Natural Resources, 1995), 35-70.

33.   Greenwood, et al., *CRS Report for Congress: Oceans and Coastal Resources: A Briefing Book*, CRS 160-161.

34.   See, for example, Lee Kimball, *The Law of the Sea: Priorities and Responsibilities in Implementing the Convention*; Roach and Smith, *Excessive Maritime Claims*, 258, 259-263.

35.   Roach and Smith, *Excessive Maritime Claims*, 259-262.

36.   See generally Kimball, *The Law of the Sea: Priorities and Responsibilities in Implementing the Convention*, 41, 55, 60, 77, 87.

37.   Roach and Smith, *Excessive Maritime Claims*, 260.

38.   Ibid., 260-262.

39.   See *Treaty Document 103-39*, 41.

40.   See Robert Friedheim, *Negotiating the New Ocean Regime* (Columbia, South Carolina: University of South Carolina Press, 1993). See also Thomas Clingan, *The Law of the Sea: Ocean Law and Policy* (San Francisco, California, Austin and Winfield, 1994), 29; World Resources Institute, *World Resources 1988-1989* (New York: Basic Books, 1988); Biliana Cicin-Sain and Katherine A. Leccese, eds., *Implications of Entry into Force of the Law of the Sea Convention for U.S. Ocean Governance*, 24-50.

41.   Michael Satchell, "The Rape of the Oceans," *U.S. News and World Report*, 22 June 1992, 67.

42.   Greenwood, et al., *CRS Report for Congress: Ocean and Coastal Resources: A Briefing Book*, CRS-146.

43.   Joyner, "Ocean Fisheries, United States' Interests and the 1982 Law of the Sea Convention," 1.

44.   Lisa Speer, "Improving International Management of Straddling and Highly Migratory Fish," in *Implications of Entry into Force of the Law of the Sea Convention for U.S. Ocean Governance*, Cicin-Sain and Leccese, eds., 47-49.

45.   Friedheim, *Negotiating the New Ocean Regime*, 168.

46.   Speer, "Improving International Management of Straddling and Highly Migratory Fish," 47.

47.   Greenwood, et al., *CRS Report for Congress: Ocean and Coastal Resources: A Briefing Book*, CRS-146.

48.   Joyner, "Ocean Fisheries, United States' Interests and the 1982 Law of the Sea Convention," 13.

49.   Speer, "Improving International Management of Straddling and Highly Migratory Fish," 47-49. See also Friedheim, *Negotiating the New Ocean Regime*, 168.

50.   *Treaty Document 103-39*, 42, 43.

51.   This list is drawn from Greenwood, et al., eds., *CRS Report for Congress: Ocean and Coastal Resources: A Briefing Book*, CRS 159-161. See also Kimball, *The Law of the Sea: Priorities and Responsibilities in Implementing the Convention*, 71-76; Joyner, "Ocean Fisheries, United States Interests and the 1982 Law of the Sea Convention."

52.   See James Wang, *Handbook on Ocean Politics and Law* (New York: Greenwood Press, 1992), 483-502; Kimball, *The Law of the Sea: Priorities and Responsibilities in Implementing the Convention*, 76.

53.   Drawn from Kimball, *The Law of the Sea: Priorities and Responsibilities in Implementing the Convention*, 71-76; Wang, *Ocean Politics and Law*, 483-502.

54.   *Treaty Document 103-39*, 48.

55.   Barbara Kwiatkowska, "Creeping Jurisdiction Beyond 200 Miles in Light of the 1982 Law of the Sea Convention and State Practice," *Ocean Development and International Law* 22 (1995): 153; Christopher Joyner and Peter Decola, "Chile's Presential Sea Proposal: Implications for Straddling Stocks and the International Law of Fisheries," *Ocean Development and International Law*, 24 (1993): 483; Evelyn Meltzer, "Global Overview of Straddling and Highly Migratory Fish Stocks: The Nonsustainable Nature of High Seas Fisheries," *Ocean Development and International Law* 25 (1994): 255.

56.   Senate, *Treaty Document 103-39*, 48-51. See generally Joyner, "Ocean Fisheries, United States' Interests and the 1982 Law of the Sea Convention," 1-17.

57.   Joyner, "Ocean Fisheries, United States, Interests and the 1982 Law of the Sea Convention," 7; Wang, *Ocean Politics and Law*, 125-28.

58.   Kimball, *The Law of the Sea: Priorities and Responsibilities in Implementing the Convention*, 75; *Treaty Document 103-39*, 46.

59.   Wang, *Ocean Politics and Law*, 163-164; Kimball, *The Law of the Sea: Priorities and Responsibilities in Implementing the Convention*, 75.

60.   *Treaty Document 103-39*, 45.

61.   Ibid., 44; R. R. Churchill and A. V. Lowe, *The Law of the Sea* (Manchester, U.K.: Manchester University Press, 1983), 208.

62.   Kimball, *The Law of the Sea: Priorities and Responsibilities in Implementing the Convention*, 72-74.

63.   See also *Treaty Document 103-39*, 46.

64.   Kimball, *The Law of the Sea: Priorities and Responsibilities in Implementing the Convention*, 64; Churchill and Lowe, *The Law of the Sea*, 119-121.

65.   Kimball, *The Law of the Sea: Priorities and Responsibilities in Implementing the Convention*, 74-75.

66.   Greenwood, et al., *Ocean and Coastal Resources: A Briefing Book*, 7, 8, 150. For a thorough treatment of these matters, see generally U.S. Department of the Interior, Minerals Management Service, *Federal Offshore Statistics: 1989: Leasing Exploration and Revenues*, OCS Report MMS 90-0072 (Washington,

D.C.: USGPO, 1990), 1-104.

67.   See Greenwood, et al., *Ocean and Coastal Resources: A Briefing Book*, 101.

68.   Ibid., 150.

69.   Ibid., 97-100.

70.   See *Treaty Document 103-39*, 79.

71.   Ibid., 79-83.

72.   Browne, *CRS Issue Brief: The Law of the Sea Convention and U.S. Policy*, CRS-4. See *Treaty Document 103-39*, 81-83, 186-91.

73.   Friedheim, *Negotiating the Law of the Sea*, 201-19. The author develops this theme more fully, noting that, "The last thing Third World leaders wanted to foster were scientists from developed States who knew more about their near-shore areas than they did."

74.   *Treaty Document 103-39*, 82-84.

75.   J. Ashley Roach, "Dispute Settlement in Specific Situations," 11-12.

Chapter Ten

MAKING UNITED STATES OCEANS POLICY

IN SEARCH OF A SOLUTION

In his 7 October 1994 transmittal letter submitting the 1982 United Nations Convention on the Law of the Sea to the United States Senate for its advice and consent,[1] President Clinton reaffirmed that previous administrations, both Democratic and Republican, have recognized that the wide acceptance of the Convention on the Law of the Sea is the cornerstone for United States oceans policy. This reaffirmation was an important first step in developing a comprehensive oceans policy for the United States.

United States oceans policy exists at several levels. Most visibly, it exists at the international level in our relations with other nations in the maritime arena. As we enter an era in which the majority of the community of nations has agreed to be bound by the Convention, U.S. oceans policy must focus on achieving an accommodation between the provisions of the Convention and other existing international agreements. A perusal of Appendices 7 and 9 gives some indication of the magnitude of this task. Similarly, future bilateral and multilateral agreements must be crafted in areas where the Convention requires, contemplates, or admits of further amplification and refinement.

At the national level, a comprehensive review of the extensive existing national legislation, particularly with respect to protection and preservation of the marine environment and acquisition and conservation of marine resources, must be conducted. This review must ensure that existing legislation is consistent with the Convention and propose new legislation, where necessary. A perusal of Appendices 6 and 8 provides a sense of the extent of this undertaking.

Finally, the interaction between, and legal framework supporting, the federal, state, and local governments in all areas of oceans use must be reviewed to determine where existing policies are adequate and where policy changes must be made.   This is particularly important because agreements made at the international level often require local implementation, such as controlling land-based sources of maritime pollution.   Additionally, federal statutory mandates regarding oceans uses may require commensurate funding to support implementation at the local level.

Current inconsistencies among federal, state, and local agencies exercising jurisdiction over marine activities can lead to inefficient or ineffective regulation of ocean space.   In the absence of specific new federal initiatives to establish an integrated planning and management regime for ocean resources, a number of coastal states have found it necessary to develop local or regional policies and plans for regulating or encouraging activities in the ocean that impinge on their territorial waters or their coasts.

THE INTERNATIONAL ENVIRONMENT

Although the 1982 United Nations Convention is comprehensive, it is not conclusive or dispositive of every aspect of United States oceans policy in the international arena.   This oceans policy must be developed and articulated in a number of ways that complement the Convention.   Historically, the policy positions of the Department of State and the Department of Defense have included at least three tiers, consisting of a vigorous Freedom of Navigation Program, promulgation of guidance to military forces, and active development and support of conventional international law addressing oceans issues. The key elements of this policy will, in all probability, remain essentially intact, though the Freedom of Navigation Program may receive less emphasis as excessive claims are rolled back in conformance with the Convention.

In the transmittal letter submitting the Convention and the Agreement, the president articulated ways in which the United States would benefit from the United Nations Convention.   While not making policy, per se, this clear statement of the benefits expected to be derived from the United Nations Convention provided a window on the current administration's intended oceans policy.   It corresponded with other recent administration decisions on oceans policy and may set the stage for upcoming oceans policy determinations.

Concurrently, additional guidance has helped shape United States oceans policy. Presidential Review Directive 12 (PRD-12), entitled "Oceans, Fisheries and Fresh Water Resources," published in May 1993, provided extensive guidance regarding the direction the administration intended to move policy in these important areas. Presidential Decision Directive 32 (PDD-32), published in January 1995, provided extensive, explicit guidance on the U.S. Freedom of Navigation Program. Presidential Decision Directive 36 (PDD-36), published in April 1995, provided general guidance on the nation's policy on protecting the ocean environment.[2] Although these three documents are either "classified" or listed for "official use only," their essential elements are contained in other, open-source documents.

Within the executive branch, other vehicles are used to announce oceans policy. The Department of State publishes various documents, such as the *Department of State Dispatch*, which articulate United States oceans policy in the context of the Convention. Various State and Defense Department officials make very regular appearances at recurring academic and legal symposia, such as those held by the Law of the Sea Institute, the Council on Ocean Law, the Center for Oceans Law and Policy at the University of Virginia, and the Georgetown University Law Center. While appropriate disclaimers are made, these presentations by high officials within the executive branch are taken as official policy. Additionally, the sum of the policy discussions at such meetings can often reveal the future of oceans policy at the national and international levels.[3]

Concerning legal divisions of the oceans and airspace, and particularly regarding excessive claims by various nations, the Departments of State and Defense have published lists of excessive claims. Because navigation and overflight rights are a primary, critical concern to the United States, this extent of governmental attention is not surprising. What is particularly noteworthy, however, is that United States executive branch documents are now being used by an increasing number of nations as source documents illustrating the excessive maritime claims of other States.[4]

At the international level, in a post-Convention environment, it is critical that the United States participate actively in international organizations with responsibility for further development of the international law of the sea; these include the International Maritime Organization, the International Tribunal for the Law of the Sea, the Commission on the Limits of the Continental Shelf, and the International Seabed Authority, among others. Representation among these disparate organizations must be coordinated, and this policy coordination must emanate from a comprehensive, national oceans policy position. With policy coordination, national expertise can flourish, and the United States will be better prepared to engage in bilateral and multilateral negotiations on the law of the sea on the most pressing issues.

There is much work to be done, but the United States must remain actively engaged, armed with a comprehensive oceans policy. For example, despite the extensive nature of the negotiations leading to the adoption of the Convention, several ambiguous and indeterminate provisions remain in the Convention's text.[5] In addition, a careful analysis of the Convention's six authentic language texts reveals that conflicting interpretations may exist among these different language texts of the Convention. The implications of these ambiguities are significant in that they allow States to argue that their particular, contradictory interpretations are valid. As one example of the magnitude of these ambiguities, a critical point of contention between the United States and the Soviet Union concerned the scope of Article 22, paragraph 1, of the Convention regarding whether the Convention allows coastal States to limit innocent passage only for navigational safety considerations, or whether sea lane restrictions may be imposed when necessary for other purposes, such as protecting national security.

Some commentators point to this ambiguity as a principal cause of the February 1988 bumping incident in the Black Sea.[6] Clearly, the United States must navigate the international oceans policy arena with a well-coordinated oceans policy position in order to effectively resolve controversies such as these.

Perhaps of more immediate concern to U.S. policy makers is the risk of being drawn into conflicts between other nations over island disputes impelled by strait baseline delimitation inconsistencies. Disputes in East Asia between North and South Korea over the Northwest Islands in the Yellow Sea, between Japan and Russia over the Northern Territories/Kuril Islands in the Sea of Okhotsk, between North Korea and Russia over their exclusive economic zone/continental shelf boundary, between Japan and South Korea over the Liancourt Rocks, and between Japan and China over the Senkaku/Diaoyr Islands, all present the potential for conflict. The United States has a number of bilateral treaties with the nations of East Asia, and these nations have not hesitated to assert the right to seek United States assistance under these treaties. For example, on 12 December 1996, Japanese officials claimed that the United States' defense pact with Japan obligates the United States to assist Japanese forces if attacked by Russia. Similarly, Philippine officials have invoked the Philippine-United States Mutual Defense Treaty to require assistance of Philippine forces in the Spratley Islands if they are attacked by any other party. Complicating these disputes in many cases is the absence of diplomatic relations among the parties or resistance to dispute resolution mechanisms.[7] These areas will demand highest level oceans and foreign policy coordination.

THE NATIONAL LEVEL

It is likely that the United States has a more extensive body of national legislation governing the oceans than any other nation. This can be seen as either positive or negative. It is positive in that this legislation has accomplished positive things, particularly in the area of protection and preservation of the marine environment. It is negative in that each individual piece of legislation addresses primarily a single issue, which leads to a suboptimized management approach and attendant conflicts among different ocean sectors, including conflicts among different users and different government agencies.

A causal factor for the current situation is the way in which oceans policy legislation evolved in the United States. Chapter 8 and Appendices 6 and 8 have addressed the evolution of this legislation. A review of this information can lead to the conclusion that this legislation grew in a nonlinear fashion, primarily in fits and starts in the post-World War II era, in response to national security or interest group concerns. Thus, in the immediate postwar era, when ownership of offshore oil and gas was of primary concern, Congress enacted the Submerged Lands Act and the Outer Continental Shelf Lands Act. In the wake of *Sputnik*, ocean science concerns dominated and laws were passed creating the Marine Sciences Council, the Commission on Marine Sciences, Engineering and

Resources, and the Sea Grant College Program. In the late 1960s and early 1970s, environmental issues began to dominate and legislation such as the National Environmental Policy Act of 1969, the Federal Water Pollution Control Act of 1972, the Marine Mammal Protection Act of 1972, the Marine Protection, Research, and Sanctuaries Act of 1972, the Coastal Zone Management Act of 1972, and the Endangered Species Act of 1973 were created. In the mid to late 1970s, in the wake of the Arab oil embargoes, legislation designed to ensure access to energy resources, such as the Coastal Energy Impact Program amendment to the Coastal Zone Management Act, and the Outer Continental Shelf Lands Act Amendments of 1978, was passed.[8]

A survey of this legislation leads to the inevitable conclusion that this legislation did not emanate in response to coordinated national policy, but rather grew in response to both the international environment and the national mood. Perhaps none of it was crafted in consideration of a comprehensive international Convention. Some of the current U.S. legislation is inconsistent with the provisions of the Convention. For example, Margaret Hayes, Assistant General Counsel for Fisheries for National Oceanic and Atmospherics Administration (NOAA), noted at a 1995 symposium that United States' fisheries law and the provisions of the Convention have a fundamental incongruence that needs to be fixed.[9]   Other national legislation affecting the oceans, such as much environmental legislation, is often single-purpose in nature, addressing only single aspects of the ocean and largely ignoring interrelationships and possible conflicts among users and resources.[10]

Mention has been made of the Reagan Proclamations establishing a 200-mile exclusive economic zone and a twelve-mile territorial sea. Although primarily designed to articulate our policies at the international level, these proclamations also have a very real, and oftentimes very immediate, domestic aspect to them, presenting yet another layer of regulation.   For example, Alaska's senior senator, Ted Stevens, has noted on numerous occasions that over half of the fish the United States consumes comes from "Alaska's" EEZ, and has been very active in demanding appropriate "considerations" for his state.   At one symposium, Senator Stevens presented a case for legislation providing additional protections to Alaska fishermen and for increased attention to the so-called "donut hole" and the impact on pollock, an important fish for Alaskan fishermen. The senator's using the keynote address at this conference—and lobbying for his state's interests—gives some indication of the complexities and pressures involved in effecting coherent national legislation regarding the law of the sea.[11]

Recurring windows of opportunity exist to coordinate national oceans policy legislation, because a large body of federal legislation affecting oceans policy, such as the Endangered Species Act, the Marine Mammal Protection Act, the Coastal Zone Management Act, and the Magnuson Fishery Conservation and Management Act come before the Congress periodically. Alternatively, comprehensive review of the pertinent federal law, under the auspices of a coordinated national oceans policy, would have a high potential to achieve coordinated, mutually supportive legislation that supports our national oceans policy at all levels.

There is cause for optimism that a higher degree of oceans policy coordination can be achieved through federal legislation. As the weaknesses of single-use approaches to ocean policy have been recognized, amendments to existing legislation, such as amendments to the Coastal Zone Management Act and the Outer Continental Shelf Lands Act have been designed to accommodate a broader range of interests and recognize the real-world interconnection of events. Thus, there are examples of legislation that has evolved to a more multi-use context and has provided for accommodation of different uses in the same spatial context.[12]

FEDERAL, STATE, AND LOCAL INTERACTION

While attention has been refocused on the international and national level, the interaction of federal, state, and local governments, and their response to industry and other interest groups, presents the most complex area in the evolution of effective United States oceans policy. Conflicts among ocean users, including government agencies at different levels, have been increasing significantly. Lawsuits have proliferated accordingly.

For example, in the controversies over oil exploration and exploitation off the central coast of California, there are numerous legal actions in effect, pitting local, state, and federal governments and multiple ocean and land interests against one another. The proliferation of lawsuits may evidence a lack of overarching national policy guidance, including inadequate devices for policy conflict resolution under the current framework for ocean governance.[13]

There are numerous reasons for friction among and between various governmental agencies and the constituencies they serve. In the almost two decades since the last of the significant national legislation on the oceans was crafted, extensive changes have taken place, including a rise in environmental consciousness, the emergence of energy use and supply issues, significant increases in ocean uses and conflicts, growth in the capacity of coastal States and territories in coastal ocean management, growth in the capacity of the marine natural sciences and in the marine social sciences, increased population growth in coastal areas and extensions of U.S. federal jurisdiction over vast ocean areas.[14]

This last area, the extension of federal jurisdiction over coastal waters, is one that promises to increase the tension between state, and local governments and the federal government absent an overarching national policy that considers the needs and aspirations of all governmental entities. Prior to the Reagan Proclamations and the 1982 United Nations Convention, individual states of the United States had jurisdiction over the waters out to three miles off their coasts. Now that the United States has claimed sovereignty over a territorial sea out to twelve miles, and exclusive resource rights in an EEZ out to 200 miles, many states are demanding what they consider to be their fair share. For example, the state of Hawaii has recently declared that state marine waters extend out to twelve miles and has written a 200-mile exclusive economic zone into the state constitution.[15] Other law-of-the-sea experts predict that as the level of activity in these expanded zones increases, especially with respect to resource exploitation, disagreements between federal, state, and local governments will intensify.[16] A national oceans policy is a necessary first step toward diffusing such contentious issues.

This is not to say that a national oceans policy will obviate all contentious issues between the federal government and state governments and local municipalities. Areas of disagreement will remain. Policy coordination at the national level, however, will likely, at a minimum, diminish expectations to reasonable levels. Importantly, dispute resolution mechanisms, perhaps guided by those in the Convention, need to be set up among and between governmental agencies to diffuse the costly and time-consuming litigation that currently envelops many of these oceans policy issues.

The evolution of a continuous and adaptive oceans policy should not be viewed as an exceptionally daunting task—only as one that has not completely succeeded. Until now, the United States has not had an oceans policy per se, but has had, rather, a series of unconnected sub-policies, for example, an offshore oil policy, a marine mammals policy, and an ocean dumping policy. What is needed is a process that will consider and tie together disparate—and potentially conflicting—policies within an overarching coordinating policy. This policy should recognize the interests at all levels of government and their sometimes diametrically opposed constituencies advocating resource exploitation or resource conservation.

The balancing of these interests is challenging. In the past, policy has oscillated between virtually unconstrained development followed by the adoption of predominantly preservationist approaches. But, an "either-or" view of development and conservation is costly and inhibits cohesive policy development.[17] Approaches must be constructed that dampen oscillation in oceans policy goals. These policies must be based on such fundamental principles as equity and stewardship of the public trust, policies that reflect an appreciation of the functioning of the ocean and its various subsystems and establish the priorities upon which the success or failure of any ocean management program depends.[18]

BASIC ISSUES IN UNITED STATES OCEANS POLICY

Many of the issues highlighted at the international, national, state, and local levels, are symptomatic, but do not get at the root of the problem—what Edward Miles, charter member of the Panel on the Law of Ocean Uses, called "the sorry state of U.S. oceans policy."[19] At present, there is no effective organizational structure at the federal level for the development and coordination of oceans policy. According to Professor Miles, and others, policy, if one can even identify it, develops only reactively on a problem-by-problem basis.[20] Indeed, ocean governance, such as it is in the United States, remains in the hands of a set of Federal agencies operating under the terms of specific, often disparate, pieces of legislation. The goals of these separate single-sector ocean governance regimes are spelled out in the individual laws creating them. As a consequence, few overarching national goals or common principles can be found in the governance schemes currently in place to manage U.S. ocean resources and interests. What exists is a series of separately based legislative initiatives and separately operated management systems, each striving to meet relatively narrow, "stand-alone" goals.[21] Because ocean governance remains on the periphery of the American political process, it is extremely unlikely that this situation will change, absent overt, proactive effort to create a national oceans policy.[22]

In essence, the rational evolution of effective United States oceans policy is impeded for three fundamental reasons: the jurisdictional split among various levels of government; the functional, sector-by-sector approach in the management of different resources and uses; and the very complexity of the oceans system itself. It is unlikely that policy integration can be achieved unless and until a commitment is made to develop a comprehensive United States oceans policy.

Jurisdictional issues remain a key factor in untangling the U.S. oceans policy dilemma. As currently constructed and consistent with the structure of federalism, three separate bands of jurisdiction divide the coastal and ocean areas. Local governments generally control shoreline use, state governments have jurisdiction in the belt of oceans from the low-tide mark out to the three-mile limit, and the federal government has jurisdiction from three to two hundred miles. These jurisdictional splits cause problems because many of the most important ocean activities traverse or affect all three jurisdictions; no effective mechanism achieves coordination among the levels of government. Additionally, the costs and benefits of oceans resources exploitation, such as offshore oil exploration, frequently fall disproportionately on different jurisdictions, exacerbating natural interjurisdictional friction.

This jurisdictional split exists not only between the different levels of government but at the federal level of government. Chapter 8 addressed the history of post-World War II oceans policy formulation in the United States, noting, in particular, the times when either the legislative branch or the executive branch was ascendant in shaping United States oceans policy. Today, while neither branch is clearly ascendant, there is disagreement on the best way to deal with oceans policy issues. Some within the executive branch favor a omnibus, coordinated policy approach with, perhaps, a cabinet-level position to direct oceans policies.[23] Conversely, other professionals working oceans policy issues within the legislative branch are more comfortable with a looser, coalition approach to working oceans policy issues. By taking this approach, they argue, "important" oceans policy legislation is easier to pass incrementally—oftentimes by attaching it as a rider on another, sure-to-pass bill—than if it was bound up with numerous other oceans policy bills.[24]

Management of ocean resources functionally, by sectors, is less than optimal. Within the offshore federal and state jurisdictions, each ocean resource and use is typically under the jurisdiction of a different agency operating under a different legislative framework. For example, one federal scheme and agency govern fisheries management, a different statue and agency manages offshore oil development, while a third agency handles water quality. This approach provides few opportunities for systematic examination of the ramifications of decisions in one sector on other sectors. For the same reasons, few opportunities exist for long-range planing for both resource use *and* resource conservation. Similarly, no streamlined mechanism exists for resolving interagency disputes.

Finally, the very complexity of the ocean system inhibits the search to effective solution of important oceans issues. The highly dynamic nature of the ocean, its mobility and fluidity, combined with the presence of complex and interdependent ocean ecosystems, make detailed predictions of the affects of an ocean-use activity exceptionally difficult, especially given our present level of understanding of ocean processes and behavior. Tying all of these factors together is, arguably, the best way to make informed, rational decisions on ocean resource exploitation and conservation.[25]

TOWARDS AN EFFECTIVE NATIONAL OCEANS POLICY

This chapter has dealt with challenges and concerns in the area of devising an effective United States oceans policy. It has not offered concise solutions to overcoming these challenges and concerns or arriving at a cohesive national oceans policy. Such undertakings defy simple prescriptions. One useful approach to beginning to take on this issue is that offered by Biliana Cicin-Sain, rapporteur for the Ocean Governance Study Group. She has listed a number of options to be considered for beginning the needed analytical work to develop a national oceans policy. Five primary options present themselves.

The first option would be congressional legislation to create a national commission to examine the entire issue of ocean governance. This commission would be similar to the Stratton Commission, whose product, the report entitled "Our Nation and the Sea," was extremely important in influencing United States oceans policy throughout the 1970s and 1980s. Such a commission would have great legitimacy and prestige, but would probably take a significant amount of time to arrive at recommendations.

A second option would be to empower a high-level group within the administration—preferably in the White House, perhaps in the National Security Council—to conduct an analytical review and to develop a national strategy. Such a group probably could move much more quickly than an autonomously chartered commission and would have the required legitimacy and high-level access within the administration. Interest in such a group by the administration, however, is not readily apparent.

A third option would be to empower an interagency task force of federal agencies to cobble together an omnibus oceans policy. Such an approach would take advantage of the oceans policy expertise extant within the Departments of State, Defense, Commerce and the Interior, among others, and would have sufficient legitimacy. However, the basic mechanisms for such interagency coordination already exist, in theory, at the executive branch level. But because of the sheer number of Executive Department agencies with at least some ownership in law of the sea issues (a total of twenty-two agencies),[26] and because these agencies may have somewhat divergent interests, it is unlikely that additional empowerment would lead to effective solutions.

A fourth option would be to create a national research council committee to conduct the analytical review and develop policy options. Focused analyses by the national research council have the potential to serve as catalysts for change in a particular policy area. This committee could have a great deal of legitimacy and prestige and would have access to a number of ocean policy experts on the two major national research council entities concerned with the oceans—the Marine Board and the Ocean Studies Board. Additionally, these studies usually take a great deal of time to complete.

A final option would be to designate a group of oceans policy experts—such as the Panel on the Law of Ocean Uses or the Ocean Governance Study Group—to conduct the analytical work and prepare the policy options. While this approach would bring together considerable expertise which has already demonstrated the ability to produce a product in a short time frame, such a group would have circumscribed access and would lack universally recognized legitimacy.[27]

The spectrum of these possible approaches indicates that there is no easy, obvious, or consensus solution to achieving a coherent and coordinated United States oceans policy. Some have called for the creation of a cabinet-level position to deal with the oceans, a Secretary of Ocean Affairs, a position that would carry sufficient bureaucratic authority to make the standard techniques of interagency coordination effective. Others have called for the interagency process to be made to work better. Some have called for the executive branch to "take charge," while others have called for the Congress to "take charge" via legislation. Without further study and analysis, it is not yet clear what the best path is. What *is* needed is a *commitment* by the administration, by the Congress, by state and local governments, by industry, and by nongovernmental actors, to recognize the *compelling need* for a comprehensive United States oceans policy.

NOTES

1.   U.S. Senate, *Treaty Document 103-39, United Nations Convention on the Law of the Sea, with Annexes, and the Agreement Relating to the Implementation of Part XI of the United Nations Convention on the Law of the*

Sea of 10 December 1982, with Annex, 103d Cong., 2d sess., 7 October 1994 (hereinafter *Treaty Document 103-39*).

2.   These documents are on file with the U.S. Department of State, Office of Marine Policy.

3.   Among those officials making frequent appearances at these symposia during the mid-1990s were Mary Beth West, Deputy Assistant Secretary of State for Oceans; former Ambassador for Oceans, David Colson; Robert Smith and Maureen O'C. Walker of the U.S. Department of State, Office of Marine Policy; the Honorable Walter Slocombe, Under Secretary of Defense for Policy; Mr. John McNeill, Senior Deputy General Counsel, International Affairs and Intelligence, U.S. Department of Defense and Chairman of the Department of Defense Law of the Sea Task Force; Rear Admiral Carlson LeGrand, JAGC, U.S. Navy, Department of Defense Representative for Ocean Policy Affairs; Rear Admiral William Center, U.S. Navy, Deputy Director for International Negotiations, Joint Chiefs of Staff; Eric Fersht, Office of General Counsel, Department of Defense; Professor Hugh Lynch, professor of naval warfare, U.S. Naval War College; and Professor Jack Grunawalt, Director, Oceans Law and Policy Department, Center for Naval Warfare Studies, U.S. Naval War College. Examples of their statements occur throughout earlier chapters.

4.   These publications were listed in previous chapters.

5.   Jonathan Charney, "Progress in International Maritime Boundary Delimitation Law," *American Journal of International Law* 88 (1994): 227. See also Ken Booth, *Law, Force, and Diplomacy at Sea* (Boston: George Allen and Unwin, 1985), 74-89.

6.   Department of State Memorandum from David Small, dated 31 August 1988, declassified 10 August 1989, referred to in William Aceves, "Ambiguities in Plurilingual Treaties: A Case Study of Article 22 of the 1982 Law of the Sea Convention," *Ocean Development and International Law* 27 (1996): 202. Aceves demonstrates the problems raised by the complex, plurilingual nature of the Convention. The 1982 Law on the Sea Convention was drafted in six authentic language texts: Arabic, Chinese, English, French, Russian, and Spanish. A State Department analysis of the Convention identified language differences in several provisions in the Chinese, French, Russian, and Spanish texts of the Convention. See also William Aceves, "The Freedom of Navigation Program: A Study on the Relationship Between Law and Politics," *Hastings International and Comparative Law Review* 19 (1996): 259. Aceves presents exhaustive documentation showing the specific differences in the various texts and demonstrating that these differences are more than a matter of semantics, but represent areas of significant potential conflict.

7.   Daniel Dzurek, "Comments on Island Disputes in East Asia" (address at the Center for Oceans Law and Policy, Center for National Security Law, and Council on Foreign Relations Seminar, *Security Flashpoints: Oil, Islands, Sea Access, and Military Confrontation*, New York, February 1997).

8.   Robert Knecht, et al., "National Ocean Policy: A Window of

Opportunity," *Ocean Development and International Law* 19 (1988): 115-127.

9.   Margaret Hayes, "Fisheries Interests in the 1982 Convention" (address at the Center for Oceans Law and Policy Symposium, *Toward Senate Consideration of the 1982 Law of the Sea Convention*, Washington, D.C., June 1995).

10.   Biliana Cicin-Sain and Robert Knecht, "Essay: A National Ocean Governance Strategy for the United States Is Needed Now," *Ocean Development and International Law* 22 (1994): 171-172.

11.   Ted Stevens, "Keynote Address" (address at the Center for Oceans Law and Policy Symposium, *Toward Senate Consideration of the 1982 Law of the Sea Convention*, Washington, D.C., June 1995), 11.

12.   See Lawrence Juda, "Ocean Policy, Multi-Use Management, and the Cumulative Impact of Piecemeal Change: The Case of the Outer Continental Shelf," in *Challenges and Issues in Ocean Governance*, David Caron, et al., eds. (Honolulu: Ocean Governance Study Group, 1993).

13.   See Knecht, et al., "National Ocean Policy: A Window of Opportunity," 129.

14.   Cicin-Sain and Knecht, "Essay: A National Ocean Governance Strategy for the United States is Needed Now," 172.

15.   M. Casey Jarman, interview by George Galdorisi, Honolulu, 31 August 1995. Professor Jarman, a faculty member at the W. S. Richardson School of Law at the University of Hawaii and a member of the Ocean Governance Study Group Steering Committee, is a noted expert on governmental legislative and regulatory interaction.

16.   Jack Archer, interview by George Galdorisi, University of Massachusetts, Boston, 29 September 1995. Professor Archer, a faculty member at the University of Massachusetts at Boston, is also a member of the Ocean Governance Study Group and has worked extensively in environmental law and its impact on state and local governments. Professor Archer points out that even though it is expected that state and local governments may make extensive claims like those of Hawaii, their legitimacy is questionable, considering court decisions back through 1947.

17.   See Biliana Cicin-Sain, "A Framework for Multiple-Use Ocean Governance for the United States" in *Challenges and Issues in Ocean Governance*, 15.

18.   See Knecht, et al., "National Ocean Policy: A Window of Opportunity."

19.   Edward Miles, "Reflections on the Political Implications of Current Ocean Governance Discussions in the U.S.: A Call to Action," in *Challenges and Issues in Ocean Governance*, 85.

20.   See Thomas Clingan, "Ocean Governance Challenges," *L.O.S. Leider* (January 1993).

21.   Robert Knecht, "International Influences on the Goals and Principles of National Ocean Governance," in *Challenges and Issues in Ocean Governance*, 28.

22.   Interview with Professor Jack Archer, 29 September 1995. Professor Archer postulates that the prospects are not favorable to move oceans governance towards the center of the political process in the near-term.

23.   Maureen O'C. Walker, "Entry Into Force of the 1982 United Nations Convention on the Law of the Sea" (paper presented at the Oceans '95 MTS/IEEE Symposium, San Diego, October 1995). Ms. Walker notes that the interagency working group, headed by NSC, is charged with coordinating the efforts of the numerous federal agencies—State, Defense, Commerce, Interior, Treasury, and others, with ownership in the U.S. oceans policy process.

24.   Rebecca Metzner, interview by George Galdorisi, Washington, D.C., 3 October 1995. Ms. Metzner, a Sea Grant Fellow and staff member for the Senate Commerce Committee, points out the effectiveness of utilizing a "bill-by-bill" approach to moving oceans policy legislation through the Congress. She cites, as one example, the 1995 reauthorizaton of the Coastal Zone Management Act. This reauthorization was making little progress even getting out of committee until it was attached as a rider to the "fast-moving" NOAA reauthorization bill.

25.   Knecht, et al., "National Ocean Policy: A Window of Opportunity," 134-135.

26.   John Norton Moore, "Observations by Former Special Representatives of the President for the Law of the Sea" (address at the Center for Oceans Law and Policy Symposium, *Toward Senate Consideration of the 1982 Law of the Sea Convention*, Washington, D.C., June 1995).

27.   Cicin-Sain and Knecht, "Essay: A National Ocean Governance Strategy for the United States Is Needed Now," 175.

President's Ocean Policy Statement, 10 March 1983

The United States has long been a leader in developing customary and conventional law of the sea. Our objectives have consistently been to provide a legal order that will, among other things, facilitate peaceful, international uses of the oceans and provide for equitable and effective management and conservation of marine resources. The United States also recognizes that all nations have an interest in these issues.

Last July, I announced that the United States will not sign the United Nations Law of the Sea Convention that was opened for signature on December 10. We have taken this step because several major problems in the Convention's deep seabed mining provisions are contrary to the interests and principles of industrialized nations and would not help attain the aspirations of developing countries.

The United States does not stand alone in these concerns. Some important allies and friends have not signed the Convention. Even some signatory States have raised concerns about these problems.

However, the Convention contains provisions with respect to traditional uses of the oceans which generally confirm existing maritime law and practice and fairly balance the interests of all States.

Today, I am announcing three decisions to promote and protect the oceans interests of the United States in a manner consistent with those fair and balanced results in the Convention and international law.

First, the United States is prepared to accept and act in accordance with the balance of interests relating to traditional uses of the oceans—such as navigation and overflight. In this respect, the United States will recognize the rights of other States in the waters off their coasts, as reflected in the Convention, so long as the rights and freedoms are recognized by such coastal States.

Second, the United States will exercise and assert its navigation and overflight rights and freedoms on a worldwide basis in a manner that is consistent with the balance of interests reflected in the Convention. The United States will not, however, acquiesce in unilateral acts of other States designed to restrict the rights and freedoms of the international community in navigation and overflight and other related high seas uses.

Third, I am proclaiming today an Exclusive Economic Zone in which the United States will exercise sovereign rights in living and nonliving resources within 200 miles of its coast. This will provide United States jurisdiction for mineral resources out to 200 nautical miles that are not on the continental shelf. Recently discovered deposits there could be an important future source of strategic minerals.

Within this Zone, all nations will continue to enjoy the high seas rights and freedoms that are not resource related, including the freedoms of navigation and overflight. My proclamation does not change existing United States policies concerning the continental shelf, marine mammals, and fisheries, including highly migratory species of tuna which are not subject to United States jurisdiction. The United States will continue efforts to achieve international management of these species. The proclamation also reinforces this government's policy of promoting the United States fishing industry.

While international law provides for a right of jurisdiction over marine scientific research within such a zone, the proclamation does not assert this right. I have elected not to do so because of the United States interest in encouraging marine scientific research and avoiding any unnecessary burdens. The United States will nevertheless recognize the right of other coastal States to exercise jurisdiction over marine scientific research within 200 nautical miles of their coasts, if that jurisdiction is exercised in a manner consistent with international law.

The Exclusive Economic Zone established today will also enable the United States to protect the marine environment. In this connection, the United States will continue to work through the International Maritime Organization and other appropriate international organizations to develop uniform international measures for the protection of the marine environment while imposing no unreasonable burdens on commercial shipping.

The policy decisions I am announcing today will not affect the application of existing United States law concerning the high seas or existing authorities of any United States Government agency.

In addition to the above policy steps, the United States will continue to work with other countries to develop a regime, free of unnecessary political and economic restraints, for mining deep seabed minerals beyond national jurisdiction. Deep seabed mining remains a lawful exercise of the freedom of the high seas open to all nations. The United States will continue to allow its firms to explore for and, when the market permits, exploit these resources.

The Administration looks forward to working with the Congress on legislation to implement these new polices.

PROCLAMATION 5030, EXCLUSIVE ECONOMIC ZONE OF THE UNITED STATES OF AMERICA, 10 MARCH 1983

WHEREAS the Government of the United States of America desires to facilitate the wise development and use of the oceans consistent with international law;

WHEREAS international law recognizes that, in a zone beyond its territory and adjacent to its territorial sea, known as the Exclusive Economic Zone, a coastal State may assert certain sovereign rights over the natural resources and related jurisdictions; and

WHEREAS the establishment of an Exclusive Economic Zone by the United States will advance the development of ocean resources and promote the protection of the marine environment, while not affecting other lawful uses of the zone, including the freedoms of navigation and overflight, by other States;

NOW, THEREFORE, I, RONALD REAGAN, by the authority vested in me as President by the Constitution and laws of the United States of America, do hereby proclaim the sovereign rights and jurisdiction of the United States of America and confirm also the rights and freedoms of all States within an Exclusive Economic Zone, as described herein.

The Exclusive Economic Zone of the United States is a zone contiguous to the territorial sea, including zones contiguous to the territorial sea of the United States, the Commonwealth of Puerto Rico, the Commonwealth of the Northern Mariana Islands (to the extent consistent with the Covenant and the United Nations Trusteeship Agreement), and United States overseas territories and possessions. The Exclusive Economic Zone extends to a distance 200 nautical miles from the baseline from which the breadth of the territorial sea is measured. In cases where the maritime boundary with a neighboring State remains to be determined, the boundary of the Exclusive Economic Zone shall be determined by the United States and other States concerned in accordance with equitable principles.

Within the Exclusive Economic Zone, the United States has, to the extent permitted by international law, (a) sovereign rights for the purpose of exploring, exploiting, conserving and managing natural resources, both living and non-living, of the seabed and subsoil and the superjacent waters and with regard to other activities for the economic exploitation and exploration of the zone, such as the production of energy from the water, currents and winds; and (b) jurisdiction with regard to the establishment and use of artificial islands, and installations and structures having economic purposes, and the protection and preservation of the marine environment.

This Proclamation does not change existing United States policies concerning the continental shelf, marine mammals and fisheries, including highly migratory species of tuna which are not subject to United States jurisdiction and require international agreements for effective management.

The United States will exercise these sovereign rights and jurisdictions in accordance with the rules of international law.

Without prejudice to the sovereign rights and jurisdiction of the United States, the Exclusive Economic Zone remains an area beyond the territory and territorial sea of the United States in which all States enjoy the high seas freedoms of navigation and overflight, the laying of submarine cables and pipelines, and other internationally lawful uses of the seas.

IN WITNESS WHEREOF, I have hereunto set my hand this tenth day of March, in the year of our Lord nineteen hundred and eighty-three, and of the Independence of the United States of America the two hundred and seventh.

/s/ Ronald Reagan

LETTER FROM THE SECRETARIES OF STATE AND DEFENSE TO SENATOR PELL, WASHINGTON, D.C., 28 JULY 1994

SENATOR PELL
United States Senate, Washington, D.C.

DEAR SENATOR PELL: We are pleased to inform you that an agreement has been concluded that will reform the deep seabed mining provisions of the United Nations Law of the Sea Convention to meet United States objections. This agreement, which Ambassador Madeleine Albright will sign on July 29, 1994, will clear the way for transmittal of the entire Law of the Sea Convention to the United States Senate for its advice and consent early in 1995.

Between now and the time that the Senate considers the Law of the Sea Convention, as amended by the new agreement, we will work with the Congress to provide complete and accurate information for your deliberations. We stand ready to provide briefings, information, background materials and any other assistance that you may require.

A comprehensive and widely accepted Law of the Sea Convention has been an objective pursued by Democratic and Republican Administrations for more than two decades. We now have an opportunity to join such a Convention. Becoming a party to the Law of the Sea Convention is in our national interest in all respects.

As one of the world's major maritime powers, the United States has a manifest national security interest in the ability to navigate and overfly the oceans freely. So too, the free flow of commercial navigation is a basic concern for the United States as a major economic power, whose economic security and well-being is linked with robust international trade.

It is our intention to explore with you and your colleagues all of the issues connected to this important Convention. We look forward to a continuing dialogue with you on this vital matter.

Sincerely,

/s/ WARREN CHRISTOPHER,
        Secretary of State
/s/ WILLIAM J. PERRY,
        Secretary of Defense

LETTER OF TRANSMITTAL

THE WHITE HOUSE,
October 7, 1994

To the Senate of the United States:

I transmit herewith, for the advice and consent of the Senate to accession, the United Nations Convention on the Law of the Sea, with Annexes, done at Montego Bay, December 10, 1982 (the 'Convention'), and, for the advice and consent of the Senate to ratification, the Agreement Relating to the Implementation of Part XI of the United Nations Convention on the Law of the Sea of 10 December 1982, with Annex, adopted at New York, July 28, 1994 (the 'Agreement') and signed by the United States, subject to ratification, on July 29, 1994. Also transmitted for the information of the Senate is a report of the Department of State with respect to the Convention and Agreement, as well as Resolution II of Annex I and Annex II of the Final Act of the Third United Nations Conference on the Law of the Sea.

The United States has basic and enduring national interests in the oceans and has consistently taken the view that the full range of these interests is best protected through a widely accepted international framework governing uses of the sea. Since the late 1960s, the basic U.S. strategy has been to conclude a comprehensive treaty on the law of the sea that will be respected by all countries. Each succeeding U.S. Administration has recognized this as the cornerstone of U.S. oceans policy. Following adoption of the Convention in 1982, it has been the policy of the United States to act in a manner consistent with its provisions relating to traditional uses of the oceans and to encourage other countries to do likewise.

The primary benefits of the Convention to the United States include the following:

• The Convention advances the interests of the United States as a global maritime power. It preserves the right of the U.S. military to use the world's oceans to meet national security requirements and of commercial vessels to carry sea-going cargoes. It achieves this, *inter alia*, by stabilizing the breadth of the territorial sea at 12 nautical miles; by setting forth navigation regimes of innocent passage in the territorial sea, transit passage in straits used for international navigation, and archipelagic sea lanes passage; and by reaffirming the traditional freedoms of navigation and overflight in the exclusive economic zone and the high seas beyond.

- The Convention advances the interests of the United States as a coastal State. It achieves this, *inter alia*, by providing for an exclusive economic zone out to 200 nautical miles from shore and by securing our rights regarding resources and artificial islands, installations and structures for economic purposes over the full extent of the continental shelf. These provisions fully comport with U.S. oil and gas leasing practices, domestic management of coastal fishery resources, and international fisheries agreements.
- As a far-reaching environmental accord addressing vessel source pollution, pollution from seabed activities, ocean dumping and land-based sources of marine pollution, the Convention promotes continuing improvement in the health of the world's oceans.
- In light of the essential role of marine scientific research in understanding and managing the oceans, the Convention sets forth criteria and procedures to promote access to marine areas, including coastal waters, for research activities.
- The Convention facilitates solutions to the increasingly complex problems of the uses of the ocean—solutions that respect the essential balance between our interests as both a coastal and a maritime nation.
- Through its dispute settlement provisions, the Convention provides for mechanisms to enhance compliance by Parties with the Convention's provisions.

Notwithstanding these beneficial provisions of the Convention and bipartisan support for them, the United States decided not to sign the Convention in 1982 because of flaws in the regime it would have established for managing the development of mineral resources of the seabed beyond national jurisdiction (Part XI). It has been the consistent view of successive U.S. Administrations that this deep seabed mining regime was inadequate and in need of reform if the United States was ever to become a Party to the Convention.

Such reform has now been achieved. The Agreement signed by the United States on July 29, 1994 fundamentally changes the deep seabed mining regime of the Convention. As described in the Report of the Secretary of State, the Agreement meets the objections the United States and other industrialized nations previously expressed to Part XI. It promises to provide a stable and internationally recognized framework for mining to proceed in response to future demand for minerals.

Early adherence by the United States to the Convention and the Agreement is important to maintain a stable legal regime for all uses of the sea, which covers more than 70 percent of the surface of the globe. Maintenance of such stability is vital to U.S. national security and economic strength.

I therefore recommend that the Senate give early and favorable consideration to the Convention and to the Agreement and give its advice and consent to accession to the Convention and to ratification of the Agreement. Should the Senate give such advice and consent, I intend to exercise the options concerning dispute settlement recommended in the accompanying report of the Secretary of State.

/s/ WILLIAM J. CLINTON

KEY FEATURES OF THE LAW OF THE SEA CONVENTION

- Coastal States would exercise sovereignty over their territorial sea up to twelve nautical miles in breadth, but foreign vessels would be allowed peaceful "innocent passage" through those waters.
- Ships and aircraft of all countries would be allowed "transit passage" through straits used for international navigation; States alongside the straits would be able to regulate navigational and other aspects of passage, but passage could not be suspended and "passage" would include overflight and submerged transit of submarines.
- Archipelagic States, made up of a group or groups of closely related islands and interconnecting waters, would have sovereignty over a sea area enclosed by straight lines drawn between the outermost points of the islands; all other States would enjoy the right of archipelagic passage (similar to transit passage), potentially through designated sea lanes.
- Coastal States would have exclusive resource exploitation rights in a 200 nautical mile exclusive economic zone (EEZ) with respect to natural resources and certain economic activities, and would also exercise jurisdiction over marine science research and environmental protection.
- All other States would have high seas freedoms of navigation and overflight in the EEZ, as well as freedom to lay submarine cables and pipelines.
- Land-locked and geographically disadvantaged States would have the opportunity to participate in exploiting part of the EEZ's fisheries on an equitable basis when the coastal State could not harvest them all itself; highly migratory species of fish and marine mammals would be accorded special protection.
- Coastal States would have exclusive resource rights over the continental shelf (the national area of the seabed) for exploring and exploiting it; the shelf would extend at least 200 nautical miles from the shore, and possibly more

under specified conditions.

- Coastal States would share with the international community part of the revenue they would derive from exploiting resources from any part of their continental shelf beyond 200 miles; a Commission on the Limits of the Continental Shelf would make recommendations to States on the shelf's outer boundaries when it extends beyond 200 miles.
- All States would enjoy the traditional freedoms of navigation, overflight, scientific research and fishing on the high seas; they would be obliged to adopt, or cooperate with other States in adopting, measures to manage and conserve living resources.
- The territorial sea, EEZ and continental shelf of islands would be determined in accordance with rules applicable to other land territory, but rocks that could not sustain human habitation or economic life on their own would have no economic zone or continental shelf.
- States bordering enclosed or semi-enclosed seas would be expected to cooperate in managing living resources and environmental research policies and activities.
- Land-locked States would have the right of access to and from the sea and would enjoy freedom of transit through the territory of applicable coastal States.
- States would be bound to prevent and control marine pollution and would be liable for damage caused by violation of their international obligations to combat such pollution.
- All marine scientific research in the EEZ and on the continental shelf would be subject to the consent of the coastal States, but coastal States would be obliged in most cases to grant consent to other States when the research was to be conducted for peaceful purposes and fulfilled specified criteria.
- States would be bound to promote the development and transfer of marine technology "on fair and reasonable terms and conditions," with proper regard for all legitimate interests.
- States would be obliged to settle by peaceful means their disputes concerning the interpretation or application of the Convention.
- Disputes could be submitted to an International Tribunal for the Law of the Sea to be established under the Convention, to the International Court of Justice, or to arbitration as selected by States party to the Convention. Conciliation would also be available and, in certain circumstances, submission to it would be compulsory. The Tribunal would have exclusive jurisdiction over deep seabed mining disputes.

NATIONAL POLLUTION
CONTROL LEGISLATION

National Ocean Pollution Planning Act of 1978: Establishes a comprehensive five-year plan for federal ocean pollution research and development and monitoring programs, and coordinates research of the Great Lakes and estuaries of national importance. Develops an information base for use in conservation, equitable distribution and development of ocean and coastal resources.

The Act to Prevent Pollution from Ships of 1980: Implements international agreement "Convention for the Prevention of Pollution by Ships" (MARPOL Annexes I-V). Prevents pollution from ships by the discharge of harmful substances or effluent.

Ocean Dumping Ban Act of 1988: Prohibits issuance of new permits for dumping of sewage sludge or industrial waste dumping (existing permittees) under compliance schedules/enforcement agreements to phase out dumping activities.

Marine Pollution and Research and Control Act of 1989: Implements the provisions of MARPOL Annex V. Prohibits the disposal of plastics at sea by any vessel within the U.S. EEZ.

Oil Pollution Act of 1990: Increases and extends civil and criminal liability and measures to increase navigation safety, new standards for vessel construction, crew licensing and manning of vessels.

INTERNATIONAL POLLUTION CONTROL AGREEMENTS

Treaty Banning Nuclear Weapon Tests in the Atmosphere, in Outer Space and Under Water of 1963

International Convention on Civil Liability for Oil Pollution Damage of 1969

International Convention Relating to Intervention on the High Seas in Cases of Oil Pollution Casualties of 1969

Convention Relating to Civil Liability in the Field of Maritime Carriage of Nuclear Material of 1971

International Convention on the Establishment of an International Fund for Compensation for Oil Pollution Damage of 1971

Treaty on the Prohibition of the Emplacement of Nuclear Weapons and Other Weapons of Mass Destruction in the Seabed and the Ocean Floor and in the Subsoil Thereof of 1971

Convention on the International Regulations for Preventing Collisions at Sea of 1972

Convention on the Prevention of Marine Pollution by Dumping of Wastes and Other Material of 1972

International Convention for the Prevention of Pollution from Ships of 1973

Convention on Limitation of Liability for Maritime Claims of 1976

Merchant Shipping Minimum Standards Convention of 1976

Protocol for the Prevention of Pollution of the Mediterranean Sea by Dumping from Ships and Aircraft of 1976

International Convention for the Safety of Fishing Vessels of 1977

Convention on Civil Liability for Oil Pollution Damage Resulting from Exploration and Exploitation of Seabed Mineral Resources of 1977

Protocol for the Protection of the Mediterranean Sea against Pollution from Land-Based Sources of 1980

Protocol for the Protection of the South-East Pacific against Pollution from Land-Based Sources of 1983

U.N. Convention on Conditions for Registration of Ships of 1986

Protocol for the Protection of the South Pacific Region by Dumping of 1986

Protocol for the Protection of the South-East Pacific against Radioactive Pollution of 1989

Convention on the Control of Transboundary Movements of Hazardous Wastes and Their Disposal of 1989

Protocol Concerning Marine Pollution Resulting from Exploration and Exploitation of the Continental Shelf of 1989

Protocol for the Protection of the Marine Environment against Pollution from Land-Based Sources of 1990

Annex IV to the Antarctic Protocol for the Prevention of Marine Pollution of 1991

Annex III to the Protocol on Environmental Protection to the Antarctic Treaty—Waste Disposal and Waste Management of 1991

Protocol on Protection of the Black Sea Marine Environment against Pollution from Land-Based Sources of 1992

Convention on Civil Liability for Damage Resulting from Activities Dangerous to the Environment of 1993

Draft International Convention on Liability and Compensation in Connection with the Carriage of Hazardous and Noxious Substances by Sea of 1996

NATIONAL MARINE AND COASTAL RESOURCES LEGISLATION

Fish and Wildlife Coordination Act of 1934: Authorizes the Fish and Wildlife Service to assist federal, state and other agencies in developing, protecting, rearing and stocking fish and wildlife on federal lands.

Saltonstall-Kennedy Act of 1939: Establishes a fund for fisheries research and development.

Outer Continental Shelf Lands Act of 1953 (including amendments of 1978 and 1985): Regulates offshore oil, gas and mineral leasing. Requires compliance with natural resource protection programs from damages associated with oil, gas and mineral development activities.

Fish and Wildlife Act of 1956: Establishes a comprehensive national fish and wildlife policy to develop measures for maximum sustainable yield to insure stability of domestic fisheries. Provides for agency consultation with the Fish and Wildlife Service whenever the "waters of any stream or other body of water are to be impounded, directed or otherwise controlled."

Anadromous Fish Conservation Act of 1965: Authorizes programs to conserve, develop and enhance federal anadromous fisheries resources.

Fisherman's Protective Act (Pelly Amendment) of 1967: Ensures that foreign fishing activities are in accordance with international fishery conservation programs, and activities do not affect endangered/threatened species.

Coastal Zone Management Act of 1972: Makes federal funds available to encourage states to develop comprehensive management programs in an effort to increase the effective management, beneficial use, protection and development of the coastal zone.

Marine Mammal Protection Act of 1972 (including amendments of 1988): Provides for long-term management, research, conservation and recovery programs for marine mammals. Establishes a moratorium on the taking and importing of marine mammals and marine mammal products.

Magnuson Fishery Conservation and Management Act of 1976: Conserves and manages fishery resources within the U.S. Exclusive Economic Zone for maximum sustainable yield. Creates eight regional fishery management councils to prepare fishery management plans for their respective regions.

Lacey Act Amendments of 1981: Prohibits commerce of fish and wildlife in violation of federal, state and international laws.

Fur Seal Act Amendments of 1983: Prohibits the taking of fur seals, with the exception of subsistence harvest by Alaska Natives.

Atlantic Striped Bass Conservation Act of 1984: Authorizes programs for the conservation and management of Atlantic striped bass.

Coastal Barrier Resources Act of 1986: Prohibits development of barrier islands within the Coastal Barrier Resources System to conserve fish, wildlife, and other natural resources in those areas.

Driftnet Impact Monitoring, Assessment and Control Act of 1987: Directs the government to assess and minimize the adverse effects of driftnets in the North Pacific ocean on marine resources.

Shore Protection Act of 1988: Requires vessels to protect coastal areas from disposal of solid waste.

South Pacific Tuna Act of 1988: Regulates tuna harvest by U.S. flag vessels within the Exclusive Economic Zones of Pacific Island Parties.

Coastal Barrier Improvement Act of 1990: Amends the Coastal Barrier Resources Act of 1986, which established the Coastal Barrier Resources System consisting of undeveloped coastal barriers and other areas located on the coasts of the United States.

INTERNATIONAL FISHERIES AGREEMENTS

International Convention on the Regulation of Whaling of 1946

Convention for the Establishment of an Inter-American Tropical Tuna Commission of 1949

Interim Convention of the Conservation of North Pacific Fur Seals of 1957

Convention Concerning Fishing in the Black Sea of 1959

International Convention for the Conservation of Atlantic Tunas of 1966

Convention on the Conservation of Antarctic Seals of 1972

Convention of Fishing and Conservation of the Living Resources of the Baltic Sea and Belts of 1973

International Convention for the Safety of Fishing Vessels of 1977

Convention on Future Multilateral Cooperation in the Northwest Atlantic Fisheries of 1978

Convention on the Conservation of Antarctic Marine Living Resources of 1980

Convention on Future Multilateral Cooperation in North East Atlantic Fisheries of 1980

Convention for the Conservation of Salmon in the North Atlantic Ocean of 1982

Eastern Pacific Ocean Tuna Fishing Agreement and Protocol of 1983

Treaty on Fisheries Between the Governments of Certain Pacific States and the Government of the United States of America of 1987

Convention for the Prohibition of Fishing with Long Driftnets in the South Pacific and Protocols of 1989

Convention on the Conservation of Migratory Species of Wild Animals of 1979

Agreement to Reduce Dolphin Mortality in the Eastern Tropical Pacific Tuna Fishery of 1992

Agreement on Cooperation in Research, Conservation and Management of Marine Mammals in the North Atlantic of 1992

Convention for the Conservation of Anadromous Stocks in the North Pacific Ocean of 1992

Agreement for the Establishment of the Indian Ocean Tuna Agreement of 1993

Convention on the Conservation and Management of Pollock Resources in the Central Bering Sea of 1994

SELECTED BIBLIOGRAPHY

Abel, R. B. "The History of United States Ocean Policy." In *Making Ocean Policy*, edited by F. Hoole, R. Friedheim, T. Hennessey. Boulder, Colorado: Westview Press, 1981.

Aceves, William. "Ambiguities in Plurilingual Treaties: A Case Study of Article 22 of the 1982 Law of the Sea Convention." *Ocean Development and International Law* 27 (1996): 187-233.

———. "The Freedom of Navigation Program." *Hastings International and Comparative Law Journal* 19 (1996): 259-326.

Alexander, Lewis. "The Cooperative Approach to Ocean Affairs: Twenty Years Later." *Ocean Development and International Law* 21 (1990): 105-109.

———. *The Law of the Sea: A New Geneva Conference*. Kingston, Rhode Island: Rhode Island University Press, 1972.

Allen, Scott. "The Elements of Seapower: Mahan Revisited." In *Ocean Yearbook 7*, edited by Elizabeth Borgese and Norton Ginsburg. Chicago: University of Chicago Press, 1988.

———. "Mare Liberum." *Naval Institute Proceedings* 109 (July 1983): 45-49.

Allison, Anthony. "The Soviet Union and UNCLOS III: Pragmatism and Policy Evolution." *Ocean Development and International Law* 16 (Spring 1986): 109-136.

Allott, Philip. "Mare Nostrum: A New International Law of the Sea." *American Journal of International Law* 86 (1990): 764-787.

Anand, R. P. *Origin and Development of the Law of the Sea*. Boston: Martinus Nijhoff, 1983.

Aspin, Les. *Annual Report to the President and the Congress, 1994*. Washington, D.C.: USGPO, 1994.

Bandow, Doug, George Galdorisi, and M. Casey Jarman. *The United Nations*

Convention on the Law of the Sea: The Cases Pro and Con, Occasional Paper No. 38. Honolulu: Law of the Sea Institute Press, 1995.

Bateman, Sam. "Build a WESTPAC Naval Alliance." *United States Naval Institute Proceedings* 119 (January 1993): 77-82.

Bathurst, R. B. *Understanding the Soviet Navy: A Handbook*. Newport, Rhode Island: Naval War College Press, 1979.

Berge, Stig, Jan Markussen, and Gudmund Vigerust. *Environmental Consequences of Deep Seabed Mining—Problem Areas and Regulations*. Oslo, Norway: Fridtjof Nassen Institute Press, 1991.

Blum, Yehda. "The Gulf of Sidra Incident." *American Journal of International Law* 80 (1986): 668-677.

Boczek, Boleslaw. "Peacetime Military Activities in the Exclusive Economic Zone of Third Countries." *Ocean Development and International Law* 19 (1988): 445-468.

Booth, Ken. *Law, Force, and Diplomacy at Sea*. London: George Allen and Unwin, 1985.

Borgese, Elisabeth, Norton Ginsburg, and Joseph Morgan, eds. *Ocean Yearbook 11*. Chicago: University of Chicago Press, 1994.

Brewer, William. "Deep Seabed Mining: Can an Acceptable Regime Ever be Found?" *Ocean Development and International Law* 11 (1982): 25-67.

Brittin, Burdick. *International Law for Seagoing Officers*. 5th ed. Annapolis, Maryland: Naval Institute Press, 1986.

Browne, Marjorie Ann. *CRS Issue Brief: The Law of the Sea Convention and U.S. Policy*. Washington, D.C.: Congressional Research Service, Library of Congress, 1995.

Brownlie, Ian. *Principles of Public International Law*. 3d ed. Oxford, U.K.: Clarendon Press, 1979.

Bull, Hedley, Benedict Kingsbury, and Adam Roberts, eds. *Hugo Grotius and International Relations*. Oxford, U.K.: Clarendon Press, 1990.

Bush, George. *The National Security Strategy of the United States*. Washington, D.C.: USGPO, 1993.

Butler, W. E. *The Soviet Union and the Law of the Sea*. Baltimore, Maryland: The Johns Hopkins Press, 1971.

———. *The USSR, Eastern Europe and the Development of the Law of the Sea*. Dobbs Ferry, New York: Oceana Publications, 1987.

Caron, David, et al., eds. *Challenges and Issues in Ocean Governance*. Honolulu: Ocean Governance Study Group, 1993.

Charney, Jonathan. "Progress in International Maritime Boundary Delimitation Law." *American Journal of International Law* 88 (1994): 227-256.

Churchill, R. R., and A. V. Lowe. *The Law of the Sea*. Manchester, U.K.: Manchester University Press, 1983, and 2d ed., 1988.

Cicin-Sain, Biliana. "Essay: A National Ocean Governance Strategy for the United States Is Needed Now." *Ocean Development and International Law* 22 (1994): 171.

Cicin-Sain, Biliana and Robert Knecht. "Implications of the Earth Summit for Ocean and Coastal Governance." *Ocean Development and International Law* 24 (1993):323-353.

Cicin-Sain, Biliana, and Katherine Leccese, eds. *Implications of Entry into Force of the Law of the Sea Convention for U.S. Ocean Governance.* Honolulu: Ocean Governance Study Group, 1995.

Clingan, Thomas. *The Law of the Sea: Ocean Law and Policy.* San Francisco: Austin and Winfield, 1994.

———. "The Next Twenty Years of Naval Mobility." *Naval Institute Proceedings* 106 (May 1980): 82.

———. "Ocean Governance Challenges." *L.O.S. Leider* (January 1993).

Clinton, William. *A National Security Strategy of Engagement and Enlargement.* Washington, D.C., USGPO, 1995.

Commission on Marine Science, Engineering, and Resources. *Our Nation and the Sea.* Washington, D.C.: USGPO, 1969.

Council on Oceans Law. *Oceans Policy News* (February 1992).

Craven, John. "The Evolution of Ocean Policy." In *The Law of the Sea in the 1990s: A Framework for Further International Cooperation,* edited by Tadao Kuribayashi and Edward Miles. Honolulu: Law of the Sea Institute Press, 1992.

Dalton, John H., Admiral Jeremy M. Boorda, USN, General Carl E. Mundy, USMC. *Forward...From the Sea.* Washington, D.C.: USGPO, 1995.

David, Steven, and Peter Digeser. *The United States and the Law of the Sea Treaty.* Washington, D.C.: The Johns Hopkins University, 1990.

Department of Defense. DOD Maritime Claims Reference Manual. Washington, D.C.: Department of Defense, Office of the Secretary of Defense for International Security Affairs, 1990, revised ed. June 1994.

———. *National Security and the Convention on the Law of the Sea.* Washington, D.C.: Department of Defense, 1994.

———. *National Security and the Convention on the Law of the Sea.* 2d ed. Washington, D.C., Department of Defense, 1996.

———. *Soviet Military Power 1983.* Washington, D.C.: USGPO, 1983.

Department of State. "Law of the Sea," *Current Policy* No. 371. Washington, D.C.: Department of State, 1982.

———. "Law of the Sea and Oceans Policy," *Current Policy* No. 416. Washington, D.C.: United States Department of State, Bureau of Public Affairs, 1982.

———. "Navigation Rights and the Gulf of Sidra." *GIST.* Washington, D.C., Department of State, Bureau of Public Affairs, 1986.

———. "Ocean Policy and the Exclusive Economic Zone." *Current Policy* No. 471. Washington, D.C.: Department of State, 1983.

———. Publication 112, *Limits in the Seas: United States Responses to Excessive Maritime Claims.* Washington, D.C.: Department of State, Bureau of Oceans and International Environmental and Scientific Affairs, 1992.

Department of the Navy. *The Commander's Handbook on the Law of Naval Operations, Naval Warfare Publication 1-14M/MCWP 5-2.1.* Washington, D.C.: Naval Warfare Publications Library, 1995.

——. *The Commander's Handbook on the Law of Naval Operations*, NWP-9A/FMFM 1-10. Washington, D.C.: Naval Warfare Publications Library, 1989.

——. *Understanding Soviet Naval Developments* (Washington, D.C.: USGPO, 1985.

Doran, Walter. "An Operational Commander's Perspective on the 1982 LOS Convention." *International Journal of Marine and Coastal Law* 10 (1995): 335-347.

Dubs, Marne. "Minerals in the Deep Sea: Myth and Reality." In *The New Order of the Oceans*, edited by Giulio Pontecorvo. New York: Columbia University Press, 1986.

Dumbauld, Edward. *The Life and Legal Writings of Hugo Grotius.* Norman, Oklahoma: University of Oklahoma Press, 1969.

Evririades, Euripides. "The Third World's Approach to the Deep Seabed." *Ocean Development and International Law* 11 (1982): 201-264.

Friedheim, Robert. *Negotiating the New Ocean Regime.* Columbia, South Carolina: University of South Carolina Press, 1993.

Galdorisi, George. "The United Nations Convention on the Law of the Sea: A National Security Perspective." *American Journal of International Law* 89 (1995): 208-213.

Galdorisi, George, and James Stavridis. "Time to Revisit the Law of the Sea." *Ocean Development and International Law* 24 (1993): 301-315.

Goldstein, Joshua. *Long Cycles: Prosperity and War in the Modern Age.* New Haven, Connecticut: Yale University Press, 1988.

Gorshkov, S. G. *The Sea Power and the State.* Annapolis, Maryland: Naval Institute Press, 1976.

Greenwood, Alfred, et al. *CRS Report to the Congress: Oceans and Coastal Resources: A Briefing Book.* Washington, D.C.: Congressional Research Service, Library of Congress, 1995.

Grotius, Hugo. *Mare Liberum: The Freedom of the Seas or The Right Which Belongs to the Dutch to Take Part in the East Indian Trade*, 1608. Translated by Ralph Magoffin and edited by J. B. Scott. New York: Oxford University Press, 1916.

Grunawalt, Richard. "United States Policy on International Straits." *Ocean Development and International Law* 18 (1987): 445-458.

Haerr, Roger. "The Gulf of Sidra." *San Diego Law Review* 24 (1987): 751-767.

Harry, Martin. "The Deep Seabed: The Common Heritage of Mankind or Arena for Unilateral Exploitation?" *Naval Law Review* 40 (1992): 207-228.

Hollick, Ann L. *U.S. Foreign Policy and the Law of the Sea.* Princeton: Princeton University Press, 1981.

———. "United States Oceans Politics." *San Diego Law Review* 10 (1973): 471.

Holloway, James. "Victory and an Uncertain Future." *U.S. Naval Institute Proceedings* 121 (1995).

Hu, Nien-Tsu Alfred, and James K. Oliver. "A Framework for Small Navy Theory: The 1982 United Nation's Law of the Sea Convention." *Naval War College Review* 41 (Spring 1988).

Ikle, Fred, and Albert Wholstetter. *Discriminate Deterrence: Report of the Commission on Integrated Long Range Strategy*. Washington, D.C.: USGPO, 1988.

Institute for National Strategic Studies. *Strategic Assessment 1995: U.S. Security Challenges in Transition*. Washington, D.C.: National Defense University Press, 1995.

Janis, Mark. *The Influence of Naval Interests on the Development of the Law of the Sea*. Newport, Rhode Island: Naval War College Press, 1975.

———. *Sea Power and the Law of the Sea*. Lexington, Massachusetts: Lexington Books, 1976.

Janis, Mark, and Donald Daniel. *The USSR: Ocean Use and Ocean Law*. Kingston, Rhode Island: University of Rhode Island Press, 1974.

Johnston, Douglas. *NATO Realignment and the Maritime Component*. Washington, D.C.: Center for Strategic and International Studies Press, 1992.

———. "Protection of the Ocean Environment: Competing Views of the Implementation Process." In *Implications into Force of the Law of the Sea Convention for U.S. Ocean Governance*, edited by Biliana Cicin-Sain, and Katherine Leccese. Honolulu: Law of the Sea Institute, 1985.

Joyner, Christopher, and Peter Decola. "Chile's Presential Sea Proposal: Implications for Straddling Stocks and the International Law of Fisheries." *Ocean Development and International Law* 24 (1993): 99-121.

Juda, Lawrence. "Ocean Policy, Multi-Use Management, and the Cumulative Impact of Piecemeal Change: The Case of the Outer Continental Shelf." In *Challenges and Issues in Ocean Governance*, edited by David Caron, et al. Honolulu: Ocean Governance Study Group, 1993.

Kapumpa, Mumba. "Reflections on Institutional Aspects and How to Facilitate Universal Acceptance of the Convention." In *Law of the Sea in the 1990s*, edited by Tadao Kuribayashi and Edward Miles. Honolulu: Law of the Sea Institute Press, 1992.

Kaufmann, William, and John Steinbruner. *Decisions for Defense: Prospects for a New Order*. Washington, D.C.: Brookings Institution Press, 1991.

Kim, Dalchoong, and Jin-Hyun Paik. "The Relation Between User States and Coastal States with Respect to International Navigation." In *The Law of the Sea in the 1990s: A Framework for Further International Cooperation*, edited by Tadao Kuribayashi and Edward Miles. Honolulu: Law of the Sea Institute Press, 1992.

Kimball, Lee. *The Law of the Sea: Priorities and Responsibilities in Implementing the Convention*. Gland, Switzerland: International Union for Conservation of Nature and Natural Resources Press, 1995.

―――. "Turning Points in the Future of Deep Seabed Mining." *Ocean Development and International Law* 17 (1986): 367-393.

Knecht, Robert, Biliana Cicin-Sain, and Jack Archer. "National Ocean Policy: A Window of Opportunity." *Ocean Development and International Law* 19 (1988): 113-142.

Krueger, Robert, and Stefan Riesnfeld, eds. *The Developing Order of the Oceans, Proceedings of the Eighteenth Annual Conference of the Law of the Sea Institute*. Honolulu: Law of the Sea Institute, 1985.

Kuribayashi, Tadao, and Edward Miles, eds. *The Law of the Sea in the 1990s: A Framework for Further Cooperation*. Honolulu: Law of the Sea Institute Press, 1992.

Kwiatkowska, Barbara. "Creeping Jurisdiction Beyond 200 Miles in Light of the 1982 Law of the Sea Convention and State Practice." *Ocean Development and International Law* 22 (1995):153.

Larson, David. "Conventional, Customary and Consensual Law in the U.N. Convention on the Law of the Sea." *Ocean Development and International Law* 25 (1994): 75-85.

―――. "Deep Seabed Mining: A Definition of the Problem." *Ocean Development and International Law* 17 (1986): 271-308.

―――. "Foreword." *Ocean Development and International Law* 11 (1982): 1-8.

―――. "The Reagan Administration and the Law of the Sea." *Ocean Development and International Law* 11 (1982): 297-320.

―――. "When Will the U.N. Convention on the Law of the Sea Come Into Effect?" *Ocean Development and International Law* 20 (1989): 175-202.

Laursen, Finn. *Superpower at Sea: U.S. Ocean Policy*. New York: Praeger Publishers, 1983.

Lee, Luke T. "The Law of the Sea Convention and Third States." *American Journal of International Law* 77 (1983): 541-568.

Malone, James. "Who Needs the Sea Treaty?" *Foreign Policy* 54 (1984): 44.

Markussen, Jan. "Commercial Exploitation of Polymetallic Nodules: Comments on Some Critical Issues." In *The Law of the Sea in the 1990s: A Framework for Further International Cooperation*, edited by Tadao Kuribayashi and Edward Miles. Honolulu: Law of the Sea Institute Press, 1992.

McDorman, Ted. "Will Canada Ratify the Law of the Sea Convention?" *San Diego Law Review* 25 (1988): 535-579.

McGruther, K. R. *The Evolving Soviet Navy*. Newport, Rhode Island: Naval War College Press, 1978.

Meltzer, Evelyne. "Global Overview of Straddling and Highly Migratory Fish Stocks: The Nonsustainable Nature of High Seas Fisheries." *Ocean Development and International Law* 25 (1994): 255-344.

Mero, John. "A Legal Regime for Deep Sea Mining." *San Diego Law Review* 7 (1970): 488-503.

Meyer, John. "The Impact of the Exclusive Economic Zone on Naval Operations." *Naval Law Review* 40 (1992): 241-252.

Miles, Edward. "Preparations for UNCLOS IV?" *Ocean Development and International Law* 19 (1988): 421-430.

Moore, John Norton, ed. *International and United States Documents on Oceans Law and Policy*. Buffalo, New York: William Hein and Company, 1986.

Morell, James B. *The Law of the Sea: An Historical Analysis of the 1982 Treaty and Its Rejection by the United States*. Jefferson, North Carolina: McFarland and Company, 1992.

Morgan, Joseph. "Constabulary Navies in the Pacific and Indian Oceans." In *Ocean Yearbook 11*, edited by E. Borgese, N. Ginsburg, and J. Morgan. Chicago: University of Chicago Press, 1994.

Nandan, Satya. "The 1982 U.N. Convention on the Law of the Sea: At a Crossroad." *Ocean Development and International Law* 20 (1989): 515-518.

Nandan, Satya, and Shabtai Rosenne, eds. *United Nations Convention on the Law of the Sea 1982: A Commentary*. Boston: Martinus Nijhoff, 1993.

National Intelligence Council. *The Law of the Sea: The End Game*. Washington, D.C.: National Intelligence Council, 1996.

Neutze, Dennis. "The Gulf of Sidra Incident: A Legal Perspective." *U.S. Naval Institute Proceedings* 108 (1982).

Nixon, Richard M. "Report to the Congress: U.S. Foreign Policy for the 1970s—A New Strategy for Peace." *Department of State Bulletin 62*. Washington, D.C.: USGPO, 1970.

———. "United States Policy for the Seabed," *U.S. Department of State Bulletin 62*. Washington, D.C.: USGPO, 1970.

Nordquist, Myron H., and C. H. Park , eds., *Report of the U.S. Delegation to the Third U.N. Conference on the Law of the Sea*. Honolulu: Law of the Sea Institute Press, 1983.

Nyhart, J. D., and M. S. Traintafyllou. *A Pioneer Deep Ocean Mining Venture*. Cambridge, Massachusetts: MIT Press, 1983.

O'Connell, D. P. *The International Law of the Sea*. Oxford, U.K.: Clarendon Press, 1987.

Oda, Shigeru. "Proposals Regarding a Twelve-Mile Limit for the Territorial Sea by the United States in 1970 and Japan in 1971: Implications and Consequences." In *Law of the Sea in the 1990s, A Framework for Future Cooperation*, edited by Tadao Kuribayashi and Edward Miles. Honolulu: Law of the Sea Institute Press, 1992.

Ogiso, Motoo. "International Cooperation in the New Sea Regime." In *Law of the Sea in the 1990s: A Framework for Further International Cooperation*, edited by Tadao Kuribayashi and Edward Miles. Honolulu: Law of the Sea Institute Press, 1992.

O'Hanlon, Michael. *The Art of War in the Age of Peace: U.S. Military Posture for the Post-Cold War World*.   Westport, Connecticut: Greenwood Publishers, 1992.

Osgood, R. E., and A. L. Hollick. *Toward a National Ocean Policy, 1976 and Beyond*. Washington, D.C.: The Johns Hopkins Press, 1977.

Oxman, Bernard. *From Cooperation to Conflict: The Soviet Union and the United States at the Third U.N. Conference on the Law of the Sea*. Seattle: University of Washington Press, 1985.

―――. "United States Interests in the Law of the Sea Convention." *American Journal of International Law* 88 (1994): 167-178.

Panel on the Law of Ocean Uses. "U.S. Interests and the United Nations Convention on the Law of the Sea." *Ocean Development and International Law* 21 (1990): 373-410.

Pontecorvo, Giuilo, ed. *The New Order of the Oceans: The Advent of a Managed Environment*. New York: Columbia University Press, 1986.

Potter, E. B., and C. W. Nimitz. *Seapower, A Naval History*. Englewood Cliffs, New Jersey: Prentice-Hall, 1960.

Powell, Colin. *The National Military Strategy of the United States*. Washington, D.C.: USGPO, 1992.

Reisman, Michael. "The Regime of Straits and National Security: An Appraisal of International Law Making." *American Journal of International Law* 74 (1980):48-76.

Richardson, Elliot. "Law of the Sea: A Reassessment of U.S. Interests." *Mediterranean Quarterly* 1 (1990).

―――. "The Politics of the Law of the Sea." *Ocean Development and International Law* 11 (1982): 9-23.

Roach, J. A., and R. W. Smith. *International Law Studies 1994: Excessive Maritime Claims*, vol. 66. Newport, Rhode Island: Naval War College Press, 1994.

Robertson, Horace B. "Contemporary International Law: Relevant to Today's World?" *Naval War College Review* 45 (Summer, 1992): 89-103.

Rolph, John. "Freedom of Navigation and the Black Sea Bumping Incident, How 'Innocent' Must Innocent Passage Be?" *Military Law Review* 135 (1992): 137-165.

Rose, Steven. "Naval Activity in the EEZ—Troubled Waters Ahead?" *Naval Law Review* 39 (1990): 67.

Sanger, Clyde. *Ordering the Oceans: The Making of the Law of the Sea*. Toronto: University of Toronto Press, 1987.

Sebenius, J. K. *Negotiating the Law of the Sea*. Cambridge, Massachusetts: Harvard University Press, 1984.

Shalikashvili, John. *National Military Strategy of the United States of America: A Strategy of Flexible and Selective Engagement*. Washington, D.C.: USGPO, 1995.

Smith, Edward. "What '...From the Sea' Didn't Say." *Naval War College Review* 48 (Winter 1995)

Stevenson, John R. "International Law and the Oceans," *Department of State Bulletin 62*. Washington, D.C.: USGPO, 1970.

Stevenson, John, and Bernard Oxman. "The Future of the United Nations Convention on the Law of the Sea." *American Journal of International Law* 88 (1994): 488-499.

Stumpf, Robert. "Air War with Libya." *U.S. Naval Institute Proceedings* 112 (August 1986): 42-48.

United Nations. *The Law of the Sea: Annual Review of Ocean Affairs, Law and Policy, Main Documents*. New York: United Nations, 1993.

———. *The Law of the Sea: Official Text of the Convention on the Law of the Sea with Annexes and Index*. New York: United Nations, 1983.

———. *1982 United Nations Convention on the Law of the Sea*, United Nations Publication, 1261. New York: United Nations, 1982.

U.S. House Committee on Foreign Affairs, Subcommittee on International Organizations and Movements. *Law of the Sea and Peaceful Uses of the Seabed*. 92nd Cong., 2nd sess., 1972.

U.S. Naval Institute. *The Maritime Strategy*. Annapolis, Maryland: Naval Institute Press, 1986.

U.S. Senate. *Treaty Document 103-39, United Nations Convention on the Law of the Sea, with Annexes, and the Agreement Relating to the Implementation of Part XI of the United Nations Convention on the Law of the Sea of 10 December 1982, with Annex*. 103d Cong., 2d sess., 1994.

U.S. Senate Committee on Foreign Relations. *Current Status of the Convention on the Law of the Sea*. 103d Cong., 2d sess., 1994.

Van Dyke, J. M., ed. *Consensus and Confrontation: The United States and the Law of the Sea Convention*. Honolulu: Law of the Sea Institute Press, 1985.

———. "Hawaii's Claim to Archipelagic Waters." In *Implications of Entry into Force of the Law of the Sea Convention for U.S. Ocean Governance*, edited by Biliana Cicin-Sain and Katherine Leccese. Honolulu: Ocean Governance Study Group, 1995.

Van Dyke, J.M, Lewis Alexander, and James Myer, eds. *International Navigation, Rocks and Shoals Ahead?* Honolulu: Law of the Sea Institute Press, 1988.

Wagner, Eric. "Submarine Cables and Protections Provided by the Law of the Sea." *Marine Policy* 19 (1995): 127.

Wallace, Michelle. "The Right of Warships to Operate in the Exclusive Economic Zone as Perceived by Delegates to the Third United Nations Law of the Sea Convention." In *International Navigation, Rocks and Shoals Ahead?*, edited by Jon Van Dyke, Lewis Alexander, and James Myer. Honolulu: Law of the Sea Institute Press, 1988.

Wang, James. *Handbook on Ocean Politics and Law*. Westport, Connecticut: Greenwood Press, 1992.

World Resources Institute. *World Resources 1988-1989*. New York: Basic Books, 1988.

Zacher, Mark, and James McConnell. "Down to the Sea with Stakes: The Evolving Law of the Sea and the Future of the Deep Seabed Regime." *Ocean Development and International Law* 21 (1990): 71-103.

Zuleta, Bernardo. "The Law of the Sea After Montego Bay." *San Diego Law Review* 20 (1983): 475-488.

INDEX

About the Authors

CAPTAIN GEORGE V. GALDORISI is Chief of Staff in the U.S. Navy's Cruiser Destroyer Group 3. He holds degrees from the United States Naval Academy, the Naval Postgraduate School, the University of San Diego, and the Naval War College.

CAPTAIN KEVIN R. VIENNA is with the U.S. Navy's Judge Advocate General's Corps. He holds degrees from the United States Naval Academy, the College of William and Mary, the University of Southern California, and the University of Virginia.

ISBN 0-275-95754-3

90000>

EAN

9 780275 957544

HARDCOVER BAR CODE